THE SEARCH

ALSO BY BRUCE FEILER

Life Is in the Transitions

The First Love Story

The Secrets of Happy Families

The Council of Dads

America's Prophet

Where God Was Born

Abraham

Walking the Bible

Dreaming Out Loud

Under the Big Top

Looking for Class

Learning to Bow

THE

Finding Meaningful Work
in a Post-Career World

BRUCE FEILER

PENGUIN PRESS

NEW YORK   2023

PENGUIN PRESS
An imprint of Penguin Random House LLC
penguinrandomhouse.com

Infographic designs by Michael Yoon, Yoon Creative LLC

LIBRARY OF CONGRESS CATALOGING-IN-PUBLICATION DATA
Names: Feiler, Bruce, 1964– author.
Title: The search : finding meaningful work in a post-career world / Bruce Feiler.
Description: New York : Penguin Press, 2023. |
Includes bibliographical references and index. |
Identifiers: LCCN 2022049262 (print) | LCCN 2022049263 (ebook) |
ISBN 9780593298916 (hardcover) | ISBN 9780593298923 (ebook)
Subjects: LCSH: Quality of work life—United States. |
Work-life balance—United States. |
Conduct of life—United States. | Success—United States.
Classification: LCC HD6957.U6 F44 2023 (print) | LCC HD6957.U6 (ebook) |
DDC 306.3/60973—dc23/eng/20230201
LC record available at https://lccn.loc.gov/2022049262
LC ebook record available at https://lccn.loc.gov/2022049263

Printed in the United States of America
1   3   5   7   9   10   8   6   4   2

Book design by Daniel Lagin

Bruce Feiler is available for select speaking engagements.
To inquire about a possible appearance, please contact Penguin Random House
Speakers Bureau at speakers@penguinrandomhouse.com.

For Pat Conroy

For writing the way

Tell me, what is it you plan to do
with your one wild and precious life?

—MARY OLIVER

I'm here to persuade you not to have a job. . . . That doesn't mean
try not to do anything.

It means try to leave yourself in a position where you do the
things that you want to do with your time and where you take
maximum advantage of whatever your possibilities are.

—BRIAN ENO

CONTENTS

INTRODUCTION: **The Work Story Project** ·   1
How to Write Your Own Story of Success

I

THE THREE LIES ABOUT WORK

1. **Lie #1: You Have a Career**   31
   The (Short) Rise and (Rapid) Fall of the Career

2. **Lie #2: You Have a Path**   57
   How Workquakes Overtook Work

3. **Lie #3: You Have a Job**   81
   The Surprising Wisdom of Work360

II

THE ONE TRUTH ABOUT WORK

4. **We All Need Another Hero**   111
   Who Gets to Be the Face of Success?

5. **The Meaning Audit**   133
   What to Do When You Don't Know What to Do

III
THE SIX QUESTIONS TO ASK IN A WORKQUAKE

6. **Who Is Your Who?**   157
   I Want to Be the Kind of Person Who _____

7. **What Is Your What?**   179
   I Want to Do Work That _____

8. **When Is Your When?**   201
   I'm at a Moment in My Life When _____

9. **Where Is Your Where?**   223
   I Want to Be in a Place That _____

10. **Why Is Your Why?**   243
    My Purpose Right Now Is _____

11. **How Is Your How?**   263
    The Best Advice I Have for Myself Right Now Is _____

CONCLUSION: **The New Rules of Success**   283
The American Dream Is Dead, Long Live the American Dreams

ACKNOWLEDGMENTS   305

FURTHER READING   309

SOURCES   311

INDEX   323

THE SEARCH

The Work Story Project

How to Write Your Own Story of Success

Brijette Peña grew up in the middle of Middle America clinging to what she thought was the American Dream.

"I come from a working-class family in Baldwin City, Kansas. We lived on Tenth Street; my grandma lived on Ninth Street; my aunt lived on Seventh Street. Ninety percent of my family lived within one mile."

Brijette's mom, a veteran, raised three children; her father, an auto mechanic, worked at the local Chrysler dealer. "He never missed a day of work in forty years. And this was Kansas, where it can be one hundred and ten in the summer and negative twenty in the winter. It put a roof over our heads, but he was deeply unhappy."

Brijette understood exactly what was expected of her. "I would be the first in my family to get a four-year degree. I would get a nine-to-five job. I would work my way up the economic ladder." But she didn't share those expectations.

"I wanted to be happy."

Brijette fell in love with plants while watering mums in a greenhouse one summer. She moved to Costa Rica to study ecology, met her future husband, and followed him to Southern California. "I was so naive, I expected to find a job quickly." Instead, she waited tables for a year and was fired "for being a terrible waitress."

"When you grow up poor, there's always that fear that you'll backslide out of the American Dream."

Brijette took some classes and volunteered at a farm that hosted schoolchildren. One day she watched a third grader pull a carrot from the ground. "He was so excited. He had no clue where carrots came from." Brijette had an idea: *I'll open a seed company!*

"It's Southern California. There are 365 days of sun. You can breed everything from avocados to mangoes. I figured, I'll grow vegetables and herbs—not to sell them, but to harvest their seeds and sell those. Again, I was so naive."

Seeding is expensive. Only two dozen seed-cleaning machines existed in the country, and the cheapest was $12,000. To save up money, Brijette took a job managing a gardening company. "I brought in a lot of business, I had a team of twenty and a company vehicle, I was making $50,000 a year. With my husband's salary from Costco, we were on top of the world."

Then, a lifequake—actually, two.

Brijette's brother, then mother, died in car accidents five months apart. Brijette spent so much time flying back and forth to Kansas that her boss brought in an employee to help her. When she returned, the employee started groping her. "He sexually harassed me constantly."

Brijette told her boss, who did nothing.

"This job was our main source of income. We had just bought a small piece of land. I needed a plan."

Brijette took her W-2 to the bank, secured a loan, and bought a white Toyota Tacoma. "The next day I walked into the office, called a meeting with my owner and entire team, and said, 'I can't have somebody that reports to me touch me, grab my ass, pull me into cubicles. Either you fire him, or I can't work here anymore.' When the owner remained silent, I handed him my keys and walked out the door."

Here she was again, on the brink of backsliding out of the American Dream.

"I made a vow that with my unemployment and my husband's salary, I had a year to make the seed company work."

Two years later, San Diego Seed Company was selling three hundred varieties—from artichoke to zinnias—and shipping three hundred thousand packets a year from Brijette's living room.

"I kept thinking of my mom. She called herself a bra burner. If she had known what was going on—and that I let it go on for so long—she would have been outraged.

"But I also kept thinking of my children. I don't have any now, but when I do, I want to be able to tell them that they don't have to be treated unfairly, they don't have to do something that makes them unhappy. Each of us gets to write our own American Dream. And the bliss that awaits at the end is being able to say, *I did everything I could to be fulfilled.*"

The Story of Your Work

This book is designed to help you write your own story about work. It grows out of an unprecedented shift in how we think about what we do. More people are taking control of their work lives.

In recent years, for the first time in history, the number of Americans quitting their jobs reached a million people a week. Buoyed by the tightest talent market in eighty years, a million marketing directors and money managers, truck drivers and tech designers, artists and acupuncturists decided they weren't doing what they wanted to be doing and opted to do something else. Many of these people did what their parents and grandparents would never have dreamed of doing: walk away from one job without have another job lined up.

Most of these decisions have been attributed to a supposed surge in resignations set off by the pandemic. But that narrative is grossly misleading. What economists call the *quit rate*, the number of people who quit their jobs every month, has risen every year except one for two decades. After reaching a low of a million and a half people following the recession in 2009, the number of monthly quitters rose to two million in 2012, three million in 2018, a record three and a half million in 2019, four million in 2020, and then four and a half million in 2022.

A third of the workforce now leaves their jobs every year.

Another third redesigns the jobs they're in. They assert more influence, work more remotely, dial back hours to spend more time with family, dial up flexibility to pursue side work that brings them purpose.

Even those who lose their jobs say they don't necessarily want to return to the grind; many would prefer more variable arrangements, even if that means sacrificing some conventional metrics of achievement.

Clearly something is happening in work that's never happened before in work.

This book is about that something. It's about a once-in-a-generation rethinking of the rules of success. A rebalancing of power away from employers and toward employees. A shift from a time when most of us were forced to bend to someone else's narrative to a time when more of us assert the freedom to write our own narrative.

Fewer people search merely for work these days.

More people search for work with meaning.

We're moving from a means-based economy to a meaning-based economy.

And this book is about learning to take advantage of this opening to get the happiness you deserve and the meaning you crave. The first step in that process: revisiting the script you inherited about work. For generations, Americans have been fed a narrow definition of success. That script was passed down by our parents, encouraged by our neighbors, reinforced by our culture. These days, more of us are turning our backs on that playbook. We're questioning its values and challenging its assumptions. We're flipping that script and replacing it with . . .

Well, we're not sure, exactly.

Turns out, we're much better at rejecting scripts than we are at writing them.

Many of us feel lost, adrift, frustrated, confused.

That leads to the second step on this journey: rediscovering your own scripture of work. A huge flaw in the myth of success we've been sold is that it gazed too exclusively and elevated too reflexively on only one type of hero and one measure of achievement. The only way to be successful is to always push ahead. *March forward! Reach higher! Get more!*

This advice is wrongheaded at best and dangerous at worst.

The most important step to being successful today is not to look forward.

It's to look backward. Peer inward. Dig deep.

When you do, what you discover is that each of us is grappling with our own internal definition of success. We have a roiling assortment of homilies, parables, truisms, and beliefs, some imprinted on us by our families and inscribed on us by our surroundings, but more chosen by us from our role models and forged by us from our wounds. The best way to understand these stories is as a kind of scripture, a sacred treasure that each of us tries to live up to even as we try to break free from it.

This book is about learning to identify that scripture. Tapping into it at the defining moments in your life so that you don't waste your time chasing someone else's dream.

You chase your own dream.

That leads to the final step on this journey: taking control of your own work narrative.

The last few years have seen a renaissance of storytelling. Through the confluence of narrative psychology, which showed that our internal narratives lie at the heart of our identity, and cognitive neuroscience, which revealed that our brains are wired to process information through narrative, we've come to accept that stories define many aspects of our lives. But for whatever reason, our work lives have been largely left out of that conversation.

The time has come to correct that imbalance. In these pages, I explore the idea that each of us has what I call a *work story*, an ongoing, unspoken narrative that we're constantly revisiting and revising in response to changes in our jobs, our families, and our lives. The freedom to rethink that story comes at a time when our work lives are more volatile than ever before. We face a never-ending barrage of interruptions—some voluntary, others involuntary; some unique to us, others shared by the entire planet; some that grow out of changes in our workplace, others that grow out of changes in our mindsets. I call these moments *workquakes*. And as I'll lay out, at any given moment, eighty million Americans are going through one.

I also offer one more thing: a set of questions to ask when you're in a workquake that maximizes the chance you get the outcome you want. As each of us goes through this process of rewriting our individual story of success, we also participate in something that's urgently overdue: rewriting our collective story of success. This new story is more complex—and more elastic—than the one we've been telling. It's more colorful—and more welcoming.

It doesn't undermine the American Dream.

It opens the door to myriad American Dreams.

This book is about how I accidentally discovered these new variations on how to think about success. And how we can achieve the version that's right for us.

"This Is Your Story; Own It"

Troy Taylor was born in what he calls "the smallest independent country in the Americas," the islands of Saint Kitts and Nevis. His mother was a college professor, his father a carpenter. "I watched the man my entire life, come rain, snow, hail, or sleet, get up every morning and get the job done." But because his mother was the primary breadwinner, when she was hired by the City University of New York when Troy was seven, the family emigrated to the Bronx.

Troy was obsessed with aviation. "I was always interested in why big airplanes could fly, but I couldn't tie a towel around my neck and fly." He enrolled in Penn State to study aeronautical engineering, and his first interview after graduating was at Boeing. "I walked into this giant room and saw all these desks in a line, and at the front was an office. My entire life flashed before my eyes. You start at the first desk, then move to the next desk, then the next, until one day you make it to the office. I thought, *I'm looking at the next thirty years of my life.* I'm not saying I'm a wildcat, but what kid at twenty-one wants their entire destiny laid out before them?"

Troy took a job at GE instead, designing satellites for NASA.

"It sounded great, and the company had a mystique. I was a rocket scientist! But the real job was learning discipline and how to break insurmountable tasks into their individual parts. That shaped how I approached my work. Even if I don't know where I'm going, I always get better at where I am."

And he did. After six years, Troy transferred to GE Electrical Distribution; five years later, after earning a master's degree in systems engineering at the University of Pennsylvania, he moved to GE Industrial Services; four years after that he was offered the job of general manager of a failing division, GE Renewal Parts and Instrumentation.

On the one hand, this job was a dead-end move, Troy said. "There's a whole lot more sex appeal in selling a brand-new, shiny widget than in selling spare parts." But his mentor, Lloyd Trotter, the vice-chairman of the company, gave him a piece of advice: "Dispel the notion that if you do a good job, the company is going to take care of you; only you can take care of yourself."

"I turned that into a motto," Troy said. "'Forget the ladder; embrace the smorgasbord.' At every turn, I either want to create something from nothing or take something from worst to first."

Over the next five years, Troy turned the worst division of GE into a $250 million profit center. His reward: a call from Johnson & Johnson inviting him to run a new clinical diagnostics division worldwide.

"On the phone, I told the CEO, *I've always been interested in medical equipment!* But internally I thought, *Can I really duplicate my success outside the fairyland?*"

Once again, he dove into the smorgasbord. And in eight years at J&J, Troy amassed a team of one thousand employees on four continents and flipped an industry also-ran into a $2 billion juggernaut.

By this point, Troy was feeling buried. "I had been running around for almost twenty years. I was worried I was becoming an absolute dick, and I wanted to make sure my children knew me before they went to college." So he walked away from the corporate world entirely. Recalling a boyhood passion for graphic design, he opened an art gallery with friends in Atlanta that specialized in underrepresented artists telling narrative stories. "I want to be a custodian for cultures that are about to be lost."

So what advice would Troy give his younger self facing that long line of desks?

"On my first trip to the United States, in 1969, I watched the moon landing from my aunt's apartment. Twenty years later, I was designing satellites for NASA. Did I experience difficulty? Tell me about it. But one thing you find among immigrants is the mentality that *yeah, this is the land of milk and honey, but you have to earn it.* So I would tell my younger self what Lloyd told me: Don't wait for someone else to tell you what to do. This is your story; own it."

Why I Wrote This Book

I never intended to write this book.

When I was nine, I was summoned to a family ritual. Awakened by my mother on a Saturday morning, I dressed in baby-blue corduroys and a white dress shirt, stepped through the sliding glass door in back of our home in Savannah, Georgia, and walked the few steps to my grandparents' house. My grandmother prepared her signature breakfast: one scrambled egg, one plate of hand-cut french fries, one glass of milk, and one Krispy Kreme glazed doughnut.

Afterward, I climbed into my grandfather's Ford, and he drove seven miles per hour through a dozen stoplights to a one-story, white brick building downtown. Inside, behind a giant oak desk, I learned to file, type, and keep ledgers as tenants delivered monthly rent payments of eighteen or twenty-two dollars. *Look them in the eye. Ask about their family. Thank them.* All while my grandfather, in his suspenders and brown oxfords, kept his hand on my shoulder and his eye on my work.

At exactly noon, we would get back into the car, and Papa would tell stories—about the first car he drove in Mississippi, the first airplane he rode in Florida, the first air conditioner he enjoyed in Georgia. The message in those mornings could not have been clearer.

Son, the most important thing in life is work.

Not family, not faith, not love.

Work.

And work in a way that was part of a long line of traditions. Of building things and making sacrifices, of handshakes and hair tonic, of masculinity and industriousness.

But while I was listening to those stories and hearing those messages, I was harboring a misgiving. I didn't dream of doing that kind of work. I didn't want to tell that kind of story.

Instead, there was another place in that one-story building that contained an alternative script of my life. It was a walk-in bank vault from the Mosler Safe Company in Hamilton, Ohio. Inside was a file with my name on it kept by my father. It contained programs from my piano recitals, stacks of letters from summer camp (Who writes twelve-page letters home from camp? I did!), and stapled collections of every poem I ever wrote.

Every Saturday of my childhood I would walk through that sliding glass door, endure those long drives, and try to detangle those conflicting strands of my identity. The earnest, dutiful, expected life; the risky, alternative, creative one. The life at the desk or the one in the vault.

The linear path or the nonlinear one.

But just as my string of Saturdays ended, I received a chilling warning. Six weeks before I graduated from high school, my grandfather, soon after learning he had a chronic disease, scribbled a note—*I cannot live a sick man*—took a pistol, and shot himself.

He might as well have said, *If I cannot work, I cannot live.*

For me, the impact of that moment was that all those straight lines I had been raised to follow became a crypt I was determined to avoid. Three months later, I boarded a train for college and took one last trip on an old-fashioned, industrial line that my grandfather would have loved into a newfangled, postindustrial world he never would have understood, where all the lines are crooked and all the sources of meaning are scrambled.

A world where work is no longer defined by giant oak desks and well-polished oxfords.

But by countless personal vaults storing vats of untapped dreams.

A world where success cannot be written for you.

Success can be written only by you.

For years I believed those tensions were unique to me. After graduating from college, I resisted pressure to go to law school or Wall

Street and instead moved to Japan to teach junior high school. Two years later, I sold a memoir about that experience. In the three decades since, I've written books, made television, given speeches. I've also survived waves of changes in the various industries where I work and endured countless moments of fear and doubt.

But I've never written about these themes. If anything, I've been drawn to topics—family, health, spirituality, meaning—that seemed far removed from the modern workplace. In the unspoken divisions of contemporary life, work involves hard skills; I specialize in soft skills.

But something meaningful shifted in the last few years. The world of work moved in my direction. With more women in the workplace and more men in the family space, once rigid divisions between work and life became more porous. The widespread adoption of work from anywhere blew those divisions to smithereens. Suddenly topics like happiness, purpose, balance, and joy became inseparable from topics like salary, benefits, productivity, and success.

Suddenly everybody went soft.

As that confluence was happening, another seismic shift was erupting in the workplace: a movement to ask, *Who gets to be the face of success in the first place?* With the lifting of long-held compacts of silence, generations of frustration came pouring into view. More and more people were finally asserting, *I want a seat at the table. I want to share my story.*

Everyone, it seems, was battling demons. Everyone had wings they wanted to spread.

These frustrations resonated with me. I was raised Jewish in the American South at a time when antisemitism was not abstract and hidden but tangible and open. I have visceral memories of my grandfather driving me around town, saying, *That bank won't lend to you; that club won't admit you; that company won't hire you.* Also, following decades of building a professional identity around being a traveler and a walker, I suddenly lost the ability to walk for a few years in my forties and developed a long-term disability when bone cancer ravaged my left femur and thigh. After having my leg rebuilt with titanium, a transplanted fibula, and screws in my knee and pelvis, I also had to rebuild my work life.

Although my internal narrative may include these challenges, I've come to appreciate in recent years that my external narrative does not. I've become much more aware of—and more grateful for—my blessings.

Still, the most valuable lesson I've learned in decades of writing about other people and cultures is the honor you pay another person by looking them in the eye, saying, *Please tell me your story.* I had just completed a massive undertaking of that nature when all these forces were converging.

Spurred by a raft of personal crises—illness, near bankruptcy, a string of suicide attempts by my father—I crisscrossed the country a few years ago collecting life stories of hundreds of Americans who'd been through wrenching life changes. I called this effort the Life Story Project.

The book I wrote about that experience, *Life Is in the Transitions,* was published just as the tsunami of change was reaching the shore. Seemingly overnight, the entire world was in a life transition. Shorn from their routines, tens of millions of people began questioning their most basic assumptions—about their relationships, their values, their beliefs. No arena of life was more disrupted than work, as unheard-of numbers of Americans started to rethink *what* they were doing, *where* they were doing it, *why* they were doing it, and with *whom* they were doing it.

Suddenly, the dominant conversation touched on all the questions I had been immersed in since those Saturday mornings with my grandfather.

Do I want to be a bit character in someone else's story, or do I want to be the hero of my own?

My story had finally merged with everyone else's.

I wanted to do something to help.

"My Friends Thought I Was Insane"

Meroë Park grew up about as far removed from the epicenters of American power as possible—on a farm in Jasper, Oregon. Her father, a Korean immigrant, was a physics professor, her mother a musician. "I grew up in a time of assimilation. My father's greatest desire was that I wouldn't stand out in any way. For my sixteenth birthday, he gave me the *Handbook of Chemistry and Physics*."

Meroë had other priorities. Her parents split when she was six, and her primary focus was holding the family together. "As a child of divorce, I always felt like a peacemaker." For college, she followed that instinct to Washington, DC, enrolling at Georgetown. After graduating, she took the foreign service exam and "went with the brand name."

She joined the CIA.

"I was worried what my dad would think. Not many people who grew up outside the United States have a great association with the CIA. But it fit with his goal of not wanting a lot of attention."

Meroë's first assignment was the agency's most coveted: a seat on the Soviet desk. She analyzed science and technology, wrote classified reports, briefed policy makers. And she hated it. "I thought, *I don't want to do this for thirty years.*"

So she did something no one thought was a good idea: she switched to management. "There are three jobs in the CIA: the spies, the analysts, and the support people. I became a support person. My friends thought I was insane. *You're leaving the most prestigious part of the agency for the least prestigious?*"

Meroë thought she could make both parts better, though. She became special assistant to the deputy director; she joined working groups; she was asked to be the chief aide to the director. Meroë faced pushback. "Many times, I'd go to a meeting with my chief of staff, who was a white man, and everyone would immediately go shake his hand, assuming he was senior." But she also experienced accommodation. When the director asked her to join his team, Meroë was pregnant with her first child.

"I told him, 'I'd love to take this job, but I have to take care of myself, too.' He told me, 'Do what you need to do.' So every afternoon, I'd go into the dining room, lie on the couch, and sleep for thirty minutes. Then I'd get up and go back to work."

No sooner did Meroë reach that pinnacle than she again appeared to sabotage herself. After a stint overseas, she returned and took over . . . payroll. "Now everyone knew I was idiotic." Her next job was even less illustrious: she ran HR. "I hadn't really managed a team that size."

But her next job proved that her unconventional choices could yield conventional results: Meroë was appointed executive director and chief operating officer of the CIA, the highest civil servant position in the agency. "I've never been a vertical person; I've always been a horizontal person. That doesn't mean I wasn't ambitious or didn't care about doing well. But I was more interested in doing whatever I was doing well than in reaching for the next big thing."

Which may be why she reached the biggest thing of all. In January 2017, in the middle of one of the most tumultuous moments in the agency's history, Meroë Park became acting director of the CIA, the first minority woman to hold that position. By trying not to have a career, Meroë ended up with one of the more distinguished careers in the history of American intelligence.

By trying not to draw attention to herself, Meroë drew the attention of the world.

"When I talk to young people, the first thing I tell them is: 'There's an updated version of the American Dream. You can be a success even if you're not the typical poster child of success.'

"The next thing I tell them is: 'Don't always focus on moving up. Look for opportunities to raise your hand—join a working group, take an unexpected position, do something that scares you.'

"The final thing I tell them is: 'You don't have to do what your parents want. You don't have to do what your colleagues want. You only have to do what you want.'

"You can be you."

The Work Story Interview

What I did was create the Work Story Project. Over the next two years, I collected the work stories of scores of Americans of all walks of life. In keeping with current trends in both popular and academic writing,

I set out to assemble as widespread and diverse a population of subjects as possible.

My primary focus was on the type of work people do. Using Department of Labor statistics, I made a bingo card of popular jobs. The card had five groupings—*life, creative, industrial, knowledge,* and *world*—and twenty-five categories, including *health, education, arts, construction, energy,* and *first responders.* In the end, I had equal distribution among all the categories. I also sought out people in a wide array of organizations—from Fortune 500 companies to startups, multinationals to mom-and-pops—as well as in a cross section of roles—from CEOs to line workers, entrepreneurs to activists.

My final list included teachers, bankers, marketers, managers, nuns, novelists, firefighters, fitness instructors, truck drivers, sex workers, safecrackers, welders, brewers, doctors, farmers, comedians, mediums, nuclear physicists, and TikTok plantfluencers.

My next focus was on demographic diversity. The individuals you'll meet in these pages come from forty states and five generations. They are evenly female and male, with a handful of nonbinary individuals. They range from high school dropouts to PhDs, with two thirds having at least some higher education. On income, while many overcame extreme poverty and others were born into privilege, as a rule I steered away from the poorest of the poor and the richest of the rich and concentrated on people who are part of the broad middle class. (For detailed demographics, see sources.)

Finally, guided by government data showing that minority workers have become the majority of new hires, as well as larger shifts in the culture that have seen Americans embrace workers of a wide spectrum of identities, beliefs, and abilities, I aimed to speak with as many people as possible from underrepresented backgrounds. These backgrounds include race, ethnicity, religion, gender, and sexual orientation, as well as physical and mental disabilities.

My goal in assembling these individuals was to create not just a more well-rounded portrait of the workplace than is common in similar accounts but also a more accurate window into where that workplace is headed in the future. In addition, my hope was that by speaking with such a wide cross section of workers in a broad spectrum of fields in all corners of the country, I might uncover clues to many of the pressing issues around work today that are normally discussed using only limited populations, from how to avoid burnout to how to master transitions to how to find your true purpose.

One more note about these individuals: They love what they do. There are paeans to people who don't like their work, and poems bemoaning drudgery. This project focuses on the opposite end of the spectrum. Just as positive psychology looks at individuals who are well-adjusted to see what they can teach the rest of us, this book looks at people who enjoy their work to see what they can teach those of us who aspire to do the same.

What I did with these people is something I call the Work Story Interview. What scholars term *life stories*—or, in the case of this project, *work stories*—differ in meaningful ways from typical journalistic interviews. They're more sweeping, more structured, and more intimate. They're also more time-consuming. Most scholarship in the field of narrative psychology includes anywhere from a handful of subjects up to a few dozen. For this book I did 155 interviews. The total number of hours was 500. Combined with the interviews I did for the Life Story Project, I have now collected in four years nearly 400 life stories, totaling 1,500 hours, whose transcripts together run more than 10,000 pages.

Each interview had three sections. The first covered the person's work history, including the values they learned from their parents, the qualities they admired in their role models, and every workquake they experienced. The second focused on their work today—from how many jobs they have to what aspect of their work they find most meaningful. The third drilled down to how these individuals navigated their biggest workquake, including the best question they asked and the best advice they received. I concluded by asking everyone what their story says about the American Dream.

Next I hired a team of ten people, and we spent a year coding these stories for 153 variables, creating a massive database of every imaginable question about work. Altogether we generated three times the amount of data I had from the Life Story Project.

My priority throughout was simple: How can I help people find more meaning through work?

"Sometimes Life Has Other Plans for You"

Trevor Boffone was the youngest of three born into a "run-of-the-mill, middle-class family" in New Orleans. His father ran a company that ferried oil along the Gulf Coast; his mother taught school. "My parents were doing well financially, but right when I was born, there was an oil crisis, and they lost everything. I grew up learning that sometimes life has other plans for you."

Trevor attended a Christian day school, where he ran track and played tennis, then enrolled at the University of Oklahoma to study film. But again, life had other plans for him. When Hurricane Katrina decimated his family's business yet again, Trevor gave up his dream of directing, returned home, and finished his degree at Loyola University in Spanish and French.

"I was always very close with teachers growing up. Plus, I was a language nerd. So when a friend told me about an opening at my high school, I called the assistant principal. They hired me the next day."

Trevor spent the next four years teaching high school Spanish and world history. He moved to Philadelphia to earn a master's degree, then to Houston to get a PhD in Hispanic literature. But as a young academic, Trevor struggled. He taught courses at Rice, dabbled in community theater, wrote some articles.

"Finally, my wife said to me, 'You've got to help out more.' The academic job market had collapsed by then, and the high school market was hardly better. I applied for twenty positions and was finally hired by Bellaire High School in South Houston."

Once again, though, life had other plans. The night before Trevor's first day of teaching, his father went into the hospital for a routine surgery, suffered a complication, and died the next morning. "It was so sudden that none of us knew what to do. I'm a mama's boy, and I didn't want to leave my mother and go back to Houston."

A week later, resigned to fulfilling his obligation, he started his new job. "I was a complete zombie; I was depressed; I was barely giving 50 percent. I felt like a total failure."

Then life showed up with other plans again—and this time, those plans came with wings.

One day after class, Trevor watched a group of freshman girls lean a cell phone against a window and record a choreographed dance.

"They weren't teaching one another the moves. Everyone just somehow knew them. It was like watching a nineties teen movie."

Trevor asked if he could join them.

"They thought my request was hilarious. They started making videos of us dancing together and posting them on Dubsmash, Snapchat, and TikTok. It was just a silly thing we did after a class—a way for me to connect with them."

The recordings went on for months; the students pressed Trevor to open an Instagram account, but he wanted to keep his personal life separate from his work life. Finally, he relented.

"That winter I opened an account called @Dr_Boffone. The students tagged me. Within a week, I had ten thousand followers; within two weeks, fifty thousand. Within two months, we were on *GMA* and our lives just blew up."

When the school year was over, Trevor returned to the academic conference in Orlando where for years he had tried to secure a job. "And for the first time, I thought, *This is not my place. My place is with those kids.* That's when I realized that we had flipped the model: They had become the teacher; I had become the student. Instead of my saving them, they had saved me."

Three years later, Trevor spends the first hour after he wakes up every morning working on his academic writing. He published a book with Oxford University Press on digital dance cultures, then started another book about TikTok and Broadway. During the day, he teaches five high school language classes and the occasional college course. At night, he volunteers to promote up-and-coming playwrights and manages his social media accounts.

"I think back on my parents losing their business—twice. I think back on what I wanted for most of my adult life—none of which I got.

What I've learned is that our dreams don't necessarily work out. But sometimes the dreams that come true are even better than the ones that don't."

The New American Success Story

Here's what I learned from the Work Story Project.

Lesson #1: The Unbearable Likeness of American Success Stories

One of the first things I did when I committed to writing a book about work was to assemble a shelf of iconic books about work. It included motivational writers—Dale Carnegie, Stephen Covey; big thinkers on economics—John Kenneth Galbraith, Peter Drucker; and seminal novelists—Horatio Alger, John Steinbeck. These books would ground me in the numerics and poetics of the American Dream.

That's when I had a horrifying realization.

Every single book had one thing in common.

The story of success we've been telling in America is terribly outdated. It's the story of only one subset of our community, seeking only one expression of our dreams. The heroes in those stories all had the same-gendered bodies, shared the same-colored faces, lived in the same-furnished homes, and chased the same-shaped careers.

Those stories defined the American Dream. That dream helped build this country, but it also helped prevent many members of this country from making their own dreams come true.

Our national scripture has been far too limiting.

Exactly how limiting? I stacked the five most influential success books of the twentieth century on my desk. The books are *Choosing a Vocation* by Frank Parsons (1909), *How to Win Friends and Influence People* by Dale Carnegie (1936), *The Power of Positive Thinking* by Norman Vincent Peale (1952), *What Color Is Your Parachute?* by Richard Nelson Bolles (1970), and *The 7 Habits of Highly Effective People* by Stephen Covey (1989).

I then turned every page and researched every person in those books. Here's what I found:

Choosing a Vocation includes 94 white men, 2 white women, no Black men or women, and no other racial or ethnic minorities.

How to Win Friends features 252 white men (including Jefferson Davis), 24 white women, no Black men or women, and 2 other minorities.

The Power of Positive Thinking showcases 144 white men (including Stonewall Jackson), 23 white women, and 5 Black people. The latter group includes 1 singer, 1 redcap, 1 "colored woman, a cook," 1 "colored maid," and 1 unnamed "wise and philosophical Negro man." No other minorities are featured.

What Color Is Your Parachute? mentions 85 white men, no women, no Black people, and no other minorities.

The 7 Habits spotlights 56 white men, 2 white women, no Black people, and no other minorities.

The total: 631 white men, 51 white women, 5 Black people, and 2 other minorities.

Those tallies mean that of the 689 stories told in these books, 7 percent are women.

Meanwhile, 0.7 percent are Black and 0.003 percent are other minorities.

It was impossible to evaluate such diversity markers as sexual orientation and disability, though there are no outward signs that any people meeting those descriptions are included.

Even Studs Terkel's landmark 1974 book, *Working*, is overwhelmingly white and has a casual racism that's jolting to today's ears. Of the 136 interviews in the book, only 8 are with Black subjects, and those include a maid, a washroom attendant, and a jazz singer; 2 are of other minorities. The N-word appears 11 times.

Before we can turn to the emerging portrait of what it means to find happiness and success at work today, we have to acknowledge and lay to rest the narrow-minded, restrictive, even cruel, depiction of how happiness and success have been portrayed in the past.

Lesson #2: The Emerging Kaleidoscope of Success Today

By contrast, the workforce today is blossoming with diversity and dynamism. The emerging face of American success is multidimensional, multilayered, and multishaped.

Multidimensional. The American workforce is changing—fast. Overall, women now hold more American jobs than men, and that gender gap is expected to grow to ten million by 2030. Also, for the first time in history, the Department of Labor reports that the majority of workers hired today are people of color, led by Black and brown women.

Multilayered. The widespread belief that our lives are divided into *work* and *life* that we all somehow try to *balance* is misleading. Even the idea of a *job* is becoming irrelevant. As we just saw with Trevor Boffone, and I'll discuss in more detail in chapter 3, 90 percent of people now say they have more than one job; most people have up to five.

Some of those jobs are ones that economists don't even count as work, yet ordinary people do.

A more accurate picture of how we spend our time includes a *main job*, a *side job*, and a *care job*, like caring for young children or aging parents. This book then introduces two new terms. The first is *hope job*—something people do in the hope that it becomes bigger, like writing a screenplay or selling jewelry on Etsy. The second is one of the larger revelations of the Work Story Project. Every person I spoke with said they spend a meaningful percentage of their time battling unseen forces. These specters include self-doubt, discrimination, money, and mental health. I call these invisible time sucks *ghost jobs*, and the stories behind them, in chapter 3, are haunting.

Finally, *multishaped*. As the stories of Brijette Peña, Troy Taylor, and Meroë Park make clear, the idea of a traditional *career* that follows a linear *path* has also been obliterated. It's not just that we have multiple sources of income and work unconventional hours (which we do); it's not even that we change roles faster and are forced to learn new skill sets sooner (which we are); it's that the very idea that our identity is based on committing to a field of work at some point and sticking with that work for decades has been irreversibly eroded.

The most valuable skill today is no longer *how to have a career.*

It's *how not to have a career.*

My data show that we go through a breathtaking number of workquakes in our lives—at least twenty. Those workquakes start earlier, continue later, and happen more frequently than most people think. As I'll show in chapter 2, more than half of these workquakes aren't even initiated at work—they begin with our families, our bodies, or our minds. Meanwhile, the number of workquakes is increasing with each generation—and is higher among people of diverse backgrounds—which means their frequency is only going to grow.

The bottom line: The traditional stories we've been telling about success no longer apply. And yet, we've not refreshed them with new stories.

Which leads to the final takeaway.

Lesson #3: Success Is a Story You Write Yourself

We need a new way to talk about work—one that doesn't generalize our experience but individualizes it. One that doesn't force us to compare ourselves to rigid standards that no longer exist but personalizes our experience for the fluid realities we all face. One that encourages us to ask—as often as we wish—*What makes me happy today? What fits my life at this moment? What should I do, as the poet Mary Oliver put it, with my "one wild and precious life?"*

Fortunately, a new approach has been emerging. It comes from a group of scholars steeped in contemporary psychology, neuroscience, and philosophy. It's called *narrative career construction.*

The premise is simple: The biggest impediment to a meaningful life is not what you don't know about work; it's what you don't know about yourself. Specifically, it's understanding the underlying themes of your life. You can bounce from job to job; you can shift from field to field; but if you don't tap into the earliest tensions, frustrations, and longings of your life—that personal scripture that's unique only to you—you'll never be happy.

The themes of that scripture stretch back to your earliest childhood. They're rooted in the values—positive and negative—you learned from your parents. They're grounded in the qualities you admired in your role models, the environments you were drawn to, the deepest tensions you've been trying to resolve since before you could think.

No one but you knows the answers to these questions.

Only you can crack your own vault.

Which is why only you can write your own story of success.

But how can you learn to do this?

There are options out there. You can hire a counselor; you can dig into the research; you can wing it.

Or you can meet the people gathered in this book and, like me, be emboldened by the richness of their experience and the courage of their choices. I think of these people as the most comprehensive informational interview ever assembled. And the collective wisdom of their stories offers something that I believe is desperately needed: a tool kit for discovering your own work story.

A road map to authoring your own life.

I lay out that road map in three sections. The first busts the three biggest lies of modern work. The second embraces the one truth. The third lays out the six questions to ask in a workquake.

To be clear, I didn't go looking for this map. But it emerged as the single most valuable takeaway from my conversations. You might be skeptical, and that's understandable. You might be thinking, *I'm not a storyteller; how can I tell the story of my life?* and that's fine, too.

But the truth is: You're already telling the story of your life. You're probably just not telling it as well as you could.

This book is the guide for the most consequential story you'll ever tell.

The story of what makes you a success.

I

THE THREE LIES
ABOUT WORK

CHAPTER 1

Lie #1: You Have a Career

The (Short) Rise and (Rapid) Fall of the Career

siah Warner grew up in Bunkie, Louisiana, population 4,656. "Whites lived on one side of the railroad tracks; Blacks lived on the other." The local post office featured a mural called *Cotton Pickers* and Isiah, indeed, picked cotton every summer.

"I was terrible at it, because you were supposed to just grab the bolls and keep on going. But I'm such a meticulous person that I would pick all the seeds out."

He made five dollars a day.

"My first mentors were those cotton fields," he said. "My hands would be bloody, and I don't like bugs. But the caterpillars would crawl all over me and cry out, *Go to college!*"

But how? Neither of Isiah's parents went to high school, and his segregated school had no science labs, no calculus classes, and only six-year-old textbooks. "The fancy would use the textbooks, and when they became outdated, they'd pass them on to us."

Fortunately, the local, historically Black university offered a full scholarship to the valedictorian of Isiah's school, and he won it. Isiah thrived in college. He met his wife and majored in chemistry. When he graduated, he accepted a job in Seattle at a contractor for the Atomic Energy Commission. He had never been on an airplane.

Once on the job, though, Isiah was stymied by discrimination and plagued by self-doubt. "I'm sure you've heard of impostor syndrome," he said. "No matter what I accomplished, I always felt like they were going to find out about my background."

Isiah told his boss he wanted to quit. But the supervisor, himself an Asian American sensitized to being an outsider, had another idea. "You need to get a PhD. When I explain things to other employees, they ask me questions. When I explain something to you, you get it the first time."

Isiah earned his doctorate at the University of Washington in three years instead of the usual five. He was offered a job at Bell Labs in New Jersey but turned it down because on the day he visited there were eight inches of snow on the ground. He opted for academia instead. "I knew if I wasn't around students, I wouldn't be happy."

Isiah moved his family to Texas A&M, where again he was denied resources, promotions, even a lab, because of discrimination. He soon left for Emory. "A small private university in a community like Atlanta that had an elite Black population was appealing."

A decade later, Isiah was lured back to Louisiana with an endowed chair at LSU. Of the school's forty highest-ranked professors, Isiah was the only Black person. LSU had given three Black people PhDs in chemistry before he arrived; he's since awarded PhDs to one hundred. He has more than three hundred eighty peer-reviewed publications and is a worldwide expert in fluorescence. He received a presidential award of excellence from Bill Clinton.

Yet when he named a group of new compounds *GUMBOS*, an

acronym for *group of uniform materials based on organic salts*, he was denounced by a reviewer. "Despite the well-known sense of humor of the author, to call these compounds GUMBOS is ridiculous."

"Now what he doesn't know," Isiah said, "is that *gumbo* is an African American word. Part of my rationale was to set an example. I'm not the kind of person who complains, but that was racism. I'm working with two colleagues—we're probably the three most prominent analytical chemists in the country of any race—to write an article about the lack of Blacks in our field."

But while chemistry is Isiah's profession, his life's work is becoming the role model he lacked as a child. The man who was mentored by cotton fields spends two thirds of his time mentoring scientists of color. "Let me explain in the words of a former student, who's now a professor. She said, 'You love working with students more than you love science.' When she said that, I was offended. But when I thought about it, I realized she was right. I love helping young people find their Yellow Brick Road. I think of myself as Dorothy."

And does Dorothy still think, *There's no place like home*?

"When I first moved back to Baton Rouge," Isiah said, "I bought a house. I wanted to impress my mother, so I invited her for a visit. She looked in all the closets, opened all cabinets, then sat down at the kitchen table. I thought she would be blown away, but she hadn't said a word. Then she leaned over. 'Son, I've spent my whole life cleaning houses. I've never even been in a house as nice as yours.' I started to cry. That's when I knew I was no longer an impostor."

Work = Numbers + Words

Perhaps our greatest failing about work is that we've left such a vital part of our lives largely to the realm of number crunchers. Economists define work as *the time and effort we spend meeting our needs and wants.* Fair enough. But talk to actual people, and they tell a far more emotional story.

The first question I asked in every interview was, *What's the first word you think of when I say work?* The answers were rich, varied, and evocative. *Passion. Purpose. Exhausted. Growth. Commitment. Pain. Serendipity. Persistence. Dreadful. Justice. Heart.*

The most revealing part of these answers: Only a few people mentioned what they do; the vast majority mentioned how they feel about what they do. Specifically, a third of people chose a word that described their work (*union, manager, music, education*), while two thirds chose a word that expressed their feelings about their work (*joy, inspi-*

First Word

What We Do	How We Feel
• Union • Crime Scene	• Pleasure • Accomplishment
• Manager • Planning	• Joy • Excitement
• Music • Comedy	• Passion • Craziness
• Forests • Education	• Fun • Inspiration
• Writing • Politics	• Pain • Heart

ration, tiresome, life). The largest single group—44 percent—used a positive word; 9 percent used a negative word.

Even considering that these are people who like what they do, the overall message is clear: the story we tell about our work is more important than the work itself.

This takeaway leads to the first lesson of the Work Story Project.

WORK = NUMBERS + WORDS

Most of the conversations we have about work revolve around numbers—hours, years, salaries, benefits, productivity, profits, output, efficiency. Yet most of the meaning we take from work comes from words—purpose, happiness, pride, connection, freedom, dignity, service.

The sad truth is that in the public discourse about work in America today, we over-rely on numbers and under-rely on words.

Too much math, not enough literature.

Let's go back to the beginning to understand how we ended up in this quagmire. And let's start with some numbers. For 95 percent of human history, work did not occupy anywhere near the sacred place it occupies today. Most people worked on the land and had no other choices. The historian Joyce Appleby notes that it took 100 percent of the working hours of 80 percent of the people to produce enough food to feed perhaps 90 percent of the population. Even then, famines were common, slavery was widespread, and starvation was routine.

Sure enough, the story that people told about work reflected this misery. The most influential story about work ever written—the Garden of Eden—was openly hostile to labor. Work was a punishment for defying the divine. Other ancient cultures were hardly more positive. The ancient Greek word for slavery, *doulevo*, is the root for both the ancient and Modern Greek words for *work*. The Roman word for *business, negotium*, means *not an enjoyable activity*. The French word *travail* (as well as the Spanish word *trabajo*) comes from the Latin word for *torture*. The English word *office* derives from the Latin for *duty*. For as long as we've been telling stories about work, work has had a bad name.

This dreary outlook existed for thousands of years, until it began to change in the premodern era. Beginning around the fifteenth century, people in the West started to believe that they could shape their own lives. Instead of being controlled by their environment, they could start to control it. They could have a say in what they did. Historian Peter Bernstein calls this moment the *invention of curiosity*. "The ability to define what happens in the future and to choose among alternatives lies at the heart of contemporary societies."

Once again, the change was led by numbers. Though we hardly remember it, the math at the heart of contemporary work was largely invented during this early modern era. Numbers were not a major part of life before 1500. There was little use of zero, no long division, and no multiplication. The fifteenth century saw the invention of double-entry bookkeeping; the sixteenth century the plus, minus, and equal signs, as well as algebra; the seventeenth century forecasting, probability, and chance. All this flowering of math was made possible by an increase in agricultural productivity that allowed people to feel less threatened by change and more willing to take risk.

These breakthroughs in math were accompanied by equal breakthroughs in literature. Traditional accounts of the emergence of capitalism often leave out this critical development: The rise of numeracy was helped along by the rise of literacy. The same span that saw all those numerical inventions also saw literary ones: the printing press, the memoir, the novel, the newspaper.

All these milestones had the same effect: they gave more people opportunities to control their own lives and more tools to do so. The rise of capitalism opened the door to work lives other than farming; the growth of cities introduced lifestyles that were more literary and cultured; the age of discovery allowed people to set off for the New World to reinvent themselves.

Not everyone welcomed these changes, of course; millions were wrested from their homelands and shipped off to the New World against their will. By the nineteenth century, though, the impact of these trends had become clear. The West shifted from being an agricultural economy to an industrial one, from Work 1.0 to Work 2.0. As work opportunities evolved, people began looking for new ways to earn money and new ways to talk about it. With those changes came a new idea—and a new word—one that had never existed before but would soon shape every conversation about work going forward.

Career.

"This Is America. You Get to Choose"

Issa Spatrisano is the third of seven children in an Irish Catholic family in Kawkawlin, Michigan. Her mother was a public health nurse. "She worked weekends, had all those children, but also taught new moms how to breastfeed." Her father drove a truck for Coca-Cola and was laid off in his fifties. "I remember that look in his eyes when he told us. It made me understand that you can't control the narrative."

Also, that she wasn't meant for a corporation.

"I love chaotic environments, but I was always the peacemaker at home. I was the one who said, 'Can't we resolve this and move on?'"

Issa liked team sports for the same reason, so she enrolled at Western Michigan University expecting to be a high school basketball coach. But during a semester abroad in Germany, she fell in love with a new, chaotic environment—international diplomacy. She triple majored in history, political science, and German studies, and when her girlfriend, Jamie, took a job in Alaska, Issa followed and applied to graduate programs. To pay off her student loans, she visited AmeriCorps. "I think I'd be good at teaching English as a second language," she told the interviewer.

"Do you have any experience?"

"No."

"Then why do you think you'd be good at it?"

"To be honest, I don't know. But you don't know, either. When's your next class? Let me go in for fifteen minutes. If I bomb, then we'll both know."

Fifteen minutes later, the students knew the difference between *I am*, *you are*, and *she is*, and Issa had a job. "Alaska has one of the most diverse zip codes in the country. Our public school has over a hundred languages. It was the perfect job for a year."

Except at the end of that year she was rejected by all four graduate schools she applied to.

"That's when my life took a drastic turn. I was standing in the classroom when a woman walked in. 'Are you Issa? I'm the director of the refugee resettlement program for the state of Alaska. Our clients keep telling me you're the best teacher they've ever had. I want you to run our education program.'"

Issa ran that program, along with a few others, for the next six years. "I quickly realized I didn't want to study international relations anymore. I love a chaotic environment; nothing is more chaotic than a refugee resettlement program." Soon she was recruited to run the entire resettlement program for the state. At thirty-two, she had a $3.5 million budget with 411 cases from ninety-five different countries.

"We teach them cultural orientation. We coach them on how to buy groceries and survive the weather. One time I picked up a family at the airport and they looked worried. 'How do you grow things here with all that salt on the ground?' They had never seen snow."

In return, they taught her about leadership. Issa hires only former refugees now. She works out of the smallest office to give others more credit. And after she pushed her clients to pursue higher education and they confessed they were worried about their English, Issa volunteered to read every paper they had to submit *for the rest of their lives*. A decade later, Issa still spends ten hours a week making sure her one-time students know the difference between *I am*, *you are*, and *she is*.

And together Issa and her clients were scripting a new narrative of the country they shared.

"In June 2013, the Defense of Marriage Act was before the Supreme Court," Issa said. "I'm a political junkie, and I woke up ready to check my computer. But people were already texting me and celebrating." She went to work intending to say nothing. "I always kept my private life to myself."

But as soon as she arrived, one of her colleagues came running up to her in the hallway.

"He was Somali, and I thought he was going to ask about a client. But he reached out and took my hands in his. 'Today is an important day for your family,' he said. I didn't know what to say. 'You know, I come from a place where discrimination is real,' he continued. 'I've seen what happens when we pit one person against another. I'm Muslim, and it's illegal in my country to have sexual relations with someone of the same sex. You get caught; you get killed. But I've been given the gift to come to this country where everyone is equal. And today your family is equal to mine.'"

Issa was speechless.

"I went to my car and started crying. That conversation changed me. I realized that by not fully being who I was that I hadn't done them right. I hadn't shown them what our country could be. Now that I'm pregnant, they're throwing me a baby shower. They say things like, 'Do we call Jamie your wife?' I say, 'You can call her Jamie. You can call her my wife. This is America. You get to choose.'"

Here Comes the Career

After undergoing no meaningful changes for millennia, the world of work underwent three massive changes in the century and a half after 1850. From agricultural to industrial (1.0 to 2.0), industrial to knowledge (2.0 to 3.0), and knowledge to network (3.0 to 4.0). While that story is fairly well-known, what's far less known—and certainly less appreciated—is that each of those changes in what we do was accompanied by an equally titanic shift in how we talk about what we do.

Each change in numbers brought a change in words.

There's no better illustration of this evolution than the rise and fall of the word *career*.

Before 1800, almost no one used that word. There was no reason to. As we've seen, most people lived where they worked, worked where they lived, and did the same thing for their entire lives.

The word *career* itself, which derives from the Latin *carrus*, or *char-iot*, was first used in the sixteenth century to refer to *running a course*, as in a racetrack. A planet careered around a sun just as a chariot careered around a track. It wasn't until the rise of capitalism that the word started to take on its modern meaning of *running the course of one's life*. Dozens of books published in the early 1800s used career to mean one's professional identity, as in your *business career*, your *literary career*, or your *political career*.

That usage grew over the next century as virtually everyone had their work lives upended. Once more, the numbers are staggering. Factories quadrupled in the thirty years after the Civil War, and their size ballooned—from an average of two hundred workers in 1865 to fifteen thousand at the first Ford factory in 1915. All of these workers had to be supervised, so an entirely new form of thought—*management science*—emerged from the work of an intense, humorless Philadelphia engineer named Frederick Winslow Taylor. The resulting boom of time clocks and efficiency metrics represented, in the words of one observer, the triumph of the *mathematized world*. It was rule by numbers.

Invention also exploded. In the seven decades before 1870, the US Patent Office recognized 118,000 inventions; in the four decades after, that pace increased twentyfold. Those patents included the backbone of a new way of life (as well as the heart of the stories my grandfather would later tell me)—the light bulb, the steam boiler, the elevator, the sewing machine, the vacuum cleaner.

Those inventions helped invert the country. As the reaper and tractor boosted farm production, droves of people fled their family farms. Eleven million Americans—nearly a third of the country—relocated from rural areas to cities in the fifty years after the Civil War; another twenty-five million joined them from overseas. The population of urban areas tripled during that period. By 1920, for the first time ever, more Americans lived in cities than in rural areas.

This upheaval created an unprecedented crisis. On one hand, cities were completely unprepared for this influx. In 1890, half the residential buildings in New York City were overcrowded tenements; homicide, suicide, and alcoholism soared. On the other hand, millions of new jobs were being created in fields that never even existed before, like communications (telegraph, telephone), manufacturing (steel, automobiles), finance (banking, Wall Street), and leisure (travel, theater).

The result was a gap: Workers needed jobs; companies needed employees. But no mechanism existed to connect the two.

Enter a largely forgotten man named Frank Parsons.

Born in New Jersey in 1854 to a long line of doctors and lawyers, Parsons himself never held a single job for very long. He was a railroad engineer, a teacher, a lawyer, and a textbook writer. He never married, and died penniless. One reason for his poverty is that late in his life, while living in Boston, he walked away from lucrative work to devote himself to the public good. He became convinced that the way Americans worked was benefiting plutocrats over workers.

With the backing of the wife of one of those plutocrats, Pauline Shaw, Parsons opened the Vocation Bureau in 1908. Its mission: to educate the underprivileged, the immigrant, and the rural refugee on the importance of making good career choices. "The building of a career is quite as difficult a problem as the building of a house," he wrote, "yet few ever sit down with pencil and paper, with expert opinion and counsel."

Parsons was not the first to have this idea. Plato had written about discovering your life's work (as long as you weren't a woman or an enslaved person); books on this topic had appeared periodically over the centuries; guides were published using quack, quasi sciences like phrenology and physiognomy—analyzing one's skull, hairiness, or voice tone—to determine suitable jobs.

Parsons's timing was better and his tools more refined. The US in the early twentieth century was awash in programs to fix social ills. These programs did everything from helping children (playgrounds and kindergartens), to workers (unions and vacations), to women (custody and suffrage). Parsons's insight was to harness this energy to help people find work; in the process he became known as *the father of vocational guidance*. In effect, he invented the career.

The Parsons method had three steps:

1. Know yourself—use a series of questions to identify your character.

2. Know the workplace—use a list of companies to identify your ideal job.

3. Make a match.

Parsons had huge blind spots. His process was designed to work only once, only on boys, and only on select industries. He pathologized indecision: anyone who didn't know what they wanted to do had a "personality problem or defect." But as Taylor did for management, Parsons scientized the career. From then on, finding a job was less about hunches and neighbors, and more about logic and objectivity.

Overnight, Parsons's approach took hold. Schools began offering career guidance; Harvard introduced the first career counseling program; and the first career training association appeared. From nonexistence a century earlier, the career quickly became the dominant way to talk about work. The next big breakthrough was the visual man-ifestation of that idea—another new invention with ruinous reper-cussions.

The *résumé*.

"I Would Give It All Back"

Eric Vélez-Villar never told anyone his secret. Certainly not when he was an army brat. Eric's father was a military police officer from Puerto Rico; his mother was a Spanish flight attendant. The two met in Ger-many, lived all over, before settling in San Juan. "I was a perfection-ist," Eric said. "I wanted to live up to my father's expectations. I just wanted him to say, *I'm proud of you*."

As a boy, Eric dreamed of becoming a pilot, and he enrolled in college to study aviation. "Then one of those pivotal moments that happens in my life." A Puerto Rican independence group launched a rocket at the local FBI office where Eric's father was working; the direc-tor decided to beef up security.

At eighteen, Eric was hired for the overnight shift. "I would go to all the desks, put confidential trash in big plastic bags, then go into the basement and shred them." On his first day, his boss gave him a speech. "If a terrorist breaks in, lock yourself in the vault. There's a revolver there for you—and a sledgehammer. Your job is to smash all the crypto equipment."

One Friday night, Eric volunteered for what he called the "worst job in the FBI," keeping watch over some copy machine repair people. An agent came in. "Hey, Eric, I just posted a job in computers. You should put in for it."

"But I don't know anything about computers."

"I can teach you computers. What I can't teach you is what you already have—being here on Friday night when no one else would."

Eric started in the IT department and four years later made the rare jump from hourly worker to agent. His first assignment was in McAllen, Texas, listening to wiretaps of imprisoned Mexican drug lords. "My Spanish language skills got me this assignment, but I swear to you, on my first night, I didn't understand a single word they said. I cried three times."

He eventually cracked their slang, transferred back to Puerto Rico, and later moved his family to Maryland to work as a supervisor at the DEA. Two years later, another pivotal event occurred: Planes flew into the World Trade Center. Eric was sent to the fifth floor of the Hoover Building in downtown Washington, DC.

"People were running around everywhere. I was told, 'Go into Room E. You see all those boxes? They're letters written to Director Mueller. Read every single one and look for tips.'"

The letters were heartbreaking, he said. *Dear Mr. Director, My name is Bob Smith. I'm a retired Marine, but I still wear a size 32. I'll do anything. Please take me. You don't even have to pay me.*

After 9/11, the FBI pivoted to become more focused on gathering intelligence around terrorism, and Eric pivoted with them. He moved back and forth to California twice. He ran the No Fly List. And in 2014, Director Mueller appointed him to run intelligence for the entire FBI, one of six top civilian jobs in the entire bureau. He had gone from the graveyard shift to the highest echelons of American law enforcement.

A few years later, facing forced retirement, Eric was hired to run security for Walt Disney Parks. He earned six times what he did in government. He was on top of the world.

And that's when the secret caught up with him.

One night, Eric and his wife were watching *Leaving Neverland*, the HBO documentary in which two men accused Michael Jackson of sexually abusing them as boys.

"'That happened to me,' I told my wife. Those words, once they came out of my mouth, I could never put them back in."

The revelation started Eric down a painful path of trying to uncover how he was groomed and abused by an older man when he was a boy; how he blamed his parents for knowing ("Didn't you notice my brothers were home all those nights and I wasn't?"), how he fought his stigma by joining the toughest organization he could find; how he channeled his shame into a desperate search for approval.

"I could be in a room with fifteen people; fourteen could be thinking, *Eric is just amazing*. But if one person didn't say anything, I was laser focused on trying to convince them. It was very exhausting."

Disney was generous. They gave him time off and helped him find a therapist. But in the end, Eric gave up his $800,000-a-year salary and moved with his wife to Arizona, where they lived on his pension.

"I look at these plaques on my wall," he said. "I was given the President's Award for Distinguished Federal Civilian Service, the highest honor the federal government can give a career employee. I would give it all back. I walked through life and would see somebody who works at a car wash or a mechanic shop. Those jobs that are honorable but don't make a ton of money. They go home to their modest houses, eat dinner, play with their kids. On the surface, they had none of what I had. Yet I envied the hell out of them.

"I used to have this traditional definition of success," he went on. "How much money you made; how much influence you had. But right now, my definition of success is to be a successful father and a successful husband and to finally, deep down, feel good about myself."

The Triumph of the Career

In 1482, a young Italian sought a job at the court of Ludovico Sforza, the Duke of Milan. Aware of the regent's penchant for war, the supplicant sent a ten-point letter boasting of his ability to design bridges, cast bombs, and build covered wagons that "shoot inflammable substances." He threw in that he could also carve sculptures in marble and bronze. "Likewise, in painting, I can do anything you want."

That supplicant's name was Leonardo da Vinci.

That letter is now considered the first résumé.

In the same way that most people never thought of their work as a career, they also never thought of writing a résumé. The few parallels that exist are descriptive letters like the one Leonardo wrote that included little more than biographical information.

Not until the mid-twentieth century did the evolution of work require such an accounting of one's work life. Again, the numbers tell a dramatic story. No sooner did factories displace farms than offices displaced factories. The front line of labor shifted from metalwork to paperwork, from people who shower after work to people who shower before. In 1900, 38 percent of the American labor force worked in agriculture, 31 percent in manufacturing, 31 percent in services. A century later, agriculture had dropped to 3 percent and manufacturing dipped below 20 percent, while service and professional workers ballooned to 80 percent. Women, whose participation in the workforce tripled, led this change.

A new language was needed. The word *economy* entered the lexicon after the Great Depression. The term *white collar*, popularized as a sneer by Upton Sinclair in 1919, became popular in the 1950s, as the bleached, starched fashion pieces became the symbol of nonmanual work. The phrase *knowledge workers*, invented by management guru Peter Drucker in 1961, came to define the age.

As before, the change in numbers and words brought with it a new way of helping people find work. Backed by a spate of quasi-scientific personality tests like Humm-Wadsworth and Myers-Briggs, as well as theories that people's work lives *developed* through a series of *stages*, a new paradigm emerged: every individual had a fixed personality, could be divinely matched with the perfect employer, and would proceed along an orderly trajectory largely defined by corporate hierarchies.

The vertical career was the only career.

It's hard to overstate the dominance of this worldview. In 1952, a third of corporations used personality testing; by 1954 the number was over 60 percent. Half of all companies screened employees' *wives*, with one in five applicants not getting offers because their spouses flunked these screening protocols. These people-sorting devices provided the scientific cover for the segregated, sexist, starched-shirt career path.

And make no mistake: a path it was. As three scholars of work characterized the new consensus, a career was "a pattern of work involving intense commitment to and continuous engagement with the occupational world, along with striving for upward mobility and achievement of external markers of success." Think about how restrictive that view is: There's no adjusting your priorities, no valuing service over money, no pulling back, even temporarily, to raise children, support a spouse, or serve your country. The only choice is *intense, continuous striving* for *upward mobility* and *external success.*

We're all rats, and we're all racing.

No single creation had more influence over this worldview than the résumé. As the field of hiring ramped up in the early 1900s, new tools were needed that went beyond forms and recommendations. Employers began asking applicants for a page containing details of their education, employment history, and skills. These documents were variously referred to as *statements of experience, business records,* or *data sheets.*

The term *résumé,* from the French for *summary,* first became popular in the 1930s. In February 1938, to cite just one example, a prospective employee would send the J. Walter Thompson Company a "short résumé of my life." After the war, the term gradually spread. The first magazine article to use the word *résumé* appeared in 1946; the first want ad in 1952; the first dictionary in 1961. Two manuals on how to write résumés were published in the 1950s, seven in the 1960s, seventy in the 1970s, and 156 in the 1980s.

This story of the résumé would be a curious sidebar to the history of work if it weren't for how profound its side effects have been. The résumé normalized—even fetishized—the linear career. One was expected to move in an uninterrupted, progressive line from school to school, job to job, from adolescence to retirement. If Parsons pathologized the otherwise normal behavior of indecision, the résumé pathologized the otherwise normal behavior of making nontraditional choices, prioritizing anything other than professional advancement, staying too long in a job or too short.

If you deviate from the norm, it will hurt your résumé.

And your résumé is your life.

To be fair, the résumé did have some benefits. As long as you made changes on an acceptable timeline, the résumé did accommodate a new development, one that Parsons would have found unfathomable: job changing. The number of books about finding the perfect job exploded from fifty in the 1960s to two hundred fifty in the 1970s. The most famous of these was *What Color Is Your Parachute?* by Richard Bolles, a genial Episcopalian priest who himself lost his job and eventually found his calling counseling other priests about finding theirs. Published in the 1970s, the book went on to sell ten million copies.

But even Bolles couldn't dent the cult of the career. Instead, what ultimately challenged it were shifts in the economy. By century's end, a host of new forces—globalization, digitization—ushered in a decline of the traditional career. The number of factory workers shrank by a quarter in the 1980s; the number of white-collar workers who lost their jobs grew by the same number in the 1990s. The days of the paternalistic company providing an endless, upward career track were over. The linear career was dead.

In its place, a host of new words joined the conversation—*downsizing, outsourcing, restructuring*—and an abundance of alternative ways of talking about work—*freelancer, free agent, flex worker.*

Another new lexicon was dawning.

"I Want People to Know You Can Talk about Anything"

Maysoon Zayid knows how to deliver a punch line. "In the Oppression Olympics, I would win a gold medal. I'm Palestinian. I'm Muslim. I'm a woman of color. I'm divorced and disabled. And . . . I live in New Jersey."

The youngest of four daughters, Maysoon was born in the Garden State to Palestinian immigrants. "My dad was a peddler who drove a Scooby-Doo van and sold electronics, bedspreads, and watches." Her mother was a medical technician.

"The doctor who delivered me was drunk, and I lost oxygen at birth. As a result, I have cerebral palsy. My brain is damaged. My muscles and nerve joints ache nonstop. I've been in chronic pain since I was conscious. Even now I can sleep only three hours a night before I wake up shaking."

Her parents never considered her a burden, she said.

"Anxieties don't exist in immigrant families. You just work. There's no, *I'm tired. I need a self-care day*. If my sisters mopped, I mopped. If they went to public school, my parents sued for me to go. They couldn't afford physical therapy, so they sent me to dance class instead. And I loved it. My school took us to *Evita* when I was eight; that's when I decided I wanted to tap-dance on Broadway."

When she was a high school senior, Maysoon performed "Wind beneath My Wings" on pointe in the school talent show. "And the crowd went apeshit for like ten minutes. There was no internet, so it couldn't go viral. But that was my Lady Gaga *A Star Is Born* moment."

Maysoon enrolled in Arizona State to study theater; after she graduated, her teacher sent her to New York to join an elite theater troupe. She had role models—Dolly Parton ("She's sparkly, multi-talented, and started an amusement park. Who wouldn't want to be her!") and Lucille Ball ("Desi Arnaz reminded me of my dad. He was an immigrant who was always yelling—not in an abusive way, but 'Oh, my God, the tomatoes are burned!'"). But none who shared her disability.

"Then I saw Richard Pryor. He was in a wheelchair; he was shaking. Yet I was listening to his story and not distracted by his disability."

Maysoon started doing stand-up; she opened for Chris Rock and Dave Chapelle. "And then 9/11 happens. Suddenly no one found Muslims funny anymore. We had forebears who had this problem—Danny Thomas and Jamie Farr—but now we were straight-up jihadists."

Then a friend called. "What do you think about doing an Arab comedy show to combat all the negative images?" They opened in a tiny club in Manhattan the following spring. "It was super grimy. A mouse ran across my foot. But the audience was wrapped around the block."

The two of them created a show called *Arabs Gone Wild* and began touring the country, reaching venues of fifteen thousand people. They were invited to the Middle East. But when the show was asked to visit Saudi Arabia, Maysoon refused to go. "I'm not going to entertain in a country where women have to ask permission to leave their house."

What seemed like the *wrong* professional move turned out to be the move that changed her life. Maysoon's decision not to go to Saudi Arabia meant she was home when NBC called and invited her to go on Keith Olbermann's show *Countdown* to talk about Saudi Arabia.

Maysoon hated her performance; the internet hated it more. "They said I was an honor killing gone wrong." But Olbermann loved her and invited her back. "He was the greatest mentor anyone can dream of having," she said. "He taught me to listen; he taught me to be prepared. And after my second appearance, he said, 'I want you to be a regular. But I'm never going to bring you on to discuss Muslim issues or disability issues. I want people to know you can talk about anything.'"

Maysoon appeared ten times a month. She was invited to give a

TED talk; she wrote a memoir; she became a recurring character on *General Hospital*. And finally, at the Arab-American Comedy Festival in 2019, forty years after she saw *Evita*, she tap-danced on Broadway.

"In that moment, I realized that the little kid longing for people who looked like me had become the person that other kids could look up to. But I didn't do it alone. Everyone who has ever opened a door or taken a chance or insisted their children go to dance class instead of physical therapy deserves credit. They were the wind beneath my wings."

There Goes the Career

The most important thing to appreciate about the world of work today is that it's meaningfully different from any world of work that came before it. We're all trying to survive in a business environment that's more global, a family environment that's more chaotic, and a stress environment that's more round-the-clock. To think of work primarily in terms of a single employer, a single profession, even a single skill set is deeply misguided.

The world is no longer linear; to expect work to be linear is a mistake.

A brief look at some numbers helps explain. In a little over 150 years, we've gone from one undersea cable running the telegraph to 380 undersea cables running the internet; in a little more than sixty years, we've gone from one satellite in the sky to 7,500; in a little beyond thirty years, we've gone from information spreading at 280 megabytes per second to 178 terabits per second—that's twenty-three million times faster.

As happened in every similar transition in the past, all this change has created millions of jobs in fields that never previously existed—AI, VR, esports, blockchain, cybersecurity, carbon scrubbing, 3D printing, autonomous vehicles, wearables, edibles, the metaverse. Is it any wonder that the average worker today holds twice as many jobs as their parents, or that three times as many people over sixty-five are working?

As the pace of life has quickened, the pace of work has quickened.

And yet, during similar inflection points in history, when the numbers around work changed, the words around work changed, too—as did the tools for how to find work. But that hasn't happened this time. We're still using outdated words and outdated tools. Neither the old-fashioned résumé nor its online facsimiles have kept up—they still rely on the reverse-chronological listings of employment. Skills tests don't work—they fail to acknowledge that our priorities shift over time and our skills evolve. Even the word *career* itself has lost value—it suggests we're all pursuing a shared dream.

In his final book, *Chronicles of a Liquid Society*, the great Italian writer and social critic Umberto Eco observes that contemporary life is marked by "the crisis of 'grand narratives.'" That remark perfectly describes the crisis of work. There is no grand narrative anymore. It's been replaced by the grandeur of individual narratives, each with its own singularity and shape.

Which is why, as paradoxical as it seems, an essential skill in crafting your own narrative of work is to spend less time focusing on work itself—or even the periods of stability when you do that work—and spend more time focusing on the periods of instability. The moments when things go wrong, when your inner voice starts to speak up, when your personal scripture begins to assert itself and suggest it's time for a change.

To understand those moments, we need yet another new word that fully captures the meaning behind all the fast-moving numbers of today.

Workquake.

CHAPTER 2

Lie #2: You Have a Path

How Workquakes Overtook Work

A t the beginning of Jerry Seinfeld's animated *Bee Movie*, Barry B. Benson, a recent graduate of "three days of grade school, three days of high school, and three days of college," who boasts "a perfect report card, all Bs!" arrives for his first day of work at New Hive City. Looking dapper in matching black-and-yellow sweater and sneakers, Barry, voiced by Seinfeld, announces, "I'm glad I took a day and hitchhiked around the hive."

After Dean Buzzwell welcomes the class of 9:15, Trudy, a guide, initiates a tour. "We know that you, as a bee, have worked your whole life to get to the point where you can work your whole life."

"Are we going to pick our job today?" Barry asks.

Trudy describes the various available jobs—pollen jock, scent adjustor, bubble popper.

"But choose carefully," she says. "You'll stay in the job you pick for the rest of your life."

"The same job for the rest of your life?!" Barry says. "That's an insane choice to have to make!"

Everyone today understands on some level that humans are not bees. Our work lives involve lots of changes. In my conversations, I brought up the biggest transformation in the history of work—Work 0.0 to Work 1.0—when humans shifted from hunting and gathering to agriculture around twelve thousand years ago. But not everyone made that switch. Some people settled in one place; they were *sedentists*. Others continued wandering; they were *nomads*. Still more wandered for a time, settled for a time, then wandered again. They were *pastoralists*.

Which are you? I asked.

One in five said *nomad*—they always keep moving. Another one in five said *sedentist*—they find what they like and stick with it. But six in ten said *pastoralist*—they start down one path, stay for a while, and then head down another. If you add nomads and pastoralists together, the percentage of people who believe that work involves a high degree of mobility is 80 percent.

Even accepting that consensus, I still believe that we underestimate the breadth, scope, and pace of that fluidity. I believe that because when I asked everyone I interviewed to count the number of workquakes they'd been through, every single person was aghast. Many were embarrassed, even apologetic.

They shouldn't have been.

The workquake is the signature unit of work today. It's the atom of the atomized work life. I started using the term *workquake* because it grows out of the expression *lifequake* I used in the Life Story Project, the first round of stories I collected that focused on the full spectrum of disruptive life events, from medical emergencies to losing a loved one. Like *lifequake*, *workquake* is value neutral. Some workquakes are voluntary (we take a new job, go back to school), others are involuntary (we lose a job, come down with an illness); some are personal (the birth of a child), others are collective (a pandemic); some begin outside the workplace (a recession), others in our heads (we get antsy and want a change).

A workquake is a moment of disruption, inflection, or reevaluation that redirects our work in a meaningful way. I collected data on three thousand such events. The two biggest takeaways: (1) workquakes are more plentiful, more varied, start earlier, run later, last longer, and touch us more deeply than most people expect; and (2) as destabilizing and scary as workquakes feel when we're in one, they're also invitations to reexamine our priorities and opportunities for growth and renewal. Above all, workquakes are de-storying events that summon us to re-story our lives.

We're going to work our way through all these topics, but let's start with some basic facts.

People usually have their first workquake long before they enter the workforce. I asked everyone, *When was the first time you imagined that something you were interested in might become something that you do?* The average age was 16.2. For people with at least one diversity marker, the answer was a full 2 years earlier than those with none—15.8 versus 17.8—suggesting what would become a theme of my conversations: The work lives of those from underrepresented communities are more volatile than their peers from more conventional communities.

Once those workquakes start, they rarely slow. The average person experiences a workquake every 2.85 years—that's 2 years and 10 months. Women go through workquakes every 2.75 years, which is 22 percent more frequently than men.

The number of workquakes also escalates by generation. Gen Xers go through workquakes 15 percent more frequently than boomers; millennials 45 percent more frequently than Gen Xers. The frequency at which millennials experience workquakes is 67 percent faster than their boomer parents—every 2.24 years compared with 3.74 years.

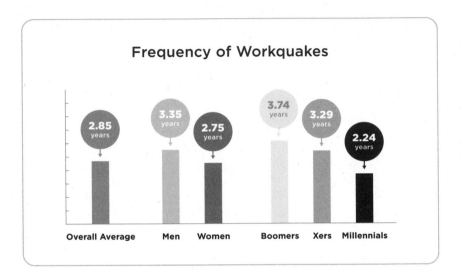

A number of explanations might account for this acceleration. People's work lives might become more stable over time; the Labor Department, for example, says that half of our jobs occur before age twenty-four. But even the department's data show that younger people are staying in jobs for shorter and shorter periods of time. Another reason might be that younger people are more comfortable with change and the growing nonlinear nature of life; data I collected from the Life Story Project indicate that people under forty change residences more frequently and change their religious beliefs more often.

Whatever the mix of reasons, the net effect is the same: the frequency of workquakes is likely to grow as the American economy becomes more dominated by workers who are younger, more female, and more diverse.

How many workquakes do we have in total? If you start the clock at sixteen and stop at, say, seventy-two, which accommodates our longer work lives, the average answer is twenty. For millennials, it's twenty-five. To put those figures into perspective: there are 234 million Americans between sixteen and seventy-two; 82 million of them are going through a workquake at any one time.

That's 35 percent of the country.

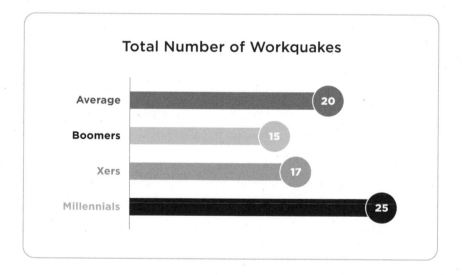

The bright, blinking warning in all these figures is that we simply must begin to think about our work lives as more unsettled and serpentine than we already do. There is no standard path anymore; we're all on a path less traveled. To master this new terrain, we need to say goodbye to some of our more beloved platitudes. That process begins with debunking the four worst pieces of advice about work.

~~Follow Your Bliss~~

Surely the most hallowed piece of wisdom about work over the last generation has been *follow your bliss*. Coined in the 1970s by Joseph Campbell, who specialized in applying lessons from mythology to contemporary life, the phrase has become a watchword of the happiness movement.

Decide what brings you joy, then go for it with single-minded determination.

The problem: This advice applies to almost no one who *is* happy at work and helps almost no one who *wants to be*. A mere one in ten people in my conversations said they followed their bliss. The rest said they took another route entirely. And yet, they still ended up happy.

Todd Krause grew up in a family of small business owners in southeastern Wisconsin. His uncles ran restaurants; his father hauled milk for a dairy; his brother started a siding company. "After being handed a sledgehammer when I was a boy and told to crawl under the hood of a truck and pound out a steering kingpin, I said no way do I want to do this for a living. It's greasy; it's dirty; you touch the wrong thing, you get burned. I wanted to sit in an office somewhere that was clean, cool, and dry."

Todd enrolled at Marquette University on a naval ROTC scholarship. He dropped the program, switched to physics, and then graduated with a degree in finance. "There was definitely a grieving process of letting go of some of those earlier dreams, but ultimately I ended up back where I started—in business."

Todd married his college sweetheart, moved to Chicago, and went to work as a pension analyst at Mercer, the largest employee benefit firm in the US. "I'd be handed a set of facts about somebody's life, read through their pension plan, then calculate what benefits they were eligible for." He was told to leave his personal life at the door. "It was 100 percent business, business, business."

He left after a few years, worked in a family office, and then jumped to an investment company that managed $100 billion in assets. He stayed for the next decade, helping assemble a management team, rebuilding their fund operations, and earning master's degrees in business and accounting. "By then I started to get bored."

After Todd and his wife adopted two children from Korea, he felt even more pressure to make money. "As the sole breadwinner, I had to provide all our income and all our health benefits." He went to work at an investment firm, but it collapsed after 9/11; he became COO of a $2 billion hedge fund management operation, but he had a falling-out with his partner; he became vice president of a Bank of America division that managed $14 billion, but he lost interest in the work.

There was a pattern to Todd's seemingly patternless work life. He'd go to a place with an impressive name on the door (Zacks Investment Management, NAV Consulting, Cortland Capital Market Services), play an increasingly impressive role (controller, director of administration, chief of operations), and then grow increasingly disaffected with the work itself.

"I got to the point where not only did I stop unpacking all my photos and personal belongings in my office, but I started taking less and less of me to the office to begin with. I was always protecting myself from becoming too committed. Work became less about making an impact and more about earning a paycheck."

Finally, when the pandemic forced him to take a break from his routine, Todd made an emotional break, too. He contacted some business brokers he knew, secured financing, and bought a residential cleaning company in northeast Indiana.

"It was a real adjustment for me—and a real improvement. I no longer work seventy hours a week; I work thirty-five. I have people from eight different countries on my team, and I gave all of them a raise. Every day, I touch the lives of forty employees, six hundred customers, and dozens of vendors and local partners—along with their families, it totals five thousand people. Instead of measuring my impact in billions of dollars, now I measure it in thousands of daily interactions."

Considering the indirect route he took back to where he started—running a small business—I asked Todd whether he followed his bliss, discovered his bliss, or made his bliss?

"For a long time I didn't think about bliss. I was an accountant, and being happy wasn't how I thought about work; I was a provider. But what I discovered is that being unhappy at work began to affect my health. I finally got to the point where I realized I needed to make my own happiness, or I would be unhappy forever."

I asked everyone I interviewed a series of questions about the wisdom of identifying what brings you happiness and then pursuing that objective with all your might. Few supported the premise.

For starters, most people begin working as teenagers, when they have little idea of their passion. Using my bingo card for categorization, the most common first jobs were in food and beverage, followed by retail, childcare, and education. Only 11 percent of these people were working in the same field when I spoke with them.

That pattern changes little as people enter young adulthood. I asked everyone, *Is what you're doing today something that you dreamed of doing as a child, a teenager, or a young adult?* Only 38 percent said yes. Sixty percent said no. Meroë Park had no idea she was going to run payroll when she joined the CIA; Brijette Peña had no clue she would start a plant seed company. One of the main reasons *follow your passion* is bad advice is that what your passion is today is unlikely to be what your passion is in the future.

Finally, I asked everyone directly what I asked Todd Krause: *Did you follow your bliss, discover your bliss, or make your bliss?* Only 12 percent said *follow*. Eighty-eight percent chose another option. Of those, *make* was most popular, as how Eric Vélez-Villar had to keep making new dreams as he moved through different roles at the FBI, then Disney, before stepping down to work on his mental health; followed by *discover*, as how Issa Spatrisano discovered a passion for helping refugees after her first love, European studies, was foreclosed to her. Some people chose a combination, but even including those answers, the number of people who said they followed their bliss was still only 16 percent.

By even the most generous interpretation, only one in six people who self-identify as being happy at work said they followed their bliss to get there; the vast majority took another route entirely.

~~Make a Ten-Year Plan~~

OK, so you don't need to follow your bliss, but you definitely need to follow your plan. Everybody knows that advice is true.

Not so fast.

Some people do make plans and follow them, of course. They set out to become doctors, or astronauts, or center fielders for the New

York Yankees, and they succeed! But for far more people, even the best plans go awry. Unannounced events pop up, unforeseen figures appear, unanticipated changes occur. I call these experiences—and the life-changing workquakes they trigger—*butterflies*. They're both the heroes of the nonlinear work life and the enemies of the ten-year plan.

Cathy Heying grew up in a large Catholic family in a small Iowa town. "I'm the youngest of seven; my dad was the oldest of thirteen. I have eighty-three first cousins." Cathy's father drove a gas truck for Amoco; her mother became a disability activist after her first child, born with Down syndrome, was denied Communion. "What I took from her is that it doesn't matter if you're raising six other kids; if there's a fight to be had, you have the fight."

After earning a social work degree, Cathy moved to Kentucky to work with the Christian Appalachian Project. Feeling unwelcome, she and her girlfriend decided to relocate to Denver, but they couldn't afford a car, so they bummed a couch for a few months in Minneapolis. Looking for work, Cathy stopped into Saint Stephen's Catholic church.

"The first thing I saw was a rainbow sticker, and I burst into tears."

She stayed for the next nine years. Cathy loved the church's inclusive politics, but the diocese didn't, so the church had to spin off its social justice arm. Cathy followed, working at a residence for Indigenous women and a shelter for single men. She earned a master's in ministry and bought a motorcycle. Her life was finally stable.

That's when her butterfly appeared.

"One thing that happens at churches all over the world is that people show up and ask for money. But I had people in my office who all told some version of the same story. *I work on this side of town. I have a second shift on the other side of town. I don't get off until eleven o'clock at night and there's no bus service. But my car is broken down and I can't afford to repair it."*

One night, Cathy was smoking outside the shelter when a man named Sidney came up to her. He pointed to his car and asked her to help him push it to a new parking spot. "It was his residence," she said. "When he filled out forms, he listed his address as 1994 Nissan Maxima Drive." Sidney made $203 a month on government support; fixing his car cost $50 an hour. "That might as well be a million dollars," he said.

"I kept thinking, *Minnesota is joked about as being the land of ten thousand nonprofits. We are generous and hardy souls. Somebody needs to do something about this.*

"That's when it hit me," she continued. "This was my burning bush moment. Just total clarity that that somebody was me."

Yet Cathy had a problem: she knew nothing about car repair. But she is her mother's daughter, after all, so Cathy, in her late thirties and already with two degrees, enrolled in a two-year, $18,000-a-year, full-time program at Dunwoody College of Technology to earn an associate's degree in automobile maintenance.

"I had no business being there on a number of levels," Cathy said. "For starters, I was a middle-aged lesbian in a classroom of fourteen eighteen-year-old boys. I had no idea what to do with eighteen-year-old boys when I was an eighteen-year-old girl, much less twenty years later."

Also, her background was in social services. "Does the carburetor really want to change?" she joked.

Cathy struggled. She cried on a few occasions and cursed on a few more. But a teacher took her under his wing, and two years later, Cathy marched across the stage. Then she scraped together funding, formed a board, and opened Lift Garage, which provided automotive repair for needy residents at $15 an hour. In its first ten years, Lift served 1,300 customers, completed 3,000 repairs, and saved customers more than $1.1 million. Cathy was named a CNN Hero.

All because of her butterfly.

"His name was Sidney. He lived on Nissan Maxima Drive. And he's why I'm here right now."

The Magna Carta of the nonlinear age is an obscure academic paper written in 1972 by MIT meteorologist Edward Lorenz. Lorenz's butterfly had appeared ten years earlier when he observed the uneven movement of clouds outside his office window. Unable to identify their pattern, he started running calculations and crystallized the idea that not everything in life is regular and periodic; many things are irregular and nonperiodic. A friend recommended the title "Does the Flap of a Butterfly's Wings in Brazil Set Off a Tornado in Texas?"

The name stuck, and by the time Jeff Goldblum uttered it two decades later in *Jurassic Park*, the *butterfly effect* had gone mainstream.

But does such irregularity apply to work, perhaps the preeminent arena of life that has long been in the thrall of long-term thinking, org charts, multiyear plans, and hierarchical rows of desks?

The answer is yes.

I asked everybody in my interviews who the butterfly was in their story. *Who or what triggered the moment when your work veered from the expected path to the unexpected?* Everyone had an answer.

Half said a person—a teacher, a coworker, a neighbor, "a random guy in a restaurant who handed me his business card." Alton White, the only boy in a Cincinnati home filled with girls, had just performed in the church choir at age twelve when a woman approached him: "Alton, oh my God, you have a gift." He rode her encouragement to a ten-year run as Mufasa in Broadway's *The Lion King*. Dan Gallagher had two butterflies. The first was being called by God in his twenties to enter the priesthood; the second, twenty years later, while working in the Vatican as the pope's chief Latinist, was falling in love with a colleague, which led him to leave the priesthood, start a family, and become a classics professor at Cornell.

A quarter of people said their butterfly was an experience—the death of a loved one, a class they took in college, a diagnosis. Lauren Nichols was nine years old when one of her neighbors in the Florida Everglades murdered his wife and mother-in-law and then turned the gun on himself. "I always wondered what would bring someone to end another life. I knew I needed to work in a field that allowed me to help protect others." Lauren went on to work in national security at the Department of Transportation.

Ben Chancey was running a thriving windshield repair company in Houston with twenty-eight employees when the pandemic forced him to shutter his operation. "Feeling like a houseplant" at home, he reevaluated his life. "I realized how complacent I'd become, how I didn't find the work fulfilling anymore." Ben enrolled in a six-month renewable energy training program and doubled his income as a wind turbine repair specialist at MFG Texas.

The final group said their butterfly was a thing—a movie, lecture, a snapping turtle. Sonali Dev was a technical writer for a pharmaceutical company in Illinois who loved dissecting Bollywood movies with her best friend. When she came down with tuberculosis and was holed up at home with a 102-degree fever, Sonali asked her husband to pick up a book from the library. He came home with *Rosehaven* by Catherine Coulter, "an old-style medieval romance."

"Ten years you've been married to me, and you think this is what I read?"

But then she began reading and stayed up all night. "*Oh my, this is delicious!* I thought. And I have a moment in my feverish state when I know exactly why I'm here on earth."

Today Sonali is one of the country's most widely read writers of Indian American romance novels.

Butterflies come in all shapes and at all times. But the critical detail is that they come at all. When they do, the most important thing is not to follow your plan just because you have a plan.

It's follow your butterfly.

~~Keep Your Personal Life out of Your Work Life~~

The next piece of advice that everyone agrees on these days is to set strict boundaries between work and life. On the surface, who can disagree with this counsel? After all, who among us couldn't do a better job of ensuring that our work lives don't encroach on our personal lives? Now that more of us are working from home, the imperative to wall off our work lives is even greater, right?

Wrong.

The happiest people do the reverse: they understand that their lives are inseparable from their work. For starters, our lives before we even start working play an enormous role in our ability to find happiness at work. From Troy Taylor wanting to fly airplanes as a boy to designing airplanes as a grown-up, to Isiah Warner feeling unmentored as a child to mentoring students as an adult, we all carry our childhood longings into our adult choices.

Every day is Take Your Childhood to Work Day.

That influence only grows as we age. A stirring conclusion of the Work Story Project is that the single biggest influence in our decisions about work—from what jobs we seek to what jobs we accept to what jobs we quit—is our life outside of work. More than half of all workquakes don't begin in the workplace at all; they begin with our families, our bodies, our mindsets.

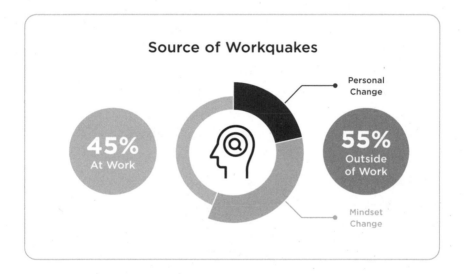

I call these events *nonwork workquakes.* They're still workquakes in that they redirect our work lives, but they're also lifequakes in that they redirect our broader lives, too. Among women and diverse workers, the number of nonwork workquakes is even higher, which suggests that the very idea of separating life from work is a legacy of a time when the workplace was dominated by white men and someone else took care of the laundry, the kids, and the aging parents.

Today, the smartest people know that you can't wall off your work from your life because no wall is strong enough to withstand a health crisis, a relationship crisis, a family crisis, or an identity crisis.

And sometimes that crisis can make us better at our jobs.

Wendy Chisholm grew up in Idaho Falls, Idaho. Her father was a nuclear engineer; her mother was a primary caretaker. "I've always been open about having an emotionally abusive upbringing, because it shaped every decision I made about work."

Wendy's first nonwork workquake occurred when she was twelve and her father brought home a computer. She started programming, mastered BASIC and Pascal, and earned a scholarship to study computer science at Elmhurst College outside Chicago. Once there, she had the next of her nonwork workquakes.

"One of my psychology professors asked me to tutor a student in statistics. I was a very helpful person, so I agreed. But what I didn't know was that the student was blind. I had never been around a blind person before, and I had no idea how to teach advanced math to someone who couldn't see."

So Wendy got creative. "I used Legos to teach bar graphs; I used a stylus to generate braille scatterplots. And the whole time I kept thinking, *There's got to be a way that computers can help with this problem.*"

The student passed his class; Wendy had a new direction. She started volunteering with autistic adults; she became a Special Olympics coach. "My first job out of college was as a computer programmer at the University of Chicago. One day my officemate says, 'Have you read this article in *The Chronicle of Higher Education*?' It was about a professor in Wisconsin whose sole purpose was to develop technology to help people with disabilities."

Wendy went to work with the professor, earned a master's degree in industrial engineering, and joined a team of forty at the World Wide Web Consortium at MIT whose job was to write protocols to make the internet more accessible. The group scripted the first adaptability guidelines covering everything from speech recognition to screen magnification. "I never really thought of the impact I was having; I thought of the problems we were trying to solve."

Then, her next nonwork workquake happened.

Wendy got married and had a son. "At the time, I thought I would take six months off and go back to work, but I decided I wanted to be a mom for a while." She took consulting gigs with Google and Adobe; she cowrote a manual called *Universal Design for Web Applications*; she moved to Seattle with her husband and son.

She also suffered postpartum depression, stopped drinking, and, after feeling as if her husband was not being as supportive as she hoped, got divorced.

"It was basically the worst time of my life. But also the best, because I finally got the help I had needed for a long time. I went into therapy; I was diagnosed with an emotional disability. I credit my son for forcing me to change."

And four years later, when Wendy was ready to return to the workforce, she was hired by Microsoft to run a program called AI for Accessibility, which gave out $25 million to support technological solutions aimed at helping the more than one billion people worldwide with disabilities.

"When I was in college, I was always the only female in my classes. I remember being in the lab one day, and the guys were all collaborating on this big project. One of the guys sits down next to me, pulls the keyboard from my hands, and starts typing. I'm like, 'Dude, I can program, too, you know.'

"For most of my life, I felt like I had to hide my femininity," she continued. "I wore baggy clothes and tried to act masculine in order to be taken seriously. But when I became a mom, I finally had enough. I realized that if I wanted to be myself at work, I first had to work on myself at home. Only then could I be who I wanted to be."

Wendy is not alone. A majority of all workquakes begin outside of work—55 percent. The largest percentage of these nonwork workquakes involves a change in our mindsets. Our interests evolve, our priorities adjust, our purpose shifts.

Derrick Ray had been a deep-sea fisherman in the Bering Sea for twenty-five years, including two seasons as a star on TV's *Deadliest Catch*, when he felt the industry had become too overregulated for his taste. "The government instituted a quota system; 186 corporations divvied up the fishery. The joy went out of it." Derrick moved to Hawaii, bought a coffee farm, and returned to Alaska every summer to lead tourist cruises.

Andrew Gauthier was making mindless celebrity and cooking videos as the head of content at *BuzzFeed* in Los Angeles when he watched a charged Supreme Court nomination hearing focusing on sexual harassment. "That was a big moment for me. It inspired me to go into therapy and made me realize I wanted to be involved in politics." Andrew became the creative director for the Democratic National Committee.

The second category was a change in our personal lives—a family event, a medical event, a collective event. Massachusetts-born Jamie Levine was a hard-driving managing director of investment banking at Goldman Sachs when his daughter, Scarlett, was born without a third of her intestine. At first, Jamie tried to power through. He'd stay in the hospital all night, then go into work the next day; he relocated from London to Boston to be closer to treatment for Scarlett. But finally, the stress caught up with him. He was fired.

Shaken, Jamie worked on his marriage for a while, then worked on himself. A year later, he took a job as the CEO of a public biotech company in San Diego, where he could build a culture that prioritized family over ambition. "I had to strip away all the MBA stuff and become much rawer. In the process I became a better person—and a better leader." Scarlett, meanwhile, grew up to enjoy a thriving life, going to school during the day, receiving nutrition through an IV at night.

From going through a heartbreak to having a change of heart, from getting sober to getting pregnant, sometimes the most powerful workquakes begin far from the workplace. For some, the best response to one of these disruptions is to keep doing what they've been doing; for others, it's to take what they learn about themselves and do work that's more aligned with who they've become.

Always Keep Your Eye on the Bottom Line

The last piece of legacy bad advice from the linear age is that the primary benchmark for measuring success is money. Instead, sometimes what people view as a step forward actually comes with a step backward in salary. When I tried to quantify how often that happens, the results were eye-popping.

Rishi Chidananda was born in the remote Indian city of Mysore; after his father died when Rishi was three, his mother moved to Cleveland and remarried. "My mother was so afraid I wouldn't fit into

America that she hid all Hindu traditions from me so I would become westernized as soon as possible."

Her plan worked.

"I was very much focused on being as rich as possible," Rishi said, "and having as much power as possible. Bill Gates was my role model."

And he learned well. Rishi traded stocks in high school, entered the honors program at Ohio State, and landed a plum job in investment banking. "I was making six figures by the time I was twenty-one."

A big reason why was that Rishi was a master at gaming the system.

"I quickly realized it was all about impressing the bosses. I would write all my emails, wait until the bosses had left, then go out, get drunk and party, then come back at midnight and press send."

By the time he was twenty-five, Rishi was making a quarter of a million dollars. He proposed to his girlfriend in an apple orchard. The wedding was weeks away. "This was the moment when I was supposed to be happy, but I felt super alone. I was tense; I was anxious; I was unsure about everything."

Then his fiancée suggested they needed to talk.

"Before I say anything, she looks at me. 'I just want you to know that if we get married, we'll have children, we'll have a house in the suburbs, everything will be fine, but you won't be happy. You're meant to do greater things in the world.'"

With the wedding canceled, Rishi went on a three-month bender— drugs, alcohol, sex. Then his butterfly appeared.

"A cousin from India was staying in my apartment. He sat me down and said, 'If you continue how you're living, you won't be living for very long.' Then he handed me this book, *Autobiography of a Yogi*."

Written by Paramahansa Yogananda in 1946, the book describes how the Hindi mystic came to America seeking self-realization and wound up introducing the West to yoga and meditation.

"Steve Jobs read the book once a year," Rishi said. "When I read it, my life changed overnight. Suddenly I would go out with my friends to drink but I wouldn't touch the drink. I became disgusted by the drugs I used to enjoy."

Rishi told his mother he was going to India for a short visit. "I have a feeling that I will not see you for a very long time," she said.

She was right. On his first day, Rishi had withdrawal symptoms; on his third, he walked down to the Ganges. A South African monk sat down and offered to introduce him to his spiritual teacher, Swami Vishwananda. "I felt a veil drop," Rishi said.

A week later Rishi followed the swami on the Kumbh Mela pilgrimage, where fifty million people gathered. The next month he moved to Germany to join his swami's ashram. Six months later he became a monk. The man who used to value his worth by counting his bonus denounced money forever. Seven years later, he returned to New York to teach meditation and lead retreats.

"I thought I knew what made me happy," Rishi said. "It was money. It was power. But really, those were masks. They were covering my fears of loneliness and mortality. When I read the autobiography, the light flickered. Now the light has become strong again, and I can finally see my true nature—profound, otherworldly love."

While Rishi might seem like an extreme example, he's not alone in how workquakes compel us to rethink our most basic assumptions. Not just around jobs, hours, and meaning. But also around money.

In my conversations, I asked everyone to pick their biggest workquake—their *superworkquake,* I called it. I then went through more than two dozen questions about how they felt and acted during that time. One of those questions was: *Did this workquake lead to a step forward, a step backward, or a lateral step?* Ninety percent said a step forward; 10 percent said a lateral step; none said a step backward.

The next question was: *Did you make more money, less money, or the same amount of money?* Here's where the results became interesting. Half of the people who said that their superworkquake was a step forward made *less money* afterward; 41 percent made more money; 9 percent the same. Put another way: among those who said that their biggest workquake improved their lives, six in ten made the same or less money than before.

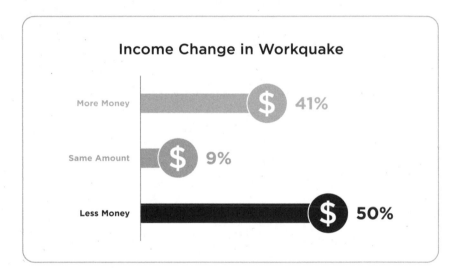

This finding goes against a century of conventional thinking about money and work. But I'm not alone in this result. While most economists have long insisted that everyone wants higher salaries, a few behavioral scientists have begun to push back on this consensus. Two researchers in Toronto, Jing Hu and Jacob Hirsh, found that if workers consider a job meaningful, they're willing to accept salaries that are

32 percent lower than for unmeaningful work. A separate study by bestselling author Shawn Achor and colleagues found that nine out of ten employees were willing to give up a quarter of their entire life earnings in exchange for work that's meaningful.

Who are the people who make these choices? They're some people that we've already met: Brijette Peña leaving her plant company for her seed startup; Eric Vélez-Villar leaving Disney for his mental health. They're Shelby Smith, who quit a lucrative job in Dublin, Ireland, selling equity derivatives for the National Bank of Canada to return to her farm roots in Iowa and open a sustainable snack company selling roasted crickets. "I wasn't building anything before; I wasn't helping anyone. I was moving around big, fictitious amounts of theoretical money, and taking a cut."

They're Divya Anantharaman, a Miami native who parlayed a degree from Pratt in Brooklyn into a job flying first class around the world designing shoes for American Eagle and Coach. After stumbling onto a road-kill squirrel while hiking in upstate New York, Divya got drawn into the world of high-end taxidermy. Three years later, after securing assignments from Tiffany & Co. and the Audubon Society, she opened Gotham Taxidermy. "The traditional career is a trap. Most people would say my move was a step backward because I took a pay cut, but to me it was a step forward in my heart and my fulfillment."

They're Caty Borum Chattoo, a nonprofit executive in Hollywood who helped legendary TV producer and *All in the Family* creator Norman Lear send his copy of the Declaration of Independence on tour, only to bail when she had a baby to take a senior job at the PR firm FleishmanHillard. "I had a fancy title and a huge office but a total bullshit job. I love to wear pink, but I had stepped into the world of beige." So she left to become the executive director of the Center for Media &

Social Impact at American University. "It wasn't glamorous; it wasn't tenured. But I had freedom."

The pace of workquakes has become so never-ending that these decisions become never-ending. That stream means that even if we opt for the supposedly safe decision this time, the law of averages suggests we'll have another chance to make the supposedly riskier choice soon enough. The net result of all this volatility is to nullify the once universal conviction that we're all on a coherent, forward-moving path in which our work always takes priority over our family, our health, and our happiness.

It's time we bid farewell to that mythical path—and to accept that a big reason such a route no longer exists is yet another assumption that turns out to be false. That assumption is the third and final lie about work.

You have a job.

CHAPTER 3

Lie #3: You Have a Job

The Surprising Wisdom of Work360

R ichard Scarry had a nonlinear work life. Born in Boston in 1919, he had no interest in the family department store, so he enrolled in business school, switched to art school, served in World War II, worked in magazines, and then published his first illustrated book in 1949. He went on to write three hundred books that sold a combined two hundred million copies.

In 1968, Scarry wrote one of the iconic books of my childhood, a portrait of the daily life in Busytown. A perfect illustration of the mid-twentieth-century American dream, Busytown was a cross between Norman Rockwell and Charles Schulz. Everybody had a job: Stitches, a rabbit, was the tailor; Charlie, a mouse, was the baker; Zip, a raccoon, was the postman, and so on. Each was traditionally gendered, gleefully happy, and gainfully secure. The only sign of the wigglyness that would soon upend such traditional roles was the tiny creature in the green felt hat who was hidden in every illustration, Lowly Worm.

Lowly Worm's job was to pose the question that gave that book its name; it's the same question I posed in this book.

What do people do all day?

The answer I heard, however, is the opposite of the one Lowly Worm heard.

Today, no one has one job anymore.

Everyone has multiple jobs.

Before we turn to the question of what's true about work today and how you adapt to it, we have one more lie to confront. That lie—that you have a job—is by far the least understood; it's also, at first blush, the least plausible. *Of course I have a job. How do you think I pay my bills?*

Still, it's true.

To understand the roots of this lie, we need to go back to the formula we started with:

WORK = NUMBERS + WORDS

Specifically, we need to dig into the one number that for the last one hundred fifty years has been the most contentious: How many hours do people work?

A forgotten feature of the agricultural economy is that there was little specialization. People raised their own food, made their own candles, cared for their own sick, and so on. John McPhee captures this bygone way of life in *The Crofter and the Laird*, his 1969 portrait of his Scottish ancestral island, Colonsay. The crofter of the title has two dozen different roles: He raises mutton, breeds ewes, grows turnips, makes cheese, collects limpets, gathers driftwood, and floats loans. He's even the constable.

For most of human history, what did people do all day? Everything!

Only since the nineteenth century have people had what we now consider a *job*. The word itself didn't even enter the English language until the sixteenth century, and then it meant only a *task*. *Job* didn't assume its current meaning of *full-time employment* until the 1850s. Those years were the heart of the industrial age, of course, and from the very beginning the single biggest tension was over how much time people worked.

Over the next century, through political pressure, union organizing, and other forms of pushback, the workday went from twelve hours to ten to eight, the workweek from seven days to six to five. Most thinkers assumed those numbers would drop even lower. Keynes said the workweek would shrink to fifteen hours; George Bernard Shaw said two; Isaac Asimov said we'd stop working altogether and only supervise machines.

Instead, the opposite happened. Americans today work longer hours, spend fewer days on vacation, and devote more time each year to labor than both our elders in this country and our peers in other countries.

But it's not just *how much* we work that's changed—*when* we work has also changed. The Busytown ideal of waking up, going to a workplace, and then leaving work and returning home to your family applies to fewer and fewer these days. Jamie McCallum, a professor at Middlebury College, has gathered impressive data on this topic. Two thirds of Americans are out of sync with this *typical* workday. Eighty percent of hourly wage-earners work atypical schedules; a majority of all workers check their work emails at night; a quarter of us do work between 10:00 p.m. and 6:00 a.m.

Still, even these numbers fail to capture what I believe is one of the biggest revelations of my conversations.

The average person has up to five jobs.

I asked everyone in my conversations a simple question: *How many jobs do you have?* The average answer was three and a half. A quarter said five or more.

At first, I was surprised by these numbers. The more I probed, the more surprised I became. What people consider to be a job these days is not at all how most economists use the term. From Merriam-Webster to the Department of Labor, the classic definition of a job is *work performed for money.* Even by this definition, the majority in my cohort— 63 percent—have more than one job.

The full picture is even more complex.

The emerging way that people use the word *job* goes well beyond paid work. If anything, it's closer to the original definition of a *job* as a task. This definition already appears as the second meaning in many dictionaries, and in effect we've repopularized it. In this usage, a *job* is a *responsibility,* a *duty,* an *obligation. It's my job to organize the holiday party at work this year. It's my job to serve on this nonprofit board. It's my job to put my children to bed so my partner can study for that second degree.*

Some of these newfangled jobs do, in fact, pay. People run errands for TaskRabbit, host Airbnbs, DJ at weddings. But almost everyone performs additional work that they consider to be a job for which they aren't paid—in many cases, they actually pay out of pocket for the privilege. They care for the elderly, coach ice hockey, tutor, mentor, protest, podcast.

Add these paying and nonpaying jobs to our primary jobs and we're all crofters these days!

Your instinct might be to dismiss some of these roles as *not really a job,* but that's missing the point. *The people who do them think of them as jobs.* In a sense, this view has been building for decades. As early as the 1970s, feminist scholars argued that unpaid household labor should be counted as a job. But today we need to go even further. We need to accept that in the battle between work and life, work has essentially won. We don't just *work* at our workplaces, we also *work* on our relationships, *work* on our parenting, *work* on our bodies, *work* on our social media profiles.

In a world where everything is work, every role is considered a job.

Instead of bemoaning this new way of thinking, we should think about it the way most people do—as a way to wring more meaning from our work. Naturally, some people take these extra jobs because they want or need more money—to pay for college, to cover the mortgage, to replace those worn-out tires. But far more take these extra jobs because they want or need more fulfillment—they want to give back, express themselves, experiment with entrepreneurship.

What I found in posing the Lowly Worm question is that people choose to have multiple jobs in large part so they can have multiple ways to cobble together the meaning they want from life.

OK, this job may not be fulfilling, but I get some of what's missing from this other job.

Gosh, I was just offered a dream job, but my kid's on the travel soccer team this year and I have to move my mom into an assisted living facility, so that's my job for now.

Wow, this new job is great on paper, but the amount of time I have to spend being twice as good as everyone else feels like a job unto itself.

I call this new world where everyone is constantly assembling and reassembling their own full circle of jobs *Work360.* Learning to master its rules is an essential life skill. That skill begins with understanding the five jobs everyone has and what role each one plays in your 360 degrees of meaning.

Main Job

The first of the five jobs seems like an easy one. It's your primary job. Everyone has one of those.

Well, it depends on what you mean.

I asked everyone what sounds like an easy question: *Do you have a main job?* The answers were surprisingly complex. For some, their main job was their primary source of income; for others, their primary source of time; for others, their primary source of meaning.

And for others, it's almost impossible to tell.

Morgan Gold knew from an early age that he wanted to draw comic strips. Born in Marlborough, Connecticut, to a father who was a special ed teacher and a mother who was a drug and alcohol counselor, Morgan idolized Matt Groening, the creator of *The Simpsons*, and dreamed of working at *Mad* magazine. In high school, he sold a comic strip about a sarcastic rabbit who smokes cigarettes and curses a lot to an alternative weekly.

"He wasn't necessarily a surrogate for me, but he was certainly what a fifteen-year-old boy would find funny."

Morgan earned a joint degree from Tufts University and the School of the Museum of Fine Arts, Boston, then moved to a trailer park outside of Hartford and tried to make a documentary about his neighbors. They kicked him out of the community. "My directing career was over before it started."

A friend offered him a gig making corporate videos, which led to a job running communications for the CEO of the Hartford insurance company, which led to being recruited by TIAA-CREF as a vice president of branding and advertising, which led to a job as the managing director and head of marketing for ProShares, a $65 billion investment company in Bethesda, Maryland.

"Cash ruled everything in my life," Morgan said. "I went from living in a trailer park to living in a rat-infested apartment in Hartford, to thinking, *Wow, I can buy a crazy town house in Washington, DC!* As soon as that happened, I realized, *Whoa, this life kind of sucks.*"

Morgan tallied all the ways his work made him unhappy. "I spend my days sitting in meetings, I'm not creating anything, I'm responding to pissed-off emails from the CEO. I thought, *I gotta find a hobby.*"

What he found was farming. "I began reading books about regenerative agriculture, learning about permaculture, starting one garden in my front yard and two in my back." Morgan was married by this time; his wife, Allison, had just finished dual master's degrees in public health and nursing. With roots in New England, the couple bought a 150-acre run-down dairy farm in northeast Vermont as a getaway.

"The house needed a lot of work. I planted a bunch of chestnut and mulberry trees. I figured that's a crop I could manage from afar."

But once he put his hands in the soil, Morgan didn't want to pull them out.

"I always wanted to be a storyteller. I said to Allison one night, 'What if we start a farm and document everything on YouTube? I bet by the time we have stuff to sell, we'll have enough viewers to buy the stuff.'"

Allison was game. She found an opening as a nurse practitioner in a medical nonprofit serving the northeast corner of the state; Morgan took a job doing marketing for a small insurance company. "It was a shift in trajectory, but I wasn't making the move for status."

Five years later, Gold Shaw Farm was "more of a farm startup than an honest-to-goodness farm," Morgan said. He sold horse feed, raised ducks, bred goose eggs. But his YouTube channel, on which he hosts twice-weekly comic videos with names like "A Day in the Life of Toby the Guard Dog" and "Our Freakishly Huge Duck (This Is Not NORMAL)," was a smashing success. He had 700,000 subscribers and 200 million views. *The New York Times* labeled him the public face of a new genre of homestead infotainment, Chore TV.

"I usually get up around 4:35 a.m., start editing, then let the animals out and do my chores," Morgan said. "By eight thirty I'm showered, doing Zoom calls for my insurance job. I kick off around five thirty, get the animals fed and locked away for the night, have dinner, then work on my children's book about my dog."

He basically has three jobs, he said—his marketing job, his farm, and his content creation.

"I'm good at the storytelling; I'm less good at the farming. The day job makes the other two possible."

Trying to figure out what is a main job these days is harder than it appears. Scholars traditionally defined a main job as *work performed on a fixed schedule, at the firm's place of business, under the firm's control, and with mutual expectation of continued employment.* Almost every part of this definition has melted away. Schedules have become more flexible, remote work more viable, continued employment more suspect. Beyond those variations, what some economists call *jobless jobs* have become more plentiful—from on-call work to contracting to gigging to collabbing.

All of these changes have led to the same result: Americans likely spend less time at a main job than at any time since *jobs* became the norm two centuries ago. By some measures, only around half of us even have a main job anymore. In my study, the number was 39 percent.

These numbers are a reminder that while long-standing norms

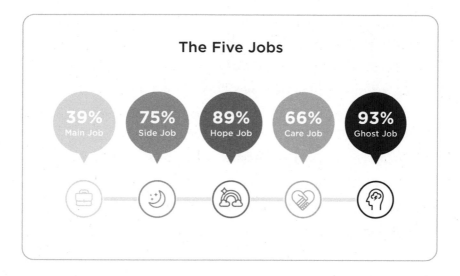

The Five Jobs

39% Main Job | 75% Side Job | 89% Hope Job | 66% Care Job | 93% Ghost Job

have been eroded, updated norms have been slow to replace them. In the case of main jobs, as their numbers decrease, the stigma against *not* having one will surely also decrease. In turn, the social acceptability of forgoing a main job altogether will rise. In the work smorgasbord of the future, more and more people walk past the mains and fill up on sides instead.

Side Job

Side jobs are the most talked-about alternatives to main jobs, but they're neither the most common nor the most demanding. What they are, for most of us, is a hedge, whether that hedge is designed to bring in more money, more meaning, or more options for the future.

Sometimes they even bring us all three.

Kirsten Green was born in Tuscaloosa, Alabama. Her father sold corporate uniforms; her mother was a school administrator. "I grew up in a middle-class lifestyle, and my parents made it clear that you shouldn't work for a paycheck, you should work for purpose. My dad would take us to a housing project on Christmas Day. 'Think about what you got for Christmas. Now look at what they're playing with. Don't ever forget that someone else would be grateful for what you take for granted.'"

Kirsten enrolled in the University of Alabama to study premed, then switched to criminal justice, moving on to earn her master's degree. Her first job was teaching criminology at a historically Black college in Tennessee.

"My smallest class in college had a hundred people; my largest class in Tennessee had thirty. My goal had always been to change a little piece of the world. Now I knew every student's name. I met their parents. And when they suffered, they came to me, which is why a six-foot-four football player cried on my shoulder after his mother died."

By her second year, Kirsten was running the department; after five years she was hired away by a college in Alabama. She was thriving, but she was also uneasy.

"Something was missing, and I didn't know what."

Then, out of nowhere, a text.

"It was from a relative's fourteen-year-old."

There's something I need to tell you.

"My stomach just dropped," Kirsten said. "I called her immediately, and she announced, 'I'm pregnant.' My first response was, *Oh, crap. Her daddy's going to kill her.* I immediately launched into Mama Bear mode: *How are you feeling? How far along are you?* Then, to calm down, I called my best friend. 'Are you sure it was consensual sex?' she asked. I realized I hadn't even put on my criminal justice brain."

The daughter, it turns out, had been raped by a fellow student. As a criminologist, Kirsten hesitated advising the girl or her parents to press charges on a juvenile, but when the family learned he had raped two other students, the daughter agreed to testify, and the attacker was jailed.

The daughter, meanwhile, announced that she had prayed on it and wanted to keep the baby. "And I want you in the delivery room to help me," she told Kirsten. Once again, Mama Bear kicked in. Kirsten timed contractions; she spoke affirmations. "And once all the beauty and hard work of motherhood had prevailed, the daughter turned to me and said, 'I think you would make a great doula.'"

Now it was Kirsten's turn to pray on it.

"I told the Lord that this wasn't in my plans. And you know what they say, *Tell God your plans . . .*"

Kirsten again went to work. She watched videos; she took classes; she earned her license. And she hatched a plan to open a birth center. Not only did her side job redirect her life, it also redirected her main job. Kirsten switched her PhD topic to the importance of offering nurseries to incarcerated pregnant women, which her research showed reduced recidivism.

"God really had the last laugh," she said.

The idea of a side job is hardly new. In the 1800s, following the potato famine in Ireland, many farmers lost their land. Some of those outraged farmers waged guerilla raids against the new owners, killing their cattle. Because those raids were conducted at night, they became known as *moonlighting*. From that ignominious start, *moonlighting* evolved to mean *performing any second job at night*.

In the twenty-first century, moonlighting has been eclipsed by another term with criminal roots, *side hustle*. Derived from the Dutch word *husselen*, which means *to shake*, *hustle* entered popular usage in the 1920s meaning *swindle* or *shake down*. From this start, *side hustle* came to mean *scam* and, later, the less judgmental *second job*.

Although *side hustle* is trendy these days, I prefer *side job* because while this phrase doesn't include leisure activities like fishing or gardening, it does include unpaid activities that many people also consider jobs, like preparing meals at the homeless shelter or serving on the board of the co-op.

Whatever you call this work, it still contains a whiff of two-timing. That's unfortunate. Hudson Sessions, an assistant professor at the University of Oregon, has found that side jobs can bring extra stress, but they also bring heightened meaning. Counter to what employers fear, side jobs also make employees happier and more productive at their main jobs, especially when the roles differ. A graphic designer who calligraphs wedding invitations on the side may feel burned out, but if her side job is welding or being a notary public, she'll recover faster and feel more creative at her design job.

Side jobs are especially helpful in easing people's path to self-employment. Half of all side jobs involve entrepreneurship. They allow someone to either experiment with self-employment while supporting themselves with a main job, as happened with Morgan Gold, or sustain themselves with self-employment by using the side job for extra cash, as happened with Sang Kim, a lawyer who left Goldman Sachs to become an interior designer but also took on a few legal clients. In both cases, the side job provided the primary source of meaning while the main job provided the primary source of cash.

How many people have side jobs? Three quarters in my study. Anooj Bhandari, a corrections specialist for the City of New York, had two side jobs—coaching storytelling at the Moth and being a member of the Neo-Futurists theater troupe. Bouy Te, a real estate broker in Virginia, had three side jobs—substitute teaching, serving on a county board, and helping an organization that encourages Asian Americans to get involved in politics. Sonia Gutierrez had no primary job but four side jobs—running a computer center in South Fayetteville, teaching college, serving as the first woman of color on any city council in Arkansas, and selling salsa using her mom's recipe under the brand Salsa for Change.

Lauren Nichols was so worried that her boss at the Department of Transportation would be unsettled by her side job as a medium that she never told him. But when her boss's deceased wife visited Lauren in a dream to deliver "a very specific message," Lauren warily approached him.

"I described the exact place where his wife died, with blood all over the laundry room floor. Then I told him that she held out her hands and had M&M's in them. His mouth dropped. 'That was our thing,' he said. 'Whenever I was sad, she would give me M&M's. It was her way of saying I love you.'"

Lauren was sure he was going to fire her; instead, the opposite happened. "Now he asks me about my mediumship all the time; he told our colleagues at the British Ministry of Defence, and they all believe that my psychic work benefits my government work."

Which is exactly what side jobs often do.

Hope Job

As popular as side jobs are, they're still not the most common alternative jobs. That distinction falls to another kind of job that I heard about so frequently I eventually gave it a name: a *hope job*. A hope job is work that people do in their spare time—like writing a children's book or selling blueberry muffins at the farmers' market—that they hope develops into something bigger.

Nearly nine in ten people have a hope job, suggesting that even people who are happy with their main or side jobs have other jobs they imagine would make them even happier.

Michael Running Wolf is part of the Northern Cheyenne and Lakota tribes. His father was an artist, his mother an engineer. "My mother was basically a genius. But she grew up in the wrong time both as a woman minority in tech—her professors called her *squaw*—and during a period when the government attempted to sterilize Indigenous women."

Michael was raised in a government home in Birney, Montana, population 108; his house had no electricity, toilets, or telephones. He spent half his year in a tepee. "I longed for big cities and gadgets, but I always feared the loss of culture. How can we carry our people's knowledge into the future when children prefer being on TikTok?"

Michael attended Montana State University, where he earned a BS and MS in computer science. He worked for IBM and Lawrence Livermore National Laboratory, before returning to Montana with his wife, Caroline, a member of the Crow Nation, to pursue side-by-side PhDs. That's when he happened into a hope job.

The Madison Buffalo Jump is a limestone cliff near Bozeman that Native Americans used for two thousand years to trap bison. When the site was threatened by a housing development, defenders of the historic site struggled to explain its significance. Michael stepped up. "I designed some augmented reality, threw up some geo tracking, re-created lost artifacts like hide scrapers, and allowed people to have a relationship with their past."

The housing development was canceled.

Michael went on to use similar techniques to help fight the Keystone Pipeline. While engaged in that work, he stumbled into a little-known calamity. Machine learning cannot translate most Indigenous languages, which rely more on morphemes that have ambiguous meanings than Western languages, which rely more on words that have concrete meanings. "It turns out there are only a handful of people in the world working on this open problem, which affects more than five hundred million people, most of whom will soon be cut off from advanced computing."

For the next five years, while working on one of the most elite AI teams in the world, building Alexa at Amazon, Michael labored on this hope job. He started a nonprofit; he begged for grants. "I felt all alone. It was a hope job because I would have loved to do it full time, but I couldn't get anyone to support us."

Finally, the urgency became too great. Michael decided to walk away from his dream job at Amazon to take a subsistence job at a university, which would give him more time to focus on his hope job. The logo of his effort: a digital buffalo running toward the jump.

In 2009, two doctoral students at Penn State were chatting about their work. Kathleen Kuehn, a self-described avid jigsaw puzzler, music lover, and dill pickle connoisseur, was researching amateur reviewers on Yelp; Tom Corrigan was researching amateur bloggers. They discovered that their subjects had something in common: they were doing unpaid work because they hoped it would lead to paying work in the future. The two coined the phrase *hope labor*.

While that term never really took hold, it perfectly captures the work that Michael and others do every day. I began asking all my subjects whether they had a *hope job*. Eighty-nine percent said yes.

Four in ten hope jobs were in media—writing a memoir, creating a comic book series, starting a podcast. Laura Delarato, a creative director at *Vox* in Manhattan who once sold high-end sex toys, was working on a book about body positivity and sex. Harmit Malik, a first-generation geneticist in Seattle, was writing a sci-fi novel about fossilized viruses.

One in four hope jobs was in the arts—making jewelry, acting in community theater, performing burlesque. Kelly Lively, a nuclear scientist at the Idaho National Laboratory, was honing her skills as a stand-up comedian. Karléh Wilson, a housing analyst in Louisiana, opened a Patreon account to support her dream of becoming a jazz singer.

One in five hope jobs involved starting businesses. Kara Young, a supermodel who appeared on the cover of *Vogue* at nineteen and later

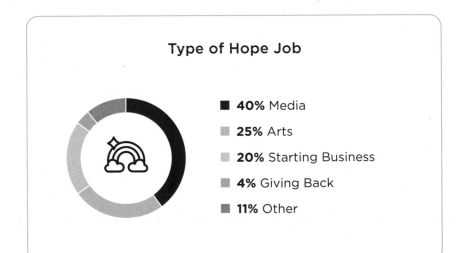

Type of Hope Job

- **40%** Media
- **25%** Arts
- **20%** Starting Business
- **4%** Giving Back
- **11%** Other

became a correspondent for Fox News, opened a cosmetics line. Susan Venturelli, a cop for Amtrak in Chicago, sold charcuterie boards, cookies, and what she called *crack brownies*, because of their addictive nature, at the farmers' market.

As this dazzling range suggests, hope jobs inspire the best in us. They bring us emotional rewards in the present, even if they never bring us financial rewards in the future. In many ways, hope jobs are a symbol of the full circumference of Work360 in that they reveal how prominent unpaid work has become to our identities. We are willing to replace free time with work time if we believe it will make us happier today and perhaps bring us even more happiness in the future.

Care Job

The fourth job in the Work360 circle is the opposite of looking toward the future. It's all about the here and now. It's a job that involves taking care of someone else, whether that's a child, a parent, a neighbor, or a mentee. And for most people, even though that work is done with love, it definitely feels like a job.

Nygil Likely grew up in Grand Rapids, Michigan, in a home that included a mom, no dad, all four grandparents, and several uncles. All the adults worked. "The first thing my grandma always said was, 'If you start something, you have to finish it.'"

When Nygil was in seventh grade, his school faced a wave of bullying. The principal set up a peer mentoring program in which students were trained to help mediate conflict; she asked Nygil to run one of the groups. He loved it. After high school, Nygil went to work for the YMCA in youth programming, while also earning a BA and MBA.

He stayed in that job for a decade, jumped to Job Corps, and then moved to a local university as the head of student services.

"I was so energized. I was married by this time, I had good work-life balance."

Then a butterfly appeared.

Nygil is Baptist; his wife, Kieychia, is Pentecostal. They had been attending a nondenominational church but were unhappy, so they returned to his childhood church, where they were married. "Immediately I began to feel God calling me to ministry."

Nygil approached the pastor, who encouraged him to become a deacon, which allowed him to administer Communion. But even that role didn't satisfy his yearning.

"Eight months in, I finally heard God say, *You're called into preaching.* The pastor said, 'I've been waiting for you to get to the message.'"

Nygil earned his ordination and was hired as the head pastor at Friendship Missionary Baptist Church. He performed this job on nights and weekends, because he still had his main job in higher ed. First at a college in Chicago, then at a university in Grand Rapids, and finally as a vice president of Lake Michigan College, where he ran advising and residential life. On top of both of those roles, Nygil and Kieychia had a biological son; they adopted the son of one of Kieychia's relatives, who had addiction problems; then they took in two more children from Nygil's side of the family, whose parents also battled addiction.

The fatherless boy who grew up in a multifamily home now was the father of his own multifamily home.

The boy who was told to always finish whatever he started now had three different jobs—vice president, pastor, and father.

"I think they're all care jobs," he said. "When I first heard God calling me, my pastor preached a sermon out of Jeremiah. The scripture said we should all be clay in the hands of the potter, but the pastor said we should all be potters. That message broke me. Even with all our shortcomings, we are called to roll up our sleeves and go to work helping to mold people."

We are all called to care.

In recent years, we've become so enamored of the conversation around *work-life balance* that we've forgotten that life itself is fundamentally unbalancing. The idea that work and life are in tension is actually a positive outcome of having more women working—and more women studying work. For decades, researchers found that men tended to keep their nonwork lives separate from their work, while women rarely did.

But those norms have been changing. The number of women who are primary breadwinners today is close to 50 percent, while the number of men who are more involved in parenting is even higher. One outcome of this change is that the language of work has migrated into the family. Most parents view large parts of child-rearing as a *job*. Economists can grouse at this usage, but pollsters have consistently found that parents view many aspects of parenting—from preparing meals to planning playdates to prepping bath time—as chores to be managed and jobs to be divvied up.

And it's not just child-rearing that's become infused with the language of work. Thirty million Americans provide unpaid labor to an adult over fifty, from aging parents to infirm spouses to grown children. Family Caregiver Alliance, which tracks this issue, says Asian Americans perform these jobs more than whites, Blacks more than Asian Americans, and Hispanics more than Blacks.

This gamut of personal obligations helps explain why two thirds of my cohort said they had a care job. Just under half of all care jobs involve family members, from children to parents to grandchildren. Susan Venturelli, for example, in addition to her cop duties and brownie selling, spends one day a week as the primary caretaker of her grandson.

But more than half involve non–family members. Issa Spatrisano, the Alaska refugee director, spends ten evening hours a week editing the papers of her former clients. Marcus Bridgewater, a TikTok plant-fluencer who makes videos relating botany to a meaningful life, was the part-time caretaker for his elderly neighbor. Kirby Metoxen, a full-time council member of the Oneida Nation of Wisconsin, had a side job as the vice president of a birdseed company, a hope job breeding show horses, and a care job as a sobriety coach, which, as a former alcoholic, was the job that meant the most to him.

Julian Vasquez Heilig is a Stanford PhD, the author of fifty peer-reviewed articles on public schools, and the dean of the University of Kentucky's College of Education. After a colleague refused to take his call, saying he didn't have time for someone so junior, Julian vowed to always make time. He created a widget on his calendar for anyone to schedule a fifteen-minute call. "I just got a tweet the other day from a parent, 'My son just told me he spoke with you about his high school paper. I can't believe you did that!'"

Care jobs rarely make us money; they usually make our other jobs harder. But we spend so much time doing them because the meaning they provide to our overall identity is disproportionate to many of the other jobs we have.

Ghost Job

The last of the five jobs is the most invisible. It's the one we rarely share with others. Yet it's the one we most need to get better at if we expect to find happiness at work.

It's a ghost job—something so powerful, scary, and haunting that addressing it feels like a job.

It was one such ghost that led Chely Wright, at what was otherwise the pinnacle of her work life, to stand in the foyer of her East Nashville home with a 9-millimeter revolver in her mouth.

Chely grew up in Wellsville, Kansas, "a town where no one had much, and we were on the poorer end of that," she says. Her father was a construction worker, her mother a stay-at-home mom. Chely knew as a little girl that she wanted to sing on the Grand Ole Opry.

"When I was four, I disappeared one day. My family dispatched a search party and discovered me in a nursing home, surrounded by people in wheelchairs, singing 'Frankie and Johnny.'"

When she was eleven, Chely started playing piano in honky-tonks and trumpet in graveyards. "I played taps in over a hundred military funerals." When she was sixteen, she took a summer job performing in Branson, Missouri. When she was eighteen, she moved to Nashville. Her classmates gave her a necklace and said, "Wear this on the Opry one day." Within a year, she did.

But Nashville was chock-full of hopefuls, and Chely struggled. She worked in a shoe store; she sang backup for Dolly Parton's longtime partner, Porter Wagoner; she managed to land a record deal. But her first six singles and two albums flopped. So Chely approached the legendary hitmaker and Elvis's onetime keyboard player, Tony Brown, to produce her next record. Their first single, "Shut Up and Drive," cracked the top fifteen; their first album hit number one.

"I was making more money than anyone in my family ever imagined."

But all this time, Chely was harboring a secret.

One night, she went drinking with the rising country star John Rich. Out of the blue, he asked, "You're not gay, are you?" "I took a deep breath and said, 'No, John, I'm not.' He said, 'Good, because that ain't right. Country music ain't gonna stand for that.'"

Chely was lying.

"I was aware from early on that I was different," she said. But in the deeply churched culture of Kansas and Nashville, she tried to block out the truth. "Every day of my life, I'd pray, *Dear God, please don't let me be gay.* I also saved every dollar because I knew I could lose it all in a second."

Now that second appeared to be here.

The next morning Chely broke up with her girlfriend of twelve years. Weeks later, she went into her bedroom and grabbed the revolver her parents had given her for safety. "I took it downstairs, where I had a beautiful, beveled mirror on this hundred-year-old mantel. The gun was heavier and colder than I thought it would be. I was surprised I wasn't crying. I had imagined this moment so many times."

But she stopped herself.

"I knew my sister would call me. She would call my best friend. And they would find me, a failure."

Chely knew she wasn't a failure, though.

She took a nap, woke up, and started praying. For the first time, she heard a response. "I didn't see a dude in a white robe or Birkenstocks. I didn't hear a booming voice. But I felt warm, and I felt hopeful. I decided that if I was going to survive, I had to share my story."

Three years later, Chely published a memoir and released a new album. "I had a book, a record, and a person all come out on the same day."

She lost half her audience, but she also gained a side job as an advocate for inclusive workplaces. She married a marketing executive she met soon after coming out. She moved to New York and had twin boys.

"What I learned from hanging out in nursing homes all those years ago is that the only way to survive is to have a map. It's how you get from five to ninety-nine. And the most important part of that map is not the thing you're worried about—in my case, the declaration that I'm gay—it's the overall picture on that map. It's the declaration that I'm a person of faith, that I grew up on a farm, that I played for troops in the Middle East, and, oh, by the way, that I love women. The only way to be happy is to create your own map, hand it to others, and say, 'Please, read this. Then you'll know my story.'"

In my earliest conversations, I didn't ask people about ghost jobs. I'd never heard of or imagined such a concept. But I kept hearing stories that suggested that everyone was haunted by some specter that made even their dream jobs otherwise nightmarish. They were plagued by impostor syndrome, exhausted by bigotry, worried about letting down their parents, anxious about relapsing into drinking.

The poet Cathy Park Hong brilliantly named such "negative, untelegenic" thoughts as *minor feelings*. Minor feelings are rarely featured in heroic stories, she said, because they "do not conform to the archetypal narrative that highlights survival and self-determination." They occur "when American optimism is essentially forced upon you."

In Hong's case, her minor feelings were related to being Korean

American. "For as long as I could remember, I have struggled to prove myself into existence. I just don't *look* the part." But she speaks for everyone when she says that patiently educating clueless people is draining. "It's like explaining to a person why you exist, or why you feel pain, or why your reality is distinct from their reality."

Minor feelings are endemic. They are relentless. But are they a job? I decided to ask.

Ninety-three percent of all my subjects said that yes, their innermost battles felt like a job. That percentage was the highest of all the five jobs I probed. And when I asked if people could quantify how many hours they spent on these jobs, 60 percent said these feelings were pervasive; their ghosts were always present. The rest said an average of twelve hours a week. That's a quarter of a typical workweek when instead of being productive, we actually feel anti-productive.

Ghost jobs are the invisible epidemic of work.

The three most common ghost jobs involve *discrimination, self-care,* and *money.* On discrimination, Alton White was wrongfully arrested

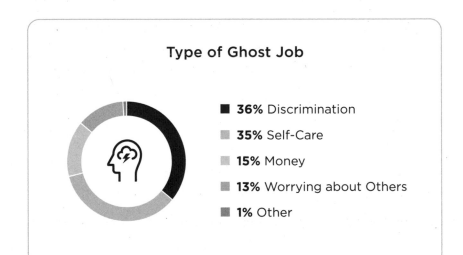

Type of Ghost Job

- **36%** Discrimination
- **35%** Self-Care
- **15%** Money
- **13%** Worrying about Others
- **1%** Other

in his own home in Manhattan while starring in *Ragtime* on Broadway. "The cops burst in, pushed me against the wall, and handcuffed me. They said, 'We got a call about some Hispanics selling drugs!' I said, 'I'm not even Hispanic. I'm Black!'" The incident made the nightly news. "*Are you fucking kidding me?* I thought. *Now I'm that guy.* At least I had the profile to fight back." Daphne Jones, who was one of the highest-ranking minority women at IBM, dealt with whispers behind her back and sneers to her face. "Being a woman in business is hard by itself; being a Black woman in STEM is impossible."

On self-care, Kelly Lively, who started out as a secretary at the Idaho National Labs and worked her way up to department manager, said her ghost job was "lack of self-confidence." Karen Noel, a bank manager for over thirty years who became a long-haul truck driver, said her ghost job was worrying—"about getting into an accident, about damaging the truck, about a bad ice storm." Wendy Chisholm, the accessibility director at Microsoft, said her ghost job was sobriety. "Having the energy to remain in a recovery program, while also being a sponsor, going to meetings, daily journaling."

On money, Cornell Scott, who lost his police officer father in New Jersey to cancer when he was four, grew up watching his dental assistant mother struggle to support her family. "Once, in sixth grade, I asked if we could order pizza; Mom gave me a look that said, *No. Don't ask again.*" After his dream of playing pro basketball in Europe was cut short by injury, Cornell coached community college, opened a youth academy, and gave motivational speeches. "I was an adult before I realized I had a horrible relationship with money. I would cry rather than ask people to pay me."

Laura Delarato, the *Vox* creative director, said that even in her thirties she stressed about earning enough to support her parents in the future. "I worry that my dad, who I barely speak to, will need me to take care of him. The same with my mother. And my brother." Laura spends ten hours a week working side jobs and surfing Zillow trying to prepare for buying a house large enough for her entire family.

Everyone sees ghosts from time to time. While the details for dealing with them may differ, one treatment has been shown to be effective against all of them: We must normalize their existence. We must bring them out of the shadows. We must see them for what they are: obstacles that prevent us from feeling whole.

"You are never a whole person if you remain silent," writes the poet Audre Lorde. "What do you need to say? What are the tyrannies you swallow day by day and attempt to make your own, until you will sicken and die of them, still in silence?"

We must break the silence.

Above all, we must accept that ghost jobs are part of a complex assortment of jobs that each of us tries to make sense of every day. A 360-degree circle of work composed of fractals of time and fragments of responsibility, each of which brings us flickers of joy and glimmers of purpose but also eats away at our confidence and undermines our dignity.

What do people do all day? They try to find meaning through all that they do.

What's the best way to do that in a world where all the old truths lie broken and shattered on the ground?

Fortunately, there is a way.

Two hundred years ago, just as the world of work was first splintering, the Scottish optician David Brewster invented a method of rearranging broken pieces of glass into brilliant patterns of color. Each arrangement would be unique, transitory, breathtaking. Brewster named his invention the *kaleidoscope*, from the Greek words meaning *observer of beautiful shapes.*

Today we need a similar new way of observing beautiful shapes. We need a tool that can help us reassemble the shattered shards of success into dazzling new arrangements that reflect our changing dreams. We need to move beyond the three lies about work.

We need one new truth.

II

THE ONE TRUTH
ABOUT WORK

CHAPTER 4

We All Need Another Hero

Who Gets to Be the Face of Success?

On a cold, Sunday dawn in October 1723, an awkward seventeen-year-old runaway from Boston, just off a rowboat on the Delaware River, walked up Market Street in Philadelphia. Dirty, bedraggled, his "best clothes" sullied by "rowing and want of rest," his pockets "stuffed out with shirts and stockings," and under his arms, not the three-penny loaf he couldn't afford but "three great puffy rolls," this "ignorant" boy-man made "a most ridiculous appearance."

That boy was Benjamin Franklin. And that moment, described in meticulous, mouthwatering detail in the opening pages of his *Autobiography*, is, in the words of legendary literary critic Harold Bloom, "the dominant visual scene in all American literature."

The reason, Bloom writes, is that when paired with another scene at the book's end, when Franklin—thirty years later, now a wealthy printer, assembly member, and confidant of George Washington—departs Philadelphia as the officers of his regiment "drew their Swords" in a manner "only proper to Princes of the Blood Royal," Franklin gives us the ultimate example of *look at me then, look at me now.*

In that juxtaposition, Bloom writes, "Franklin gave us the definitive formulation of the American Dream." It's the archetype of an individual's rise "from helplessness to power," "from log-cabin birth to self-made man," "from rags to riches."

In other words, Benjamin Franklin is the ultimate American success story.

And that, as the salty-tongued founding father might have said, is a damned shame.

What we've learned about work today is that it's in a massive state of upheaval. We face heightened instability, deeper uncertainty, and greater demands on our time but also have more freedom, more opportunity, and more options. We also have limited sources of support. Employers can't be expected to help employees find work elsewhere; elected officials have nothing to say; most of our peers are equally confused. Who should you turn to for answers?

Yourself.

The one truth about work today is that only you can provide the help you want and the direction you need.

The rest of this book is devoted to showing you how to do that. We begin with two foundational steps. The first, in this chapter, is to grapple with what we might call the Ben Franklin Problem: What is a success story anyway? The second, in the next chapter, is to ask, How do you decide what success means to you? In that discussion, I'll introduce three tools that can make that process more effective.

But first, let's explore a story that's rarely told and that goes back to that Sunday morning in 1723: the collective trauma of the American success story and how we all can escape its long shadow of pain.

What Is a Success Story?
Part I: Character Is Destiny

Who gets to decide what's a success story? Does Chris Donovan count?

Chris was born into an Irish Catholic family in Weston, Massachusetts. His father never made much money; his mother became ill with encephalitis when Chris was six. "They always instilled in us that you go out and get a good, stable job. The happiness quotient was never part of it."

Chris found that stability. After high school, he spent a decade working as a waiter and bartender, before joining the telephone company at twenty-nine as an operator. "This was before cell phones, call centers, or 911," he said. "I was the only man in a roomful of women. When you picked up the phone and dialed zero, that was me. I fielded calls from businessmen placing long-distance calls, drunks looking for a cab, people who were shot and needed an ambulance."

He stayed at the company for the next twenty-five years. Chris switched roles every few years, working as a home repairman, a computer installer, a pole climber. He volunteered at a suicide hotline and earned a bachelor's degree in religious studies. And all along, he nurtured a secret hobby.

"When I was in humanities class in high school, a girl walked in wearing sky-high platforms. I couldn't believe she could walk in them. They were like a piece of art."

Chris pulled out his notebook and started sketching.

"It was one of those moments in your life that lights a flame. I started drawing women's shoes on the back of notebooks, on envelopes, on paper napkins in restaurants. I knew there was nothing I could do with this obsession—my friends all teased me, thinking it was a fetish—so I just drew for the next thirty-five years."

He really couldn't find anything to do with his passion?

"I didn't know where to begin. My parents never taught me about saving and investing. All the shoe factories in New England had closed by then. At one point I threw all my designs in the trash. I was dating a guy at the time, and he flipped out. 'You have to save those. They're important!'"

One night Chris went to dinner with a group of men in Province-town. "They were from all over the world. One was a tie-dye artist named Steve. He had done work with the Rock & Roll Hall of Fame. I thought, *I work for the friggin' phone company.*"

Chris and Steve started dating, and, with Steve's encouragement, Chris took night courses in welding and drawing. "Then a fashion course popped up. I was the first in line. Everyone was young, tall, beautiful. I'm the short, fat, hairy guy. The teacher says, 'You must be looking for photography. That's next door.' I'm like, 'No, I'm looking for fashion.' And she starts laughing."

Chris thrived in class, but the teacher had no experience with foot-wear. Then Chris was diagnosed with prostate cancer, which required treatment. Finally, he built up enough confidence to sign up for a two-day shoe course in Manhattan. The instructor, the acclaimed designer Aki Choklat, asked everyone to draw their best shoe in sixty seconds. Afterward, he called Chris to his desk.

"Everybody else drew pastel things that looked like a potato. You did something that looked like it belongs on the runway."

Aki encouraged Chris to get a master's degree in Italy. "Steve and

I were married by then. The entire train ride back home, I kept thinking, *We have a house, we have a dog, how would we even pull this off?* But without a moment's hesitation, Steve said, 'We'll sell the house if we have to.'"

Chris put in his retirement papers, he got his first passport, and after his visa was rejected by the Italian government ("You're too old"), he eventually secured papers. At fifty-five he enrolled in Polimoda, a fashion design school in Florence.

And he bombed. Aki told him he was worried. Chris feared he was in over his head. Finally, his teacher came to his desk. "See all your classmates, those fashion vixens who worked at Saatchi? You're not them. Who were you before you came here?"

"A telephone repairman."

"Great. Be that."

And it clicked. Chris started designing shoes with fiber-optic cable, blocks of wood salvaged from construction sites, glass insulators from old telephone poles. "You can spot a Versace. You can spot a Gucci. I want you to be able to spot a Donovan."

He graduated at the top of his class.

Back home, though, no one would hire him. So Chris did what he always did: he started drawing. He entered—and won—competitions. He was invited to appear on *Project Runway*. AARP made a documentary about him. And ultimately he opened a direct-to-consumer brand, Chris Donovan Footwear. Four years later, he had three collections and twenty different styles, though he still hadn't paid himself a salary.

"No matter what happens, I've succeeded," Chris said. "Because, my God, I chased my freaking dream. I quit my job. I went to Italy. I started my own company. I'm just a success, I am."

Let's begin our discussion of the American success story by drawing a distinction between work and success: Work, as we've seen, is the combination of what you do and how you feel about what you do. It's the balance between time, effort, and money on one hand, and meaning, purpose, and happiness on the other.

WORK = NUMBERS + WORDS

Success is how that balance interacts with the rest of your life. It's how your work fulfills your overall vision of yourself; how it reflects your deepest values; how it upholds the ethos of your family, your community, your country.

SUCCESS = WORK × LIFE

If the history of work has been hamstrung by our over-reliance on numbers and our under-reliance on words, the history of success has an even worse problem: We've over-indexed on valuing work for work's sake (the *work ethic*), and under-indexed on acknowledging that the priorities we hold in life shape the priorities we hold in work. Are you primarily motivated by money, for example, or by self-expression, impact, or happiness?

Two towering figures in American mythology are largely responsible for this problem.

The first is Franklin.

The great historian of American ideas, Daniel Rodgers, reminds us that "the notion of a timeless 'American work ethic' is a myth." For large swaths of our history, work was considered toilsome while leisure was considered preferable. All that changed in the nineteenth century as getting workers to show up at factories became a national imperative. As Rodgers puts it, "the elevation of work over leisure involved not an isolated choice but an ethos that permeated life and manners." This "doctrine of the industrious life," as Rodgers calls it, pervaded churches, political speeches, children's storybooks.

The patron saint of that doctrine was the bespectacled uncle of American industriousness, Poor Richard. First introduced in 1732, Poor Richard was the alter ego that Franklin used to issue an endless stream of maxims, witticisms, and wordplays, first in an annual almanac, then in the perennial bestseller *The Way to Wealth*. And make no mistake: wealth was the point. As Richard Huber writes in *The American Idea of Success*, Franklin "made a fortune in his own lifetime—then expanded it by telling others how he did it."

Above all, Franklin took the position that success was measured in money, and money was achieved by virtue. Many of the aphorisms he quoted most often reinforce the same point: Your success is determined by who you are. The values that are most important are *industry* ("Early to bed, and early to rise, makes a man healthy, wealthy, and wise") and *frugality* ("A fat kitchen makes a lean will"), while the ones you should most avoid are *idleness* ("Laziness travels so slowly, that poverty soon overtakes it") and *extravagance* ("Waste neither time nor money").

Franklin severely narrowed the American ideal of work to the dubious proposition that character is destiny. The only way to achieve success is to have exemplary character; those without such character are doomed to failure. Both of those declarations, as we all now know, are questionable at best. On top of that, Franklin introduced a number of myths that soon became inseparable from American identity: Success is self-made, self-aggrandizing, self-justifying. And those limitations are before we ask the troublesome question of who was entitled to Franklin's vision of success: in his mind, certainly not female Americans, Native Americans, or, for most of his life, enslaved Americans.

As harmful as Franklin's contributions were, the second prince of success was far worse.

Horatio Alger is one of the more odious figures in American letters. Hardly self-made, he was the descendant of three pilgrims, a Revolutionary War general, and a member of the Constitutional Convention. His father was a Unitarian minister. After graduating from Harvard in 1852, Alger tried and failed at writing, taught in boarding schools, used illness to get out of serving in the Civil War, and eventually sought security as a pastor at a Unitarian church on Cape Cod. He abruptly left two years later, fleeing to New York at a moment when robber barons ruled and wharfs teemed with sixty thousand homeless "street urchins." Alger eagerly befriended those boys; his interest "was excited," he wrote.

In 1868, Alger published *Ragged Dick* about one of those boys, an "industrious," "generous," "honest" fourteen-year-old, in the words of the back cover, with an "aristocratic" face, who, after being bullied and robbed, still dives into the East River to save a young lad, prompting a "wealthy industrialist" to give him a "well-paying job," thus lifting him "from rags to riches." It was an instant bestseller. Alger went on to write a hundred more.

While widely read in his lifetime, Alger's books exploded in popularity in the twentieth century, when the term *Horatio Alger story* became synonymous with success. After collectively selling eight hundred thousand copies in their first thirty years, Alger's novels sold a million copies every year for the thirty years after that.

What no one knew during that span was the real reason Alger fled

Cape Cod—and likely the reason he was so "excited" to meet those street urchins in New York to begin with. In 1864, a thirteen-year-old boy at Alger's church told his parents that the new pastor had molested him. An investigation soon found that his wasn't an isolated case. Facing charges of "the abominable and revolting crime of gross familiarity with boys," Alger asked his father to intervene. The elder Alger wrote a letter begging for leniency: "I wish him to be able to enter upon the new life on which he has resolved with as little possible to prevent his success."

The letter succeeded. Alger's crime was covered up, and he found redemption in New York as, of all things, a novelist of children's literature. If we need a symbol of the warped story of success we've all been sold, I can think of no better example than a disgraced pedophile whose name embodies the American Dream and who got off scot-free for heinous crimes because of the timely intervention of Daddy.

No wonder in the early twentieth century character was displaced as the sole arbiter of success. The new ideal, though, was hardly better.

Personality.

What Is a Success Story?
Part II: The Cult of Personality

Who gets to be the face of success? Why not Alicia Rodis?

Alicia was the youngest of three girls of a Greek immigrant carpenter in suburban Cleveland and his much younger wife, a paralegal. "I grew up with my dad telling all sorts of stories about the Depression—sleeping in potato stacks and stealing watermelons to feed his family."

Alicia was bullied as a child for displaying mild obsessive-compulsive behaviors. "In seventh grade I was told I had the math skills of a third grader but the communication skills of a college student." So she gravitated to high school theater, "the island of misfit toys," as she called it.

Turned down by Juilliard, Alicia enrolled in Wright State University in Dayton to study acting and dance. "They also had this wonderful teacher, Bruce Cromer, who taught stage combat—fist fighting, sword fighting, how to punch, slap, and kick. My oldest sister was getting a doctorate in pharmacy, and my mom said, 'Your sisters may never love what they do. You will!'"

But could she support herself? After working on some regional productions, Alicia moved to New York, tended bar, developed a drinking problem, and stalled out. She would be yet another asterisk in an endless string of untapped success—if it weren't for Bruce Cromer. Oh, and the fall of an infamous sex abuser.

Alicia started teaching classes in stage combat and was asked to help out on a student film. "I had read about this woman, Tonia, who did something similar for romantic scenes. She called herself an *intimacy coordinator*. I told the director, 'Hey, you've got a sex scene coming up. I'm happy to help.'"

The director agreed. "I used the same techniques we use for street fights for the bedroom. *What's the story we're telling? What's the emotion we're looking for? When does the woman show her breasts? When does the man drop his pants?* You have to be very clinical."

After the film, Alicia reached out to Tonia, who was thrilled to have a compatriot. They wrote a manifesto and posted it on the internet. A few jobs trickled in, but not many.

"Then *The New York Times* posted its exposé about Harvey Weinstein. Overnight, the deluge began."

Alicia got a call from a producer at HBO. "God bless him, he couldn't even say the word *intimacy*. It was like he was calling a prostitute." She was invited onto the set of *The Deuce*. "How does this work?" the executives asked. "I have no idea," Alicia said. "I've never done it for TV. But here's what I know. Actors are no longer comfortable doing intimate scenes—not just lovemaking, but birthing, sexual assault, even kissing. Directors no longer feel comfortable asking actors to be naked because of guilt and shame. Everybody's so worried about lawsuits they can't perform."

She got the job.

"The sex scenes look amazing," the producers told her. HBO started sending her to other sets—*Crashing*, *Watchmen*. Finally, a legal team from the network flew to New York to meet her. "How do we get you on every set?"

"How many sets do you have?"

"Sixty."

Alicia's sister had just given her a book, *Women Don't Ask*, about how to advocate for yourself, so she was feeling emboldened. "OK, that's impossible," she said. "But why don't we go out on a limb together. Why don't you hire me full time, and I'll train a team?"

"Can you write us a proposal?"

Alicia had no idea what to charge. With no established rate for intimacy coordinators, she had been paid at the stuntman rate—about $2,000 a week. Some friends recommended an entertainment lawyer.

"So I go to this firm, and these two attorneys start trying to daughter me. *Oh, yes, what you're doing is really important.* Then they suggest

I ask for a hundred thousand dollars a year. I look at them. 'OK, wait. I work in implicit bias. I need you to pretend I'm a forty-year-old white man who is doing something that is going to revolutionize the industry. Then come back with a number.'"

The two men looked at each other. There was a long pause. Then they started laughing.

"We'll go higher," they said.

Alicia was hired to open a department at HBO. She was asked to write a book. The onetime Juilliard reject was invited to teach at Juilliard.

"Not long before I started doing this work, I was hired to be a background actor for *Boardwalk Empire*," Alicia said. "I remember being on set one day, asking, 'OK, when do I take my top off?' No one said anything, so I asked again. 'When do I take my top off?' Everyone was just dancing around it. Finally, I just raised my hand in the middle of rehearsal. 'WHEN DO I TAKE MY TOP OFF?' The director said, 'Oh, next scene.'

"When my dad came to this country from Greece," she continued, "he made it by using his hands. He built doghouses. He joined the army. He opened a small construction company. Everything was manual, uncomfortable. That physical compulsion manifested in me. The through line in my story is I enable movement. I like to think of myself as empowering people to tell physical stories. And those stories are the most powerful of all."

At the start of the twentieth century, most psychologists drew a distinction between character and personality. The former was fixed, immutable, interior; the latter was adaptable, improvable, superficial. As author Merve Emre observes in *The Personality Brokers*, character was considered the superior trait. "The very concept of having a personality was deeply, irretrievably entangled with the art of inventing and reinventing yourself."

What happened over the next fifty years is that reinventing yourself became cool. Character came to be associated with an earlier, quainter time in America, one that was dominated by Puritan homilies and agrarian frumpiness; while in the go-getter culture of the factory floor and the boss's office, the gentleman's club and the trading pit, the real ticket to prosperity was the ability to mold and market yourself, to upgrade your dress, soften your twang, sharpen your patter.

Character was dead; personality was king.

Again, two figures embody this change. The first is a mostly unremembered figure today.

Orison Swett Marden was born in New Hampshire in 1850 and rose to become the primary spokesman of success at the turn of the twentieth century. Orphaned at seven, he was hired out as a farm boy and found inspiration in self-help books. He grew up to make a fortune in hotels and write forty-five self-help books of his own. In 1897 he founded the magazine *Success*, which quickly became more popular than industry leader *McClure's*, with a staff of two hundred and a circulation of half a million.

In the magazine's early years, Marden's advice centered on the hackneyed Franklin playbook—punctuality, honesty, hard work. But as society became more urban and modern, Marden pivoted, embracing what came to be called New Thought. One part spirituality, one part psychology, New Thought stressed that intention and mental power were the keys to self-improvement. "Change the Thought, Change the Man," as Marden put it. "You must visualize yourself as the man you long to be; see yourself in the exalted position you long to attain."

Never mind that *Success* magazine failed, collapsing in debt in

1911; Marden continued peddling his ideas for the next decade, selling twenty million books and becoming what H. L. Mencken called "the most popular of American authors."

Still, even that popularity was eclipsed by the signature personality of the cult of personality.

Dale Carnegie was yet another farm boy who moved to the big city, remaking himself and the country along the way. Born in 1888 in Maryville, Missouri, to a hog and hay farmer who lost his farm, Carnagey (as his name was originally spelled) was too poor to board in the local school, so he rode a horse each way. He channeled his humiliation into oration, becoming a champion debater. His yearbook quote was "I will sit down now but the time will come when you will hear me."

After graduating, Carnagey sold correspondence courses to ranchers for a time, found his footing as a traveling bacon and lard salesman, failed at acting, sold used cars, and finally, in 1912, persuaded New York's smallest YMCA in Harlem to let him try teaching public speaking. From this start he built a national network of courses. After giving a speech at Carnegie Hall, he changed his name from Carnagey to Carnegie to take advantage of the association. In 1926 he published his first textbook; a decade later he was ready for his masterwork.

What the savvy Missouri farm boy realized earlier than most is that America in those years was made of former farm boys like him who were unsure, insecure, and eager for cure-alls. To participate in the booming consumer culture of abundance, you needed new skills. As Carnegie put it, one could "no longer put much faith in the old adage that hard work alone is the magic key that will unlock the door to our desires." Instead, successful salespeople need to sell themselves as well as their products.

The key to selling yourself was how you spoke. One forgotten casualty of America's pivot from rural to urban was that the flowery, bombastic rhetorical style of the Victorian era was left behind; replaced by a more relaxed, open, Americanized style. The chief voice guru of the nineteenth century, French opera teacher François Delsarte, had stressed pantomime, gesture, and ornate dynamics known as *harmonic gymnastics.*

Carnegie stressed the opposite, what he called *natural delivery.* To be an effective communicator, one should speak slowly—"We need not shout nor strain the voice, but we can use our every-day conversational tone and be perfectly at ease." One should connect spoken words with emotions—"Really feel what you would express and express only what you feel." One should adopt the universal secret of the personality ethic—"Smile." In effect, Carnegie did for success what Frank Parsons had done for career counseling; he introduced what he called *scientific vocational guidance.*

And it worked. Published in 1936, just as the world was emerging from the Depression, *How to Win Friends and Influence People* went on to sell thirty million copies. Carnegie single-handedly moved success away from *who* you were to *how* you packaged yourself. Unlike Poor Richard, your goal was not to be good or righteous; it was to *win* friends and *influence* people. There was nothing about being true to yourself, about fulfilling your own potential, about trying to grow and improve. Like Jay Gatsby, Dale Carnegie encapsulated the twentieth-century ideal of American bravado—*Authenticity is the most important thing; if you can fake that, you've got it made.*

But fakery can get you only so far. As the American workforce became more diverse in the coming decades, our views of success diversified as well. A new approach would be needed, one in which success was not about meeting other people's needs but about meeting your own.

Fortunately, one such solution arrived—just in time.

What Is a Success Story?
Part III: What about Me?

Maybe what we need is a new type of success story. How about Michael Smalls?

Michael was the second of five children born into a working-class family in Mount Pleasant, South Carolina. When Michael was thirteen, his father, thinking he heard a prowler outside their mobile home, went outside and shot a gun into the air. On his way back to bed, he tripped and accidentally shot and killed Michael's baby sister, who was sleeping on the sofa. "My mom ran out and started screaming, 'Oh, my child!'"

Michael's father went to prison for a time but was released when the shooting was ruled an accident; his mother, though, never forgave him. The two separated. "I immediately had to go out and help support my family." Michael mowed lawns, cut wood, picked beans, cleaned fish.

After high school, Michael washed dishes at a Captain D's seafood restaurant for a while and became a phlebotomist for the Red Cross. He eventually went to work at a factory that made car mufflers, then another that manufactured rugs. He was industrious and enjoyed working with his hands but felt stuck.

Then, a workquake.

When Michael was a boy, his grandmother built a roadside stand on US 17 to sell homemade sweetgrass baskets. Michael liked to go with her and, at age seven, learned to weave. "I was the only sibling who was interested."

When Michael reached his forties, his brother-in-law picked up the family business and would go down to Charleston to sell baskets. Michael, to make some extra cash, made a few samples for him.

"One day I went to visit him and flipped over one of my baskets. He had given me $45 for it, but he was selling it for $375. I thought, *I'm not doing that for you anymore!*"

Michael worked nights and weekends to build up some inventory and soon opened a roadside stand like the one his grandmother used to run. He didn't need a permit, he said, because baskets are the state craft of South Carolina "and the governor passed a law that we don't have to pay state taxes on them." The head of a local history museum drove by and invited Michael to sell his wares in the gift shop and teach classes. "Soon I was invited to garden clubs and tea parties in the wealthy communities of Palmetto Bluff, Hilton Head, and Spring Island."

The press picked up the story. The Weather Channel did a feature. The Smithsonian reached out. He appeared on *Good Morning America*. With so many interviews, Michael began digging into the history.

"When I was growing up, everybody thought, *I'm making baskets to survive*. What we didn't know was the story behind the baskets. The art form was actually brought from Sierra Leone in West Africa by my ancestors four hundred years ago. A lot of people don't realize that when traders went to Africa to get slaves, they didn't take random people. They took folks who were skilled at what they did."

Michael's great-great-grandmother was born into slavery in Africa; his great-great-grandfather was the same in Barbados. Shipped to America, they met at Laurel Hill Plantation in South Carolina.

"Once on the Atlantic Coast, these slaves were put to work on rice plantations. They made baskets to clean the chaff off the rice. They made baskets to take fruits and vegetables out of the fields. They made baskets to hold babies while they were working in the fields."

With all the newfound attention, Michael was able to quit his job and open a website to sell his work. "The worst part is gathering materials—the spartina grass, palm fronds, pine needles, and bulrush. I have to put on long sleeves and rubber boots and watch out for alligators and rattlesnakes." He can spend weeks weaving individual pieces, which he sells for anywhere from $60 to $3,500. The name of his company: Gullah Sweetgrass Baskets.

"Gullah is a culture. These native Africans along the coast from North Carolina to Florida all came from different backgrounds and spoke different dialects. So they created a culture that allowed them to communicate. It had its own dances; its own foods, like okra and collards. When it came to baskets, they searched the swamps for something similar to the long grasses they used at home and ended up with spartina. They called it *sweetgrass* because of the aroma."

Michael says he takes pride in continuing an art form that he first saw his great-grandmother do.

"A lot of people, when you mention success, they automatically think of money. But success is not always money. I don't wear designer clothes or live in a fancy house, but for me success is what's inside you. I'm passing on a tradition that began with slavery, and I'm turning it into happiness."

The critical thing about Michael Smalls, Alicia Rodis, Chris Donovan, or six dozen others I could have selected for this chapter is that none would have been included in any of the bestselling accounts of success that were published in the last 250 years. They simply don't conform to the standards that were used. Each hit a wall for a time, couldn't meet their obligations, battled internal doubts. All three carried heavy baggage from their parents, were late bloomers, and ultimately chose directions that weren't available to them at the outset of their lives—or, in the case of intimacy coordination, weren't even invented.

All three, you might say, are sui generis.

Except that almost everyone I spoke with would fit this description—along with almost everyone I know. There is no such thing as a generic success story anymore.

Which raises the question we should be asking: Why isn't there a definition of success that lets everyone define the idea for themselves?

In 1990, David Jepsen, the outgoing president of the National Career Development Association, the same organization that Frank Parsons dreamed up a hundred years earlier, gave a speech at the organization's annual meeting in which he declared a new vision for success: *Career as story.* Jepsen's idea grew out of a convergence of powerful forces. The first was the rise of neuroscience, which in the late twentieth century began to reveal, among other things, that our minds are wired through mirror neurons and neural coupling to process the world through stories. The second was constructivism, the philosophical movement that states people must create their own reality rather than passively accept existing absolutes.

The third was narrative psychology, the groundbreaking idea that human identity is based on the stories we tell about ourselves. Each of us has an autobiographical narrative that we're constantly rehearsing, both to ourselves and to others. When something goes awry in our lives, it's our responsibility to revise and retell that story. As Dan McAdams, the leading architect of the field, once shared with me, that story answers the questions: *Who am I? How do I fit into the world? What gives me meaning?*

In the case of work, those questions are: *Am I doing what I want to be doing? Am I becoming who I want to become? Am I living in a way that brings me meaning today—and will bring me more meaning in the future?*

One of the people in the audience listening to Jepsen's speech that day was Mark Savickas. A native of Cleveland, Savickas had grown up with a father who was born with a disability—one of his legs was longer than the other. "He was totally physically able," Savickas told me. "But no company would hire him. I always wondered, *Why are some people allowed to work?* Bruce Springsteen has a great lyric: 'Let a man work, is that so wrong?'"

Savickas went on to study the psychology of work in college, then spent nearly a decade as a career counselor, while also earning his PhD. "But when I listened to Jepsen, that was the moment that changed everything." Over the next three decades, Savickas became the undisputed dean of the professional field that he calls *career construction* and others call *narrative career counseling*. Savickas's output includes five books, more than a hundred articles, and five hundred professional presentations. He also loves to travel; he told me delightedly that he had visited fifty countries.

The essence of Savickas's philosophy is that only an individual experiencing a work crisis can resolve that crisis; the only resolution to tension is attention. "The answer is not in society," he told me. "It's not in test scores. It's already inside you."

Savickas calls this unrevealed truth your *unknown known.* "Anybody who's questioning what they're doing already knows the answer; but they don't know that they know it. The goal is to give them the tools and the confidence to unlock the story they've already been writing for years—even decades."

By empowering the individual to take ownership of their story, career construction righted an imbalance that had been in career guidance from the very beginning: it took agency out of the hands of professionals and put it back in the hands of seekers; it moved the focus from external assessment to internal assessment.

"Even when I know the answer, which I usually do within five minutes of meeting somebody, I never tell them the answer. I don't want to be powerful; I want to be useful. I tell them that they came to me for advice, but the advice must come from them."

Only you can script your own life.

What Savickas and his colleagues were doing was not just remaking how we find work; they were helping remake the very essence of success. For the first century of our country, success was about character; for the next century, it was about personality; in the new century, it would be about story. No longer do you have to be a side character in someone else's story; now you get to be the hero in your own story.

In my conversation with Savickas, I asked him whether after fifty years in the counseling profession he believed that individuals could do this work themselves. In effect, can each of us be our own counselor?

"Absolutely," he said. "And you must. As much as I'm sad to say it, counseling is a dying field. It's too white, too male, too middle class. We don't have the ear of the country." But as the workforce becomes more diverse, he said, and our definition of success becomes more individualized, the need for career construction has become even more urgent.

"People are realizing that work won't love you back. We're return-ing to a time when family, community, spirituality—those values that we used to associate with the village—are playing a larger and larger role in our work. If people are offered a job that they should want in a place that they don't want to be, they'll turn it down. No one did that before. People no longer want to meet some benchmark of success as defined by society; they want to define it themselves."

In that case, how do you decide which story of success you want to tell?

Let's turn to that question now.

CHAPTER 5

The Meaning Audit

What to Do When You Don't Know What to Do

Jessica Alba understands the vagaries of success stories. On the surface, Alba has a traditional, Lana Turner–style Hollywood narrative, from coffee shop to cover girl.

Born in Southern California, Alba grew up in a "very conservative, traditional Latin American Catholic family." Her mother, who once managed a movie theater, was of Danish descent; her father, an air force pilot, was the son of Mexican immigrants. The family moved around a lot, had little money, and leaned heavily on their religion. "I was really frustrated with the way I was raised," Alba said. "That's probably why I started working so young."

At eleven, Alba attended an open casting call in Beverly Hills and won the grand prize: a year of acting lessons. In high school, she earned modest roles in TV and commercials. After she graduated, *Titanic* director James Cameron picked Alba from a pool of a thousand candidates to play the lead in the Fox sci-fi series *Dark Angel*. She went on to be featured in a number of Hollywood film franchises, from *Fantastic Four* to *Sin City*.

Alba was, by all measures, a star: Her films grossed a billion dollars; she was named one of *People*'s fifty most beautiful people; she won an MTV Movie Award for Sexiest Performance. She also married an industry insider and became pregnant with their first child.

Which is the moment her future collided with her past.

When Alba was twenty-seven, she was washing a load of onesies she received at a baby shower. Her eyes started watering, she sneezed uncontrollably, and her hands broke out into welts. The episode triggered an even deeper reaction: bringing up memories that Alba had long kept hidden.

As a child, Alba suffered from allergies, had pneumonia multiple times a year, twice had a collapsed lung, once had a tonsillar cyst removed, and had kidney surgery—all before she was eight. "I was hospitalized several times for my asthma or related illnesses, which meant missing a lot of school and being out of sync with my classmates and teachers."

Fearful of re-creating this pattern with her own children, Alba, who had always been dismissed as something of a pretty face (she won a Razzie for Worst Supporting Actress), resolved to do something to address harmful ingredients in baby products. Three years later, along with two partners, she launched the Honest Company, a consumer goods maker that sells nontoxic household products. After a well-known shampoo sent her to the emergency room with impaired eyesight, the company introduced a beauty line, too.

Like many startups, Alba's company went through ups and downs, faced criticism and leadership shake-ups, had doors slammed in its face. But in its first five years, the Honest Company raised $100 million, grew to $300 million in annual revenue, and received a $1 billion valuation. *Forbes* pegged Alba's net worth at $340 million and featured her on its cover as one of "America's Richest Self-Made Women." The company went public six days after her fortieth birthday at a market cap of $1.5 billion.

Inevitably, some of these milestones also proved fleeting—*Forbes* admitted it overestimated Alba's net worth; the stock slumped along with the rest of the market—but even after these fluctuations, Yahoo appointed Alba to its board, proving she was more than just a pretty face; she was also a face of perseverance and reinvention.

All because at a defining moment in her life, Alba didn't just keep plowing forward; she also went dredging up her past.

She didn't just follow the script; she also followed her scripture.

"Once you understand yourself, and why you do what you do," Alba told CNBC, "it unlocks your potential."

You, too, have a scripture. Your task in the face of whatever chaos you confront is to reconnect with it—and to fulfill it.

Here's how to do that.

In 1979, the distinguished professor of English and Afro-American studies at Yale, Robert Stepto, published a landmark book called *From Behind the Veil*, in which he articulates two prototypes of Black literary narratives. The first is what he calls a *narrative of ascent*, the second a *narrative of immersion*. In narratives of ascent (e.g., Frederick Douglass), the protagonist, in order to escape oppression, goes on a ritualized journey from the symbolic South to the symbolic North, during which he or she becomes increasingly articulate and increasingly free. In narratives of immersion (e.g., W. E. B. Du Bois), the protagonist, in order to gain tribal knowledge, goes on a ritualized journey from the symbolic North to the symbolic South during which he or she becomes increasingly knowledgeable and increasingly grounded.

The most successful narratives, Stepto writes, combine both. They balance ascending and descending, emerging and immersing.

This brilliant rubric does the best single job of capturing the essence of successful work narratives that I know. Individuals, in their greatest moments of transition, combine moving upward with drilling downward.

Yet that's not the story we've been told. For the long history of the American success story, the prevailing narrative has focused almost exclusively on ascent—*rags to riches, up by your bootstraps, climb the ladder, bigger office, higher floor, larger salary, better view.*

The signature lesson of the Work Story Project is that this narrative does not capture the true experience of success. The people who are happiest and most fulfilled at work don't just climb, they also dig. They don't just barrel headlong into the future, they also burrow headfirst into the past. They unearth their roots, uncover their pains, unbury their dreams. They discover, as all heroes since antiquity have, that there is no wisdom *out there*; the truest wisdom is always *in here*.

Instead, the people who get the most out of their biggest workquakes do three things: they immerse, they reflect, and they ascend.

They excavate the past, they probe the present, and they construct the future.

I call these three acts, collectively, a *meaning audit*. When done effectively, a meaning audit is the single biggest gift you can give yourself in a moment of upheaval. To get the meaning you want, you first must identify the meaning you're wanting. This chapter explores how this process works in practice.

Excavate the Past: Perform Personal Archaeology

The first act of a meaning audit is to dig into your past. What were your earliest thoughts of work? The dream jobs you were forced to abandon? The versions of yourself that for one reason or another got cast aside along the way?

What is your underlying scripture of work that you've been scripting your entire life?

Tim Pierpont grew up in the small town of Middlebury, Connecticut. His father sold insurance; his mother was a librarian. Tim learned in fifth grade that he was adopted. "And it threw me. Something has been bothering me my entire childhood, and I could never figure out what it was."

One thing that bugged Tim was that he liked to work with his hands—doing art projects, woodworking, painting—but his parents were dismissive of his interest. "One day my mother came into my workshop in the basement. 'If you put the effort into your schoolwork that you put into your painting, you'd be an A student.'"

When Tim was thirteen, his father asked if he wanted to paint the family's white picket fence. "There must have been two hundred pickets, and he offered me a nickel a picket. I thought, *This is brilliant! I can finally get paid to work with my hands.*"

Some neighbors drove by and asked if Tim would paint their fences; suddenly he had a job during vacations. After graduating, Tim enrolled at Syracuse University and earned a degree in studio art, with a specialty in lighting. But when he took his portfolio, which combined color theory, metalwork, and sculpture, around Manhattan, everyone said, "This is amazing, but we don't know what to do with you."

So Tim returned to Connecticut and opened a painting and wall-papering company. For the next few years, he lived out his childhood dream. "Except this was southern Connecticut, which is very business minded, and painting was not acceptable work." When a girlfriend suggested he follow her to Palo Alto, California, Tim relocated and managed a ski store.

"One day I was fitting this woman with boots and she asked about my background. 'I like built environments.' 'Really? My boyfriend works in real estate at Sun Microsystems. You should talk to him.'"

Tim spent the next twenty-two years in corporate real estate. At Sun, he designed interiors and managed large projects. He loved the culture and the creativity. After marrying his girlfriend, Andrea, and having two daughters, he also appreciated that he could support his family as the sole breadwinner. But when the company went remote in 2001, he hated it. "It felt like house arrest." So he jumped to Bank of America, which he hated more. Finally he moved to Union Bank, where he stayed for six years, until his department was eliminated.

Tim had two children in college at that point; he lived in an expensive neighborhood. But he did have insurance and a small nest egg. "I started looking for other jobs in the industry, but it kept gnawing at me. *Is this really what I want to do for the rest of my life?*"

One afternoon he sat down in a coffee shop and took an inventory of his life. "I made a list of five things that were most meaningful to me, including *being part of a community*, *being outside*, and *working with my hands.*

"And then it hit me. *If I were running a painting company, I would be doing all three of those right now.*"

With Andrea's support, Tim looked at buying a franchise of

CertaPro but was turned off by the company's goal of only 70 percent customer satisfaction. So at fifty-two—thirty-nine years after his father paid him a nickel a picket—Tim opened Pierpont Painting in Marin County. He committed to hiring only documented workers, he offered health insurance, and his goal was 100 percent satisfaction.

"We compete on quality, not price."

The work is demanding, he said. The lack of financial security can keep him awake, but the biggest problem is that he's been forced to find a new friend group since his high-tech millionaire neighbors shunned him. "I've been labeled the painter guy. On a block full of Teslas, I'm the only person who drives a van with a logo on the side."

But he finally found the meaning he's been seeking his whole life.

"When I was in my twenties, I learned I could seek out my birth mom. Turns out she was young, had an office relationship with an older man, and didn't want a baby. But when I met her, I learned that she had a similar interest in art. In ten minutes, my whole life made sense. I finally understood what had been bugging me all those years. And now that I'm running this company, I'm finally back in my workshop doing what I wanted to be doing all along."

In Seamus Heaney's poem "Digging," an unnamed narrator hovers over a blank page, unable to write, his pen "snug as a gun" between his finger and thumb. The man peers through a window at his father, digging in the dirt. He admires the rasping sound of the blade, the coarseness of the boot, the cool hardness of his father's hands. *By God*, he thinks, his father could handle a spade, as could his father.

The narrator despairs that he has none of those skills. He cannot cut turf. He cannot scatter potatoes. But then he realizes that he does have a tool that can do what theirs does. He has a pen.

"I'll dig with it."

Whatever tools you've mastered in your life, you, too, can use them to dig.

The essence of personal archaeology is using the tools of emotional excavation to resurface the underlying themes that have long directed your life. I began using this term for two reasons. First, I spent more than a decade traipsing around real archaeological digs across the Middle East and North Africa and have seen firsthand how sifting through prior civilizations can produce profound insights about the present. As a wise practitioner once told me, archaeology is the best tool for looking ahead.

Second, at every major inflection point in my own life—at precisely those moments when I didn't know what to do—I found the answers I was seeking not by looking anxiously toward the future but by looking curiously toward the past. In my twenties, eager to reconnect with America after years of living abroad, I returned to my childhood love of juggling and spent a year as a clown in a traveling circus. In my thirties, feeling disconnected from spirituality, I set off on a yearlong journey retracing the five books of Moses through the desert. In my forties, as a new dad forced to stop traveling by cancer, I spent a decade exploring the foundations of modern families. And in my fifties, shaken by a string of suicide attempts by my father, I used a storytelling project I did with him to inspire the idea of collecting life stories.

In the face of every potential ending in my own life, I found inspiration by returning to my beginnings.

And I'm not alone.

I asked everyone in my conversations if during their biggest workquake they performed personal archaeology. Almost everyone said yes.

For some, doing this kind of archaeology requires conscientious reflection. Tim Pierpont, as we saw, specifically went to that coffee shop with the intention of writing down his core values. Oakland native Leah Smart, after a decade in sales at LinkedIn and a dot-com startup, had "the crawling feeling in my skin that I wanted to quit." Unsure what to do, she started meditating and journaling. "I called it subconscious unblocking. *What stories was I told about money and success?*" The process led her to remember a third-grade teacher, who gave her the attention she was missing from her workaholic father. "I realized I wanted to care for others like she cared for me." She switched to professional development at LinkedIn and started a side job as a life coach.

For others, doing archaeology means using creativity. Nate Venturelli, a third-generation welder in Indiana and a member of United Steel Workers Local 12775, wrote a country song about his grandfather called "Union Man." When the song was picked up by local radio, Nate began a hope job performing at local clubs on weekends. Daniel Minter, who was born on a farm in southern Georgia, became a Caldecott-winning illustrator and was twice commissioned by the US Postal Service to design stamps. But after relocating to Maine in his fifties, he began exploring his roots. "It was all about finding my purpose in the story within me." He cofounded Indigo Arts Alliance in Portland for underrepresented artists.

For still more, doing archaeology requires making time and space. Sabrina Bleich, the daughter of Israeli and Hungarian immigrants, grew up infatuated with what she called "incredible but flawed" Hollywood women—Lena Dunham, Amy Schumer, Tina Fey—but after a series of dead-end jobs in her twenties, she put herself through a reboot. "I get into these moments where there's too much noise—like a person who always has the TV on. I needed to turn off the noise and ask myself in a perfect world what would I be doing." Her next job was in international acquisitions at Discovery Channel.

Cindy Edwards, born in the "fruitcake capital of the world," Claxton, Georgia, grew up enthralled with fashion and beauty. "I love eye shadow. I love primping. I love it all." In her twenties, she walked away from a promising job in PR to become a stay-at-home mom. But after becoming an empty nester, Cindy reconnected with her first love and cofounded a natural skin care line called Sapelo made with Southern ingredients—gardenia stem cells, magnolia oil, palmetto honey.

By far the most vivid story of personal archaeology I heard came from Ariel Daunay. Ariel was born in the mango jungles of Saint Croix. "I grew up surrounded by violence. I was gang-raped at eleven."

When local humanitarians heard her story, Ariel was sent to North Carolina on a high school scholarship. But she didn't fit in, so she cleaned houses for a while, worked on a boat for a decade, and after caring for her dying mother, fled to the jungles of Hawaii, where she began a ten-year journey of recovery, healing, and bodywork. Today, Ariel is one of the world's leading somatic healers, based in Santa Fe, working with everyone from CEOs to abuse victims to addicts. "No matter how much a person might say, 'I'm separate from my story,' you're not. It's in your nervous system. I can touch you in a certain place, and *boom!* an entire part of your history that you tried to forget comes out. If you want to do work that is rich and fulfilling, you have to allow that story to escape."

I asked Ariel whether this process involves ascension or immersion.

"It's a combination," she said. "It's like a phoenix rising out of the ashes, but you have to go into the ashes first."

"And how would you respond to someone who says, 'But I'm just an accountant. Or a schoolteacher. Or an electrician. Your process doesn't apply to me.'?"

"I would say, 'If that's your narrative, keep going.' But I would also say, 'At some point, your story is going to catch up with you. You're going to wake up one day and say, *Wait a minute. I'm not happy anymore. What was that woman saying about my story being inside my body? I'm getting close to that feeling now.*"

Probe the Present: Know Your ABCs

The second act of the meaning audit is to probe your present. What are your priorities right now? How is what matters to you today different from what mattered to you two years ago, or five, or ten?

Specifically, is your primary focus yourself, your loved ones, or your community?

Wei-Tai Kwok was born to Chinese refugees who met in Philadelphia. His father became an engineer for the VA; his mother raised three children. "My dad was very grateful to America; he stayed in one job his entire life because of loyalty. I think that idea got stuck in my head."

Wei-Tai's childhood hero was Richard Nixon. "He and I had the same birthday, and since I was born in America, I grew up thinking I could be president. I wanted to be him."

Rejecting his mother's insistence that he play violin, Wei-Tai became an OK pianist, a pretty good tennis player, but a great debater, winning the Virginia state championship. Still, his father insisted he seek out a family friend, a doctor at Harvard, who scolded him. "Wei-Tai, in your lifetime, China will become the most important country in the world. You don't speak Chinese; you better learn."

Wei-Tai started studying Mandarin in high school; two years later, when China opened up to the world and Wei-Tai was an undergraduate at Yale, he began leading American tours of the country. After graduating, Wei-Tai moved to Shanghai and worked at a law firm. He moved back to the States to join a startup that grew to become Silicon Valley's top Asian ad agency, serving Apple, Disney, and Wells Fargo. Wei-Tai stayed for seventeen years, the last seven as CEO.

One Saturday morning in 2006, his wife, April, announced, "Hey, I hear there's this good movie out by Al Gore on climate change. Let's go watch it."

"So she drags me to the theater," Wei-Tai said. "It's basically a two-hour PowerPoint."

But it sent Wei-Tai into a spiral of personal archaeology.

"I had studied energy in high school. The national debate topic my sophomore year was 'Should America promote energy independence?' My partner and I argued that America should go solar."

By the time the movie was over, Wei-Tai was in a full-on workquake.

"I walked out of the theater and said to my wife, 'You know, honey, if what we saw today is true, we don't have a hundred years to solve this problem. We have only thirty. Our kids are six and nine. By the time they're old enough to help, it will be too late.'"

For the next four months, Wei-Tai spent every night on his computer, educating himself. "And everything I read said the same thing, 'Our political leaders don't do shit.' It made me so angry. I kept thinking, *I have to do something.* I would go to these meetings where we argue about square corners versus round corners, then come home, brush my teeth, look myself in the mirror, and ask, *What did you do today to be part of the solution to climate change?* And every day I had the same answer. *Nothing.*"

So Wei-Tai did the one thing that was unacceptable in his family narrative: be disloyal to his employer.

He also did the one thing that was most urgent in his own narrative: be loyal to something bigger than himself.

Wei-Tai quit his job. Over the next decade, he worked at China's largest solar company, at an American renewable energy firm, at a publicly listed solar panel company, and at a kinetic energy startup. Still frustrated with his limited impact, he finally decided to open his own green energy consultancy and take the one step he vowed never to take. Fifteen years after concluding that politicians "don't do shit," Wei-Tai approached the city council of Lafayette, California, a community of twenty-five thousand northeast of Oakland, and he was chosen over five others to fill a slot made vacant by a resignation.

The disillusioned boyhood fan of Richard Nixon had become a politician.

"I did a lot of soul-searching in order to decide, *I'm willing to take a pay cut. To go from being a seventeen-year veteran to being a newcomer in a field I knew nothing about.* What I realized is that I'm not happy if I'm just doing something that makes money but that's worthless to society. I feel this obligation, maybe from my parents, to do something good for this country. America can be problematic, but I feel very loyal in trying to help America be better."

If we go back two hundred years, to the birth of the industrial era, most of the ways humans gave themselves meaning were fixed. People had to do what their parents wanted them to do, live where their parents wanted them to live, believe what their parents wanted them to believe, and love whom their parents wanted them to love. Today, that dynamic has flipped. Most of us can do what we want to do, live where we want to live, believe what we want to believe, and love whom we want to love.

But as wonderful as this turnabout has been, it's also brought downsides. Foremost among them: We get paralyzed by choice. We get writer's block trying to write the story of our lives.

A big part of the Life Story Project, my first round of stories, was trying to understand how people navigate this abundance of choice. What I found is that we have three building blocks of identity, three levers we tug and push throughout our lives to maintain our sense of balance, purpose, and joy. I call these three elements the *ABCs of Meaning.*

The *A* is *agency*—what we do, make, or create; our sense of autonomy, freedom, and mastery. For many of us, our sense of agency comes from our work. In narrative terms, our *A* is our *me story.*

The *B* is *belonging*—our relationships, friends, loved ones, and colleagues. For many of us, our sense of belonging comes from our families. It's our *we story.*

The *C* is *cause*—a calling, a mission, a purpose; a transcendent commitment beyond ourselves that makes our lives worthwhile. For many of us, our cause is our higher sense of giving back. It's our *thee story.*

All of us have all three of these elements inside us. I think of us as like Lady Justice, carrying three scales instead of two, in which we're constantly trying to balance and rebalance these various strands of our identity. But here's what I've also learned: each of us prioritizes these sources of meaning in different ways. I'm an ABC, for example. I'm a writer so I'm very agentic, I'm a very committed family member and superinvolved dad, but cause is less important to me. My wife, Linda, is a CAB. She helps entrepreneurs all day, so she's very cause oriented; she's a cofounder and CEO, which means she's highly agentic; but outside of family, relationships are less important to her.

What I've learned in exploring these themes for years through my interviews is that we adjust our priorities during life transitions; we *shape-shift*, as I call it. Maybe we've been working too hard and want to devote more time to giving back; maybe we've become run-down from raising children or caring for aging relatives and want to do something for ourselves; maybe we've become burned out from serving others and want to focus on our own loved ones for a while.

In my new round of interviews, I wanted to learn how these sources of meaning shape our decisions around work. I first asked everyone, *What is your order of ABCs, and what percentage do you allot them?* Half of all arrangements were unique, a reminder of how much variety there is in how we assign meaning in our lives. Overall, cause came in first with 40 percent, followed by agency with 31 percent, and belonging with 29 percent. That means the average was CAB. For me, the biggest takeaway in this finding is that in the emerging workforce of the future, purpose is likely to be higher in importance than traditional narratives of success have long suggested.

Next, I was curious whether people adjust their priorities in work transitions. Nearly eight in ten said yes. As to which direction they shift, the majority—54 percent—moved away from agency, with the rest split evenly between moving away from belonging and cause. As for what direction they moved toward, the same number—54 percent— moved toward cause, while 31 percent moved toward belonging and only 15 percent toward agency.

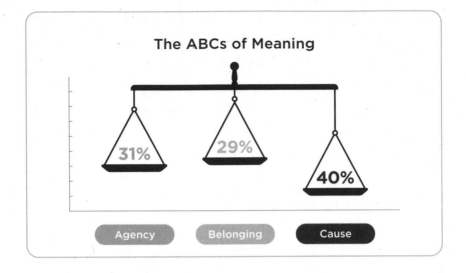

Let's be clear what these numbers are telling us: in the inflection points in our work lives, when we take stock of who we are and what we want most out of life, Americans consistently reduce their focus on personal achievement and increase their focus on serving others, connecting with loved ones, and making a greater impact on the world.

Who are these individuals?

They are people like Wei-Tai, who said that he left his CEO seat and became a foot soldier fighting climate change, a move that took him from ABC to CAB, because he was "not interested in sitting in a room looking at pieces of paper all day." They're Harmit Malik, the Seattle geneticist who said that when he was younger he was a classic ABC who believed his legacy would be "scientific achievement and selfish accomplishment," but after having a neuroatypical son, shifted to BAC because, he said, "It became very clear that my main legacy was going to be the people I trained and the family I helped raise."

They're Aaron Quinn, a second-generation Oakland firefighter who, after struggling with addiction and burnout, adjusted his priorities from ACB to BCA and now spends ten hours a week training recruits "to take care of their mental and physical health." And they're Laura Delarato, the *Vox* creative director, who after seeing the way women in the workforce develop self-hatred, shifted her emphasis from ABC to CAB. "I realized I don't need to belong. I'm happy to do my own thing. But what I do care most about is for women to stop hating themselves. Now that I'm a woman in power, I can hire plus-sized talent, I can hire women producers, I can hire nontraditional voice actors."

Workquakes, by their very nature, are destabilizing events. Some of us want nothing more than to return as quickly as possible to the firm ground we previously occupied. But far more of us seek a different ground entirely. The best way to know which choice is right for you is to know your ABCs—and know how they might be changing in real time.

Construct the Future: Ask the Kipling Questions

The third part of a meaning audit is to construct the future. Use the insights you gleaned from your personal archaeology and your assessment of your ABCs and begin to create a narrative for what comes next.

All while accepting, as any storyteller must, that you can't always control that narrative.

Laura Spaulding is very direct about her life. "I had a terrible upbringing. My father worked as a DEA agent and created an environment that made my life miserable. My mother was just weak. The most important thing in my childhood was getting out of those surroundings."

As a high schooler in Tampa, Florida, Laura poured herself into soccer, hoping to win a scholarship. When she came up short—and her parents refused to contribute to her tuition—Laura started over in the military. "I chose the army because I wanted to be uncomfortable."

Her first deployment was to Fort McClellan, Alabama. About five months in, the commanding officer took to the barracks loudspeaker one night and began calling out names. "Everybody's looking at one another, like, *What the fuck?*" One by one, he called each woman into his office and asked her to name who they thought was gay. When Laura refused, he said that someone had identified her.

"It was 1993. Bill Clinton had just signed 'Don't Ask, Don't Tell.' I said, 'We're in a barracks with twenty-eight women. We've had no days off. What are you talking about?'"

He didn't care. Based on one accusation, Laura was charged with an Article 15 offense and thrown into the stockade. She was given an ultimatum: Accept a dishonorable discharge or face court martial and up to five years in jail. "I chose the latter. Because one, I'm bullheaded, and two, I had no place to go. They gave me one phone call a week, and I didn't even use it, because I could never call my family."

Still imprisoned two months later, Laura changed her mind. She signed a confession, was stripped, given civilian clothes, and handed a manila envelope with the word HOMOSEXUAL stamped on the front. A cellmate who was in the same position invited her home to Michigan. With no options, the two took out a map, put on a blindfold, and threw a dart. Wherever it landed, they would go.

So Laura moved to Knoxville, Tennessee, and started over for a second time. She worked two jobs and used food stamps to pay for college, studying criminology. After graduating, she took the first offer she could get, with the Kansas City Police Department. She patrolled housing projects, then transferred to undercover narcotics.

"Women had never done undercover before, but because I came from a toxic environment, I was determined to prove I could do it. I disguised myself as a prostitute, wore the same outfit every night for two years, never did my hair, and blacked out my teeth with nail polish. I was going into crack houses alone, with no wire and no gun, so I had to make sure my acting was very, very good."

But when her department got a new boss, a nepotistic hire who was young, unqualified, and bigoted, she knew her days were numbered. "If you're a gay man, you're at the bottom of the hierarchy. If you're a gay woman, as I am, you're just one step up from that."

Once again, Laura began a process of self-examination. "I realized I kept repeating the same cycles, putting my future in someone else's hands." She also remembered that she had an entrepreneurial streak as a girl. "When I was growing up, every time I got a Christmas or birthday present, I would resell it to my friends for a profit. In sixth grade, I bought a box of Blow Pops at Sam's Club for four dollars and sold them for a quarter a piece. My family really frowned on those activities."

Laura enrolled in an MBA program at night and, when she was done, quit policing altogether and restarted her life for the third time in ten years. She returned to Florida, sold medical centrifuges to make money, and opened a crime scene cleanup company on the side called Spaulding Decon. "I was turned down by every bank, so I had to take out a home equity loan for $15,000, which I used to buy a HEPA vacuum, personal protective equipment, and biomedical containers."

Today, Spaulding Decon has thirty-seven franchises in eighteen states. Laura hosts a YouTube series called *Crime Scene Cleaning* that has eight hundred fifty thousand subscribers. Her job is to clean up what she calls the nastiest messes—decomposing bodies, meth labs, bloody homicides, hoarders.

"Sometimes the mess is so bad—ten thousand magazines, five hundred soiled diapers—that instead of paying me to clean their house, people sell it to me for fifty cents on the dollar, and I flip it."

And at fifty, a single mom, and finally "not worried about what other people think" of her, Laura was imagining yet another restart. "I can't be the only woman who's experienced what I have. I want to open a platform to elevate women. I want to say, *If I can persevere, you can persevere.*"

As Laura suggests, and story after story shows, each of us reaches, at multiple times in our lives, existential crises around work. These superworkquakes don't just upend our work lives, they upend our entire identities. They're meaning vacuums that invite us both to revisit the underlying themes of our lives and begin to reconstruct them.

A meaning audit is the most effective response to a meaning vacuum. It's the process of moving from passively suffering to actively solving. As we saw with Tim Pierpont's decision to start a company, Wei-Tai Kwok's decision to walk away from a company, and Laura Spaulding's decision to remake herself time and again, that process involves deep emotional work. Finding meaning in your work life is not as simple as beefing up your résumé, identifying job openings, and going on interviews. If anything, those steps are the last part of the process.

The real work is what precedes those steps. In 2013, the psychologist Roy Baumeister of Florida State University, along with colleagues Kathleen Vohs, Jennifer Aaker, and Emily Garbinsky, published a milestone study called "Some Key Differences between a Happy Life and a Meaningful Life." Happiness is largely "present-oriented," they write; animals can be happy. Meaning is about "linking past, present, and future"; only humans have that capacity. The primary tool to do that, they write, is storytelling.

"It's the story that stitches together past, present, and future."

If only there were a simple, easy-to-remember method to help all of us write better stories.

There is.

In April 1900, the English writer Rudyard Kipling, a few years shy of winning the Nobel Prize, published a short story in *Ladies' Home Journal* called "The Elephant's Child." The story would later be included in *Just So Stories*, the collection of bedtime tales he composed for his daughter Justine, which earned its name because if Kipling misplaced a word, Justine would open her eyes and insist it be placed *just so*.

"The Elephant's Child" ends with a poem called "I Keep Six Honest Serving-Men." It begins:

I keep six honest serving-men;
(They taught me all I knew)
Their names are What and Why and When
And How and Where and Who.

These six questions, invoked as far back as antiquity, came to be called the *Kipling questions* and were soon being taught in writing classes around the world as the best way to construct a good story. In a surprising twist of personal archaeology: not until mentioning this rubric in my conversations did I recall that I had a poster from *The*

New York Times on my bedroom wall as a teenager that featured these questions.

What I found in asking people about how they navigated their biggest workquakes is that these were the questions people were already asking. And no wonder. *Who, what, when, where, why,* and *how* have helped storytellers craft better stories for centuries; they can help us today.

The rest of this book explores how to use these questions to write the story of success you need. Each chapter is devoted to one question. In keeping with the structure of the meaning audit, each question is broken down into three subquestions: one about the past, one about the present, one about the future. The question about the future is posed in the form of a fill-in-the-blank answer: *I want to be the kind of person who* _____ , *I want to do work that* _____ , *I'm at a moment in life when* _____ , and so on. In the conclusion, we'll put all these statements together to create a rough draft of your work story right now.

The famed virologist Jonas Salk once observed that solutions come from asking the right questions, because the answer already exists. "You don't invent the answer; you reveal the answer."

The same is true for the story of your work life.

When you don't know what to do, do this: these are the six questions to ask in a workquake.

III

THE SIX QUESTIONS TO ASK IN A WORKQUAKE

CHAPTER 6

Who Is Your Who?

I Want to Be the Kind of
Person Who _____

Ayad Akhtar is an American playwright and winner of the Pulitzer Prize who wrote a novel called *Homeland Elegies* about an American playwright named Ayad Akhtar who wins the Pulitzer Prize. The novel mixes fact and fiction—"It's me, but it's not me," Akhtar the author has said of Akhtar the character—so it's impossible to know for sure whether any particular scene is real or made-up. But the truth is, all of us face this ambiguity in the stories we tell, especially the ones about our upbringings.

Which is why one scene in the novel is so affecting. Akhtar's mother, trapped in a loveless marriage with a doctor who's having an affair, finds refuge in books. "I never truly felt loved by her," Akhtar writes. "I saw now that the source of my life's work—reading, literature, theater—was in part the pursuit of something as simple as my mother's gaze, a gaze she gave happily to books."

Surely it wasn't a coincidence, he writes, that he, too, sought comfort in books. "Wasn't I seeking her attention? Isn't that what I really wanted as I would sidle up to her warm body on the couch as she read, a book of my own in hand?"

The first reality we have to confront as we start to construct a healthy story about work is that we're not the only characters in those stories. Each of us takes into consideration a wider array of *whos* than we think. Our dramatis personae, as playwrights call it, is amazingly complex. Duncan Watts, a sociologist at the University of Pennsylvania, writes, "We like to think of ourselves as individuals, capable of making up our own minds about what we think is important." But it's never really that easy. "We rarely, if ever, make decisions completely independently and in isolation."

In the case of work, our scriptures teem with parents, grandparents, teachers, neighbors, coaches, bosses, lovers, spouses, exes, children, grandchildren, even pets. Like Horton, none of us hears a single *who*. We all live in a roaring *Whoville*.

The first question to ask in a workquake is *who are these whos*, what are they trying to say to you, and which ones should you prioritize at this moment?

Judy Cockerton spent her whole life surrounded by *whos*. Born into a sprawling ranching family in Walnut Creek, California, Judy grew up engulfed in aunts, uncles, grandparents, and cousins. "Everyone invested in everyone else's well-being." Judy's mother was a stay-at-home mom; her father trained firefighters. They passed on the family's creed of caring for others. "Once, we were driving to Disneyland, and my dad saw a train that had caught on fire. He pulled to the side of the road, jumped out of the car, and ran to help the rescue team."

Judy's biggest *who*, though, was her grandmother. "She was born in Bakersfield in 1892. When she was ten, her father got a covered wagon and moved all their sheep to a ranch near Sacramento. She raised nine children and two grandchildren."

When Judy was in junior high school, she met her next *who*: the little brother of her best friend had hearing loss. "I just wanted to learn everything about that world." Judy enrolled at Lewis & Clark to study special education. She married a photojournalist named Arthur, moved to Boston, and started teaching.

Then she gave birth to her own children, who redirected her life once more. With her roots in West Coast ranch country, Judy was appalled by all the plastic toys in East Coast suburbs. "I decided to open a specialty toy store and serve families that way." She concentrated on high-quality products—Thomas the Tank Engine, Playmobil, Radio Flyer. "If my kids wanted anything from Toys 'R' Us, they went with Arthur. If they wanted quality, they came to me."

Her stores were named Best in Boston. Judy's life was settled.

Then a new *who* appeared—actually, two.

"Arthur always brought home the most interesting articles because he was a newspaperman. One night he slides this article across the dinner table. 'I think you should read this.' It was about a five-month-old boy who was in foster care. In the middle of the day, the foster mom goes down the street to pick up her kindergartener. When she returns, the baby's been kidnapped."

Judy's own children were teenagers by this point; they were putting their dishes in the sink and heading out. "Guys, could you come back for a minute?" Judy said. "I think we need to have a family meeting." By the time the meeting ended, the four of them had decided to become a foster family. Judy and Arthur went through a training program; when it was over, they were told to sit tight, they could be waiting for months.

The next day the agency called. "I was in the store making the toys look pretty. The woman said, 'I have two beautiful little sisters. They're five months old and seventeen months old. Will you open your home for them?'"

Judy was dumbstruck. "We didn't have our certificate. We didn't have supplies. Our extra bedroom was full of tools. I called Arthur in a panic. *What should we do?*"

They accepted the offer. Judy was so desperate that she did the one thing she vowed never to do. "I drove directly to Toys 'R' Us. I found a saleswoman in the diapers aisle and told her I was going to become a mom of two infants in two hours. She looked at me. 'You're going to need another cart.'"

Judy filled three carts with diapers, formula, car seats, and high-chairs. "Three minutes after I got home, the social worker drove up; Arthur zoomed in to take pictures; and we started a new life."

But the thing about *whos* is, they don't stop changing your life once you meet them.

Judy was eager to learn everything she could about foster care. While rocking her babies to sleep, she started reading and quickly drew two conclusions. "One, how broken the system was. Two, how most Americans would like to help, but asking them to become parents is simply too much to ask."

Judy had an idea. She requested a meeting with the head of children and families for the Commonwealth of Massachusetts. "His name was Harry Spence. I didn't know this at the time, but he was legendary."

Judy described her dream: she wanted to build an intergenerational community where young families who raised foster children would live alongside older adults who would provide additional love, talent, and wisdom. "Imagine how absurd this situation was. I own a toy store. I've been a foster parent for *six weeks*. I walk into this guy's office and announce I want to reenvision foster care in America. I actually used that language! I was so naive."

Spence was not naive, though. He knew exactly how impossible her dream was.

"And he leans across the table and says, 'Yes, please.'"

Harry Spence became Judy's ultimate *who*.

Judy sold her stores. She opened a nonprofit. She started driving around Massachusetts "finding out who was who." She raised $15 million. And four years later she opened Treehouse in Easthampton, Massachusetts; it included a dozen town houses for families, four dozen elder cottages, and multiple playgrounds and playing fields, all built on a horseshoe-shaped road. Fifteen years later, two dozen communities across the United States were copying her model.

The girl who had looked up to her grandmother for raising a multigenerational family had created a rubric for multiple generations to raise families together.

"I was born on May 11," Judy said, "which is often around Mother's Day. When I was eight, we were at a huge park to celebrate my grandmother, because she was the matriarch. My sister turned to me. 'Aren't you unhappy that nobody's paying attention to you?' I said, 'No, I want to *be* her.'"

And what lesson did she most take away from her grandmother?

"Never ask, *Who's paying attention to me?* Always ask, *Who needs me?* We are here to serve."

Who needs you? Who inspires you? Who haunts you? Who drives you?

Who brings you closer to *who* you want to be?

Who is your *who*?

The following three questions will help you find out.

Past: What Were the Values of Work You Learned from Your Parents?

The first place to start is with the first *whos* in your life and what they taught you about work.

In a series of letters in the 1880s, the Russian playwright Anton Chekhov introduced what would become one of the more quoted principles in the history of theater: "If in Act 1 you have a pistol hanging on the wall, then the pistol must fire in the last act." While Chekhov's gun is most often used as advice to writers of plays, it actually works even better in reverse as advice to writers of life stories.

If a pistol fires in the last act, then someone must have hung it on the wall in the first act.

The first question to ask in a workquake is, *What were the values of work that your parents hung on your wall when you were young?*

Today, everyone accepts on some level that our earliest memories shape our later lives. Yet we rarely incorporate those memories into our work narratives. A central part of writing a constructive work story is to integrate your childhood suffering into your adult success. As the psychoanalyst Hans Loewald observed, the goal is "to turn our ghosts into ancestors."

In my conversations, I asked everyone two questions about their ancestors: First, *What were the prominent values or virtues of work that you learned from your parents?* Second, *What were the prominent down-sides or shadows of work you learned from your parents?*

The answers to the first question were instructive; the answers to the second, definitional.

Let's start with the first.

Two thirds of people said that the primary value they learned from their parents was hard work. Dan Gallagher, the Catholic priest turned classics professor, said he admired the discipline of his middle-class father, who sold gasoline in Pittsburgh. "He basically worked nine to five and carried a briefcase. I thought that was pretty neat, so I got my own briefcase, basically a crayon box stuffed with paper. I decided that my office was the front yard, so I would carry my briefcase to the sycamore tree, open it up, and since I didn't know what my dad did, just start drawing."

Andrew Gauthier, who went from being an indie filmmaker to the head of video at *BuzzFeed* to the creative director of the DNC, said he learned from his parents to always keep working. "My dad was an oil painter and an illustrator; he took two days off every year—Christmas and the Fourth of July. My memories of him were that he was always in front of an easel on deadline. What I took from that is you always work really, really hard, you make money wherever you can, and you never complain."

The next biggest group said that they learned from their parents to love what you do. Shelby Smith, the daughter of Iowa farmers who moved to Dublin to play pro basketball and landed a high-six-figure job trading equity derivatives for the National Bank of Canada, walked away to return home and raise crickets for roasting. What she learned from her parents was that work should be enjoyable. "If you love what you do, you don't have to take a vacation. That's why I left a well-paying job for self-employment. My grandmother started a successful company in her forties."

The final group said that they learned from their parents the importance of being true to yourself. Morgan Gold, the Connecticut-born aspiring comic book writer who became a financial services executive before opening a farm in Vermont, noted that both of his parents had changed professions. His father was a special ed teacher who became an HR professional; his mother was a nurse who became a drug and alcohol counselor. "They both were going down a path, then made a pivot. Looking in retrospect, I guess I've done something very similar."

What's striking about these stories is that the values we learn from our parents are not static and they're not gospel; we might take one lesson from our parents at a certain time in our lives, then another later. Which is why it's so critical to revisit these questions in a workquake.

The same is true for the downsides we learn from our parents, which, it turns out, we have a tendency to repeat.

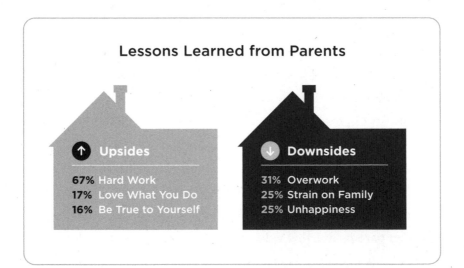

Lessons Learned from Parents

⬆ Upsides
- **67%** Hard Work
- **17%** Love What You Do
- **16%** Be True to Yourself

⬇ Downsides
- **31%** Overwork
- **25%** Strain on Family
- **25%** Unhappiness

A third of people said that the biggest drawback they learned from their parents was the risk of overworking. Marcus Bridgewater was born in Orlando to immigrant parents. "The men in my family didn't have a lot of time for emotions. They were strong and worked hard but were hurt by all the pressure to pay bills and put the family first. The downside for me was that I had to learn to take care of myself." Trained as a set designer, Marcus today runs a wildly popular wellness platform under the name Garden Marcus where he posts videos about self-care through botany from his six-hundred-plant garden in North Houston to three hundred thousand Instagram followers and seven hundred thousand TikTok followers.

Aaron Krause was raised in Philadelphia by parents who were "very well respected, extremely hardworking, and monster overachievers." His father was a cardiac surgeon, his mother a pediatrician; his sister grew up to become a federal judge. "I was absolutely the black sheep. I liked sports, hanging out with friends, and couldn't stand reading." Aaron's father was a stickler for money and made his son buy his own toys. "He gave me a list of things I could do for money. Clean your room—one dollar. Wash the car—ten dollars. My thirteenth birthday present was 'Son, congratulations, from now on you buy your own underwear.'" His father also kept the house so cold that to avoid getting out of bed to turn off the lights, Aaron used casters, dental floss, and a pulley to jury-rig an over-the-ceiling switch.

That tinkering paid off. Aaron went on to open a car-detailing company, which led him to realize that the pads people used to buff cars were inferior. So he patented and started manufacturing a buffing pad that he sold to 3M for tens of millions of dollars. Aaron then took some of the leftover materials in his shop and concocted a smiley-faced sponge with finger holes for eyes and a knife cleaner for a mouth. He called his invention Scrub Daddy. When it flopped on QVC, he launched it on *Shark Tank*. The company grew to half a billion dollars, making Aaron, well, a monster overachiever who mimicked the hardworking style of his parents.

A quarter of people said the biggest downside they learned from their parents was the strain that working put on their family. Curtis Basina, a gas station owner and member of the Red Cliff Band of Lake Superior Chippewa in Wisconsin, said he inherited a work ethic from his math teacher father that was so extreme that it "interfered" with his life. "My wife, until recently, went on vacations without me because she told me repeatedly that there really is more to life than work." When Curtis and his wife finally took a trip together, they stopped at a roadside craft distillery for a drink; it was there he got the idea to open Copper Crow, a vodka and whiskey distillery on the shores of Lake Superior, the first Native-owned distillery in the country.

Another quarter of people said that watching their parents do work that made them unhappy encouraged them to seek work that was meaningful. Jeff Cadry was raised in suburban Saint Paul, Minnesota, by a father who was a banker and a mother who was a schoolteacher. Because his mother had summers off, the family moved to the lake region, leaving his father with a three-hour commute. "What I took from that was you spend a lot of your life either working or commuting, so you better do something that you're passionate about." Today he's the chief forester—and a part-time ski instructor—at the Yellowstone Club in Big Sky, Montana.

The strong message in all these answers is that we don't write our work stories on a clean slate. Our upbringings shape our choices much more than we often admit. The purpose of asking yourself both the upsides and downsides you learned from your parents is to summon your skeletons out of the closet and bring them into the light. Those skeletons are already weighing on you; you'll make better decisions if you sit them at the table along with the rest of your *whos* and have an open and frank discussion.

Present: Who Is Your Waymaker?

The next part of identifying *Who is your who?* is to identify *Who is your dominant who right now?* It could be a parent, a lover, a spouse, a mentor, a newborn, a boss.

Or it could be a figure who comes into your life at just the right moment and opens a door for you to pass through.

A *waymaker.*

Shardé Davis grew up in a single-parent household in San Diego after her parents divorced when she was four. Shardé's mother, a kindergarten teacher, was her primary caretaker. "As a child, I was a young Black girl in a predominantly white, affluent community. I never had words to articulate who I was."

Shardé's childhood hero was Rachel Green, the character on *Friends* played by Jennifer Aniston. Because Rachel was a buyer at Bloomingdale's, Shardé set her sights on doing that, too. At the University of California, Santa Barbara, Shardé joined various organizations, took her academics seriously, and started to get noticed.

"I had a meeting with my mentor, Dr. Michael Young, the vice-chancellor, in my second quarter. He asked me, 'What do you want to be?' I said, 'I want to be a buyer at Bloomingdale's.' He laughed. 'No, Shardé, that's not what you're going to do. You're going to be an academic.' Then I laughed. 'No, Dr. Young, that's not going to happen. I don't even like to read or write.' He said, 'I see you being president of a university someday.'"

The next year, the dean of social sciences recommended that Shardé apply for the McNair Scholars Program, a federal initiative to help college students from underrepresented backgrounds prepare for graduate studies. "During the interview, the committee asked me what I wanted to do. I told them, 'I want to be a buyer at Bloomingdale's.' They laughed. 'No, you're going to be an academic.' I was like, *Where are you people coming up with this stuff?!* I was going to turn them down."

Instead, Shardé went on to win the Steven H. Chaffee Award for Excellence in Research for her thesis exploring divorce in Black families. "That's when I realized, *My gosh, this work is amazing!*" She stayed on at Santa Barbara to earn her master's degree, focusing on what she calls "the strong Black women collective," how female friendships form the backbone of Black communities. The teenager who had been inspired by *Friends* now made friends the inspiration of her academic specialty.

For all her success, though, Shardé was one of only four minorities in a graduate program of forty people, which left her feeling isolated and insecure. "There were a whole bunch of white people studying whiteness, but nobody was studying Black womanhood, Black families, and Black cultures."

Then another *who* stepped in. Shardé's adviser transferred to Iowa and suggested that Shardé follow her. Suddenly Shardé found herself in a community that encouraged her academic interests. She went on to earn her PhD, investigating speech patterns in Black female friend circles, and, at the unheard-of age of twenty-five, published an academic theory of how Black women, often negatively pressured to be strong, channel those frustrations to strengthen one another. When Shardé entered the job market, she was snatched up by the University of Connecticut and nominated for tenure.

When I asked Shardé how she could have been so wrong about her destiny and all those strangers so right, she used an expression from the church. "When I tell my story, I say that Dr. Young *spoke over me*. He laid hands on me. He used what we call prophetic words. The same happened with the dean. In the church, we talk about God using people as instruments. All these experiences were divine timing; they were spirits pushing me so that my steps could align with God's purpose."

And they weren't the last.

Not long after the Black Lives Matter protests erupted, Shardé was watching television and feeling frustrated. "I kept thinking, *Racism exists in law enforcement, but it also exists in academia.*" She was sitting on her couch one day when she had an idea. "*Maybe if I use narrative, I can bring about change.*" So she shared a personal story on social media and attached the hashtag #BlackInTheIvory.

"That was a Saturday night. The next morning a friend called me at 6:00 a.m. 'Shardé, get up! People are using your hashtag.' The rest of the day, #BlackInTheIvory just blew up. It was on the top twenty hashtags in the United States by Sunday night. By Monday morning, I can honestly say that my life had changed forever."

Shardé, who once dreamed of being a buyer at Bloomingdale's, found herself as the face of a movement to change the conversation about diversity in the ivory tower. While it's too soon to tell whether she will eventually become the president of a university, it's certainly not too soon to say that the vice-chancellor who made that prediction was prescient. The door that he opened in her mind became the barrier that she broke down.

"I needed people," Shardé explained. "I needed someone to show me what I couldn't see. When he spoke over me, it was the first time someone saw the golden thread in me in a way that allowed me to see it for myself."

In his influential 1978 book, *The Seasons of a Man's Life*, the Yale psychologist Daniel Levinson talks about *transitional figures*, people who come into our lives and help move us from one realm to another. The crucial function these figures play, he says, is "to support and facilitate *the realization of the Dream*." Begun in the 1960s, Levinson's study included forty men, all between thirty-five and forty-five, all living in the Northeast, all American born. Eighty-eight percent of his subjects were white.

These demographics might help explain why Levinson said transitional figures are "almost exclusively male," "often situated in a work setting," and "usually older by half a generation." The ideal transitional figure, he concluded, is like a "responsible, admirable older sibling."

My conversations robustly confirm that we all have transitional figures in our work lives.

They equally robustly contradict every other aspect of Levinson's conclusions.

Our transitional figures are not exclusively male, they're not only found in the workplace, and they're not always older. Instead, in a mark of how much gender diversity there is in the workplace, how much our nonwork lives now influence our work decisions, and how much we've all come to accept that the young can teach the old, our influences come from all parts of our lives—from the *Call of Duty* chat room to the addiction support group—and from all ages, from babies who demand our attention to spouses who need us to bring in more money while they start a new company.

At any moment, anyone you know can be the *who* that redirects your life.

The key is what message they have to deliver and whether you'll be open to hearing it.

I began calling these figures *waymakers* after one of my subjects used that term. Cherie Scott emigrated from India to Canada when she was sixteen. Having been in a girl band in Mumbai, Cherie split for New York City as soon as she could to study theater. Carrying only one piece of luggage and $750 stuffed in her bra, Cherie entered her dorm room. "My roommate was this absolutely gorgeous, fake-tan girl named Trish whose father was a professional golfer from Palm Springs. She and her mother were unpacking an entire array of Bath & Body Works green apple lotions and candles."

Cherie heaved her suitcase onto the bed and opened it up. "And, oh my God, I smell all the spices from my mother's kitchen. After I had gone to bed the night before, my mother had toasted all her masalas, put them in satchels, and slid them into the top of my suitcase. Trish and her mother said, 'What's that smell?' I was so humiliated I wanted to die."

She threw everything in the trash.

Twenty years later, after Broadway never came calling, after an endless slog singing on cruise ships and at amusement parks, after marrying her record producer, nursing him through cancer, moving to Maine, and working in event planning, and after becoming a mother herself, Cherie was devastated by the death of her mom. "I instantly thought back on that moment in my dorm room—and I cried. That was my mom's way of saying, *I don't care what you do with your life, how big of a star you become, whose wife or mother you end up being, you will always be my daughter and I hope you never forget it.*"

Cherie went into the kitchen that night and began cooking her mother's recipes. She had to buy new equipment, new ingredients, and, of course, new spices. It took her a year to perfect the taste. When she did, she decided to open a gourmet sauce company called From Mumbai to Maine. "I realized I needed to teach my children about their heritage. I needed to give myself new purpose. I needed to continue my mother's story. She was my waymaker."

Like Cherie's mother, some waymakers are inspirers. Chris Donovan, the telephone operator, was inspired to pursue shoe design by meeting his future husband, Steve, the tie-dye artist. Mary Scullion, a first-generation Irish immigrant, was a postulant in the Sisters of Mercy in Philadelphia when she heard the legendary social activist Dorothy Day give her final address. "She taught me that work can be transformational." Mary went on to cofound Project HOME, a support group for people experiencing homelessness that earned her a place on *Time* magazine's 100 Most Influential People in the World.

Some waymakers are enablers. Caty Borum Chattoo was a comedy groupie and underling at a Los Angeles think tank when she talked her way into a meeting with *All in the Family* producer Norman Lear, who created a job for her as senior director at his foundation. "Norman is one of the great enablers of talent. He has a long history of spotting talent, putting people in positions of responsibility, then getting out of the way. I'm not even a famous person and he did that for me. We'd go to meetings at a big talent agency, a $15 million donor would ask a question, and Norman would say, 'I think Caty should answer.' I was silly and irreverent and kind of bold headed, but Norman helped me discover a whole new brightly colored version of myself." Caty is now the executive director of the Center for Media & Social Impact at American University; she created the Yes, and . . . Laughter

Lab, an incubator for comedy and social action; and when the University of California Press published her first book, *A Comedian and an Activist Walk into a Bar*, the foreword was written by Norman Lear.

Shellye Archambeau was a junior in high school in her working-class suburb of Los Angeles when she had "that obligatory conversation with a guidance counselor about college." The counselor asked what she liked to do. "That's easy, I like being in clubs," Shellye said. "I like leading them." The counselor asked what she wanted to do after college. "I don't care. I just want a job where I can keep the thermostat at seventy-two degrees, I can eat out at restaurants, and I can travel, because those are all things I can't do right now."

"Well, in that case," the counselor said, "I think you should go into business."

Shellye asked what you call someone who leads a business.

"When the counselor said CEO, I decided right then and there that I wanted to be a CEO." Shellye earned her undergraduate degree from the Wharton School at the University of Pennsylvania. When she learned that most CEOs start in sales, she took a sales job at IBM, followed that with executive positions at Blockbuster and Northpoint, and at forty-one, became the CEO of MetricStream, a governance and risk compliance firm based in San Jose with $350 million in annual revenue.

Some waymakers are confronters. Colin Bedell was born on Long Island to parents who divorced when he was young. His mother, a nursing home aide, moved the children to North Carolina, where Colin struggled. "I was a closeted boy growing up in the South, asking questions no eleven-year-old should be asking: *Why are some people happy and other people aren't? Why do certain people get along and others don't? Why don't my parents get along?*"

Colin had passions—beauty, fashion, spirituality—but with no idea how to support himself, he enrolled at SUNY Stony Brook to study law. The first day of junior year, his older brother was driving him to campus. "He pulls the car over and says, 'Listen, no one in the family is going to tell you this, so let me be the first: Cut this shit out. You definitely don't need to go to law school; you need to go to the city. Do things that light you up. Put on your angel wings like the Victoria Secret fashion show you love so much.'"

Colin dropped out, went to work at Sephora for a while, and enrolled at Parsons, where he became valedictorian. "I gave the speech in front of the queen, Diane von Furstenberg." But after losing his job at a clothing warehouse, he started posting horoscopes on the internet under the brand name Queer Cosmos. On the day his unemployment ran out, Colin signed a book contract. Five years later, Colin was writing weekly horoscopes for *Cosmopolitan*, doing readings for clients around the world, and advising sleep brands and dating apps.

We all have ghosts; we have demons. But we have angels, too, and we have waymakers. Figures who show up at critical junctures in our lives and speak *to* us, speak *at* us, and speak *over* us.

Who is your waymaker right now? What are they trying to tell you? And are you willing to listen?

Future: I Want to Be the Kind of Person Who _____

The final step in appraising *Who is your who?* is to pull together what you learned from the *whos* of your past, along with what you're hearing from the *whos* in your present, and begin to formulate a direction for *who* you want to be in the future. A bedrock of narrative career construction is that only you can do this work. Only you can decide what messages you need to heed and what direction you'd like to move.

In the case of *Who is your who?* I asked everyone to complete this sentence about what they learned about themselves during their biggest work transition.

I want to be the kind of person who _____.

Some people learned to embrace risk. Julian Vasquez Heilig was on a linear trajectory from earning his PhD in education policy at Stanford to working at the US Department of Education in Washington, DC, to becoming an associate professor at the University of Texas, when he decided to veer off course and start a blog about hot-button school issues. "I grew up lower middle class; my mother always said, 'Work hard but work smart.' Beginning when I was eight, I always thought, *What am I doing now that is going to make me successful in the future?* The blog was the first thing I did that went against that spirit. I could have offended someone or said the wrong thing. But if you want to have impact, you can't be fearful. I realized I was in a moment when I wanted to leave bravely." In five years, Julian's blog was read by a million people in two hundred countries, and after becoming a full professor at California State University, Sacramento, he was named dean of the College of Education at the University of Kentucky.

Some learned to venture out on their own. Tye Caldwell was born in Lexa, Arkansas, near the Mississippi River. His father was a truck driver; his mother raised farm animals. "We couldn't afford the barbershop, so one day I saw a pair of shears lying around and offered to cut my brother's hair. *I'm a good artist. I'll do it!*" Soon he was cutting his family's hair, his teammates' hair, his teachers' hair.

After high school, Tye moved to Dallas, earned a cosmetology degree, and began working in a salon. "I paid $125 a week to rent a chair. My first week I grossed $175." Within a few years, he was grossing $1,800 and opening his own shop. When a visiting stylist offered to rent a chair from him, Tye developed a side job matching traveling stylists with empty salon chairs.

"After a while, I thought, *There must be a service out there that does this, like Uber or Airbnb.*" When he found nothing, he decided to build it himself. A friend introduced him to a venture capitalist in Silicon Valley. "When I told her my idea, there was a click on the phone. I thought she hung up. 'Sorry, I dropped the receiver. This is a billion-dollar idea.'" Seven years later, ShearShare was in 646 cities and 11 countries. Tye and his wife were featured in an ad for Google. They were profiled in *The Wall Street Journal*. The press nicknamed their company Hairbnb.

"I realized I was in a time in my life when I should stand on the shoulders of my ancestors and build something that I could be proud of."

But some learned things about themselves they never knew. New York City native Wynne Nowland grew up in Queens, attended college in New Rochelle, and then moved to Long Island to sell insurance. Wynne stayed with the same firm, Bradley & Parker, for the next thirty-four years, the last five as CEO, building it to $120 million a year in premiums.

But as stable as that work life was, Wynne had an unstable personal life, burning through three marriages. Until, at age fifty-six, Wynne went through a nonwork workquake. "I would say it began when I was eleven, feeling like I didn't fit. I was in a boy's body, but I wanted to be playing with the girls." Wynne compartmentalized those feelings for decades, but as society became more accepting of such feelings—and Wynne grew more confident at work—taking action became more realistic.

"I left the office on a Wednesday. I had a couple of surgeries on Thursday. I was back in the office two weeks later." Having presented for decades as a man, Wynne now presented as a woman. "My privilege made my transition much easier. I could afford to go to the best surgeon. I retained a stylist in Manhattan. And of course I had great insurance!"

Wynne also had the support of all eighty employees—all except a few, that is.

"The day I came back, I sent an email to the entire staff. That softened the shock, I think. I had a couple of people hug me and wish me luck. I have this employee who's slightly to the right of Attila the Hun, and, of course, he turned out to be amongst the most supportive. One woman complained to HR about the bathroom issue. I'm tall, and she worried that if I wore heels, I could look over the dividers. Our head of HR informed her of my rights under New York law, and she's been welcoming ever since."

But Wynne's real worry was clients.

"I was most nervous about a well-known company on the Eastern Seaboard. The CEO is on TV all the time. He's a tough, cantankerous man in his seventies. I wrote him a very personal email; he usually answers pretty fast, but it couldn't have been two minutes later when an email arrived. *This changes nothing. Our relationship can only grow stronger.* The next day, I'm sitting in my office, when my admin comes in with this box. It's from the same guy. A bottle of Dom Pérignon."

What did Wynne discover about herself through this experience?

"I learned that I want to be the kind of person who lives authentically."

Of all the answers to *Who is your who?*, learning to be your own *who* may be the most fulfilling of all.

CHAPTER 7

What Is Your What?

I Want to Do Work That _____

I n January 1956, a senior at the Wharton School at the University of Pennsylvania submitted a thesis in a seminar on real estate. The seventy-five-page paper wasn't due until the last day of class, but the student submitted it on the first day of class. "The professor told me that many students over the years had told him that they would do this, but no one ever had," the student later wrote.

The name of the paper was "Construction of a Low-Cost, Semi-Finished House." The preface begins with the following statement:

> I have chosen this semi-finished house as a topic for my research, because I feel that we have "grown-up" together. As both a summer employee of the Home Loan Company and a year-round spectator of its operations, I have followed the development of this building process throughout my adolescent years. Also, I expect to become an officer of the company upon my graduation from the University of Pennsylvania, so I wanted to acquire greater insight into its functions by making this study.

The author of that paper was Edwin J. Feiler Jr. Eight years later he became my father.

Between those two dates, my dad graduated from college; served two years in the navy; married Jane Abeshouse, an artist and art educator from Baltimore; moved back to Savannah; and went to work alongside his father in the aforementioned Home Loan Company. Over the next sixty years, my father and his father built more than a thousand affordable homes for families that my father identified in his research had been underserved in the building boom of the postwar South.

During his long, sometimes painfully up-and-down work life, my father also constructed multifamily housing, renovated historic homes, and built an assisted living facility. He also nearly went bankrupt, testified before Congress, and lobbied for other homebuilders. Baffled by this mishmash as a child—*Why can't you have* one *job, like my friends' dads?*—I once asked my dad what he *did*.

"Shelter," he said.

Fifty years later, I can still remember the shock of that answer. The beauty of that answer.

Shelter.

One of humanity's most basic aspirations. One of life's most basic needs.

Today, I think of my father's response as probably the best answer I've ever heard to the second of the Kipling questions about work: *What is your what?*

The essence of building a narrative work identity is telling a story about what you do. As we saw in the last chapter, that story has a broad cast of characters; as we'll see in the next two chapters, it also has a specific time and a specific setting. The heart of that story, though, is the plot. It's the actions you take, the things you create, the services you perform.

The *what*.

As we know by now, that *what* will surely not be a single *what*. It will be an ever-changing mélange of *whats*. But whatever those *whats* are at any given moment, they're a collective response to an underlying need that you've been nursing for years. The purpose of asking *What is your what?* is to identify both the deep-seated longings that drive your choices and the immediate needs that will guide your next steps. Only when you pinpoint those unspoken motivations will you achieve the meaning you're looking for.

Beverly Jenkins was the oldest of seven children born into a tight-knit family on Detroit's east side. Her father was a custodian who earned a teaching degree, then taught in the schools he used to clean; her mother was a full-time mom and even more full-time reader. "Libraries were segregated in Detroit, so she could use the books in the building but not take them home. She read to me in the womb in that library."

Beverly's role models were teachers. "My mom once asked my elementary teacher if it was OK that I was devouring the newspaper. 'Beverly's going to college. Let her read what she wants!'"

The teacher was right, as Beverly went on to enroll at Michigan State. But what the teacher may not have foreseen is that once Beverly got there, she quickly rebelled. "I partied. I protested. I smoked pot. It was the Summer of Love; I was a Negro hippie. It was, *Free your mind and your ass will follow.* I was raised so strict; I broke my parents' heart."

In Beverly's junior year, a friend told her about an opening at the campus library. "All I ever wanted was to work in a library, so I blew off my exams and started working full time." She spent the next thirty years as a librarian—first at the university, later at Parke-Davis, a subsidiary of the pharmaceutical conglomerate Pfizer. She married a union organizer and had a daughter. "I was content. I was making a good wage. I was driving a sports car."

But Beverly was also nurturing a hope job that she had learned from all those books.

"When I was working at Michigan State, the library had a full set of *The Journal of Negro History*, which was founded in 1916 by Carter Woodson, the man who invented Negro History Week, the forerunner of Black History Month. On my lunch hour, I would take armfuls of those journals down to the Red Cedar River that runs through campus and read them. My boss even let me bring home all the historical novels before I cataloged them. 'As long as you don't spill Coca-Cola all over 'em,' he said."

Inspired by all those stories, Beverly began to write. "Toni Morrison said if there's a book you want to read and it isn't in the marketplace, write it yourself. So that's what I did."

For her subject, Beverly chose the secret love life of a buffalo soldier.

Buffalo soldiers, Beverly explained, were members of two Black cavalry regiments in the United States Army who roamed the West in the decades after the Civil War. Their main opponents were Native Americans, who gave them their nickname because their dark, curly hair resembled a buffalo's fur. The regiments were required by law to be led by white officers and were saddled with aging horses, broken-down equipment, and inadequate supplies.

"Those Colored soldiers had saved the Union during the war. The government wanted to thank them, so they let them wreak havoc from the Canadian border to the Rio Grande. They had the lowest level of drunkenness, but the highest level of badass."

Beverly spent more than a decade writing her manuscript. When she finished, it was "seven hundred pages of heat. You opened the covers and steam came out."

And not a single person knew what to do with it. Not the editors Beverly solicited, the agents she contacted, the writers she shared her manuscript with. "The market was totally closed to African American novelists. I didn't know this at the time, but of the fiction published since 1950, only 5 percent were by writers of color. Publishers don't think we read."

Then Beverly found her *who*.

Vivian Stephens was a fact-checker at Time Life when she picked up a Harlequin romance in 1978. Raised in sheltered Houston, she was mesmerized. After being hired by Dell Publishing to start a romance line when no one else wanted the job, Vivian went on to revolutionize the romance industry, dispensing with dusty English handmaidens, insisting writers drop in details from *The Joy of Sex*, and bringing in Latina, Asian American, and Native American writers. In 1984, Stephens published the genre's first Black author, Elsie Washington, whose book *Entwined Destinies* depicts a Black journalist falling in love with a Black oilman.

When Beverly tracked her down a decade later, Stephens was working as an agent. "I sent her this raggedy manuscript. Probably had Coca-Cola all over it! There were no slaves. No white savior. The Blacks saved themselves."

And Stephens managed to sell it . . . for $2,500, minus the commission, plus a rewrite. "I got the call on my husband's birthday." Forty years after devouring those newspapers as a girl, twenty years after inhaling those *Journals of Negro History* in her lunch hour, Beverly became a published author. Avon released *Night Song* in 1994, with a shirtless, mustachioed Sergeant Chase Jefferson on the cover, holding a breathless, tight-bodiced, "strong-willed ebony beauty," Kansas schoolteacher Cara Lee Henson, in his arms.

Critics loved it. *People* ran a five-page spread. The Smithsonian declared it the first Black historical romance ever published. And readers gobbled it up. "Black women had been waiting for this forever," Beverly said. "A woman wrote me, 'I picked up the cover and said, *Oh, my God, it's two Black people!* Then I looked at the back and saw it was written by a Black woman! I sat down in the bookstore right there and started reading.'"

In the next twenty-five years, Beverly would go on to write forty more books, including contemporary romance, small-town fiction, and young adult. She won the lifetime achievement award of the Romance Writers of America, an organization that had been started by Vivian Stephens.

"When my mother would go to the segregated library when she was pregnant, she would read me classics from the Harlem Renaissance— Langston Hughes, Zora Neale Hurston. When she first gave me cloth books and I would put them in my mouth, she'd say, 'Eat those words, baby! Eat those words!' Now I'm the one filling up those shelves with words.

"The best thing about my job," she continued, "is passing on that love of books. It's reading to kids in schools; it's talking to young writers of color who hit me up on Twitter."

So what is her *what*?

"It's community. That's the thread in my life. Always trying to make the path wider."

What is *your what*? What is the animating idea that has undergirded your dreams for years? What is your *shelter*, your *community*, your _____?

Here are three questions to help you find that answer.

Past: Who Were Your Role Models as a Child?

When Beverly shared with me the story of selling her first book, I shared with her one of my all-time favorite stories. It involves Pat Conroy, the larger-than-life novelist of *The Prince of Tides* and *The Great Santini*. Pat was born in Atlanta to a sadistic father, a marine corps fighter pilot, and a romantic mother, who read him *Gone with the Wind* at bedtime and begged him to ignore the bruises they both received from her husband. Pat attended eleven schools in twelve years before finding stability—and basketball glory—in Beaufort, South Carolina, just across the Savannah River from where I grew up.

Encouraged by a high school English teacher to pursue his mother's love of storytelling, Pat went on to self-publish a book of reminiscences about his tough-but-sentimental commanding officer at the Citadel. The indefatigable author then drove across the Southeast handselling copies to booksellers. Turned down by the Peace Corps, Pat went on to teach for a year at a two-room schoolhouse on Daufuskie Island, just south of Charleston, where all the students spoke Gullah. He was fired for his unorthodox pedagogic techniques, a humiliation he turned into the caustic, delightful memoir, *The Water Is Wide*.

At the urging of friends, Pat didn't self-publish that manuscript but sent it instead to the agent Julian Bach in New York. When Bach called with the news that Houghton Mifflin had offered $7,500 for the book, Pat replied, "Hell, I can get it printed cheaper in Beaufort."

"Pat," Bach replied, "do you understand? That's what they're going to pay *you*."

I know this story because I grew up idolizing Pat Conroy. He lived where I lived, did what I dreamed of doing, and transformed the isolated corner of the world where we both grew up into a world of color and art. Most of all, he always led with his heart.

Pat was my role model.

In 1957, Robert Merton, the man known as Mr. Sociology, published a landmark study of medical students at Columbia University, in which he showed that younger doctors consciously emulated the older doctors around them, even if they didn't actually know them. The younger doctors mimicked their elders' habits, behaviors, and values. Merton was drawn to this subject because he had done something similar in his own life. Born to Russian immigrants, Meyer Schkolnick, as he was named, picked up magic by emulating his sister's boyfriend. Told he needed a stage name, Meyer selected Merton from his hero Merlin and Robert from another hero, the French magician Jean-Eugène Robert-Houdin, who also inspired the stage name of Harry Houdini.

The name stuck, and three decades later, Robert Merton paid homage to the influence of such magical figures by coining the term they still carry: *role models*.

Role models are among the most valuable building blocks of narrative career construction. The reason: choosing your model is your first choice about work. Mark Savickas told me that if you can ask only one question to someone who's struggling with what to do, it should be, *Who were your role models as a child?* He adds these additional questions for clarity: *Other than family, whom did you admire growing up? These role models can be people you knew, people you didn't know, even fictional figures like superheroes or characters from your favorite books or movies.*

Role models are deeply instructive because they're not blueprints we inherit, they're blueprints we choose. We *take in* characteristics from our parents; we *take on* characteristics from our role models. The first is passive; the second is active. And it's in that act of election—specifically in articulating the traits or values we most admire in our choices—that we reveal what's most important to us. Our role models' lives become the road map for the roadblocks we struggle with.

While the question of what you learned from your parents is a *who* question, the question of what you learned from your role models is a *what* question because *whom* you admire is not important; it's *what you admire about them* that's important.

What is their what? becomes the first clue to *What is your what?*

I asked two questions about role models in my interviews. The first was, *Who were your role models as a child?* The second was, *What qualities did you admire in them?*

One observation that Merton makes about role models surprised me: many of the figures the young doctors mirrored weren't just strangers, they were celebrities. That distance meant that the young doctors had only "partial" or "limited" knowledge of their role models' lives. A similar dynamic was true with Pat Conroy and me; I didn't meet him until I was well into my twenties, when I was already a published author. (That meeting and the ones that followed remain a highlight of my professional life.)

Merton's insight remains true today. Half the role models my subjects mentioned were celebrities—Muhammad Ali, Madame Curie, Carol Burnett, Keith Haring. Thirty percent were professionals—pastors, pilots, politicians. The final 20 percent were teachers or coaches.

The values that people admired in their role models were similarly spread out, including authenticity, creativity, and dignity. The

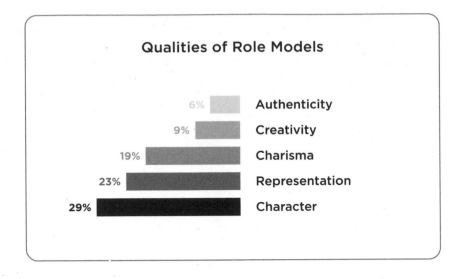

top three categories were *character, representation*—as in representing a certain group that the mentee belonged to—and *charisma.*

Among those who said *character* was Annabelle Manalo, a one-time college basketball star in New Orleans, who left her husband, a Tennessee Titan, because she didn't want her daughter to believe she was "only an NFL wife," earned a PhD at Vanderbilt University in cell and developmental biology and became an expert in genetics. Annabelle's role model was Michael Jordan. "Not because he was always the best, but because he *wasn't* always the best. He didn't have the red carpet laid out for him. What he had was a great work ethic; he demanded to be taken seriously and encouraged me to do the same."

Ken Tang, a refugee from Vietnam who grew up in Arizona, found inspiration in the writings of John Wooden, the coach who led UCLA to ten national championships in men's basketball. "I admired the way he mentored people, which inspired me to become a second-grade teacher." When Wooden was ninety-two, Tang waited in line for his autograph at the Los Angeles Times Festival of Books. "When I told him what he meant to me, he got up, walked around the table, and gave me a piece of advice, 'Your students are going to know how to read, write, and do arithmetic. Your job is to make sure they grow up to be contributing members of society.' That advice changed my whole philosophy from being a drill-and-kill teacher to focusing more on how I made these children feel."

Among those who said representation, Sonali Dev, the novelist, said her role model was Jane Austen. "Every book I read had no female agency. Jane Austen was the first author wherein the heroines had self-worth. The women wanted to be happy and didn't depend on the men for happiness."

Courtland Savage grew up in a "down-South, Bible-Belt type of Black family" in Mount Holly, North Carolina. He dreamed of becoming a pilot but had no idea if that was remotely possible. "I literally went to Google and searched *Black pilots*. I would just print the pages of random air force pilots and tape their pictures on my wall." Courtland became a fighter pilot in the navy and later started a nonprofit called Fly for the Culture, which supports young people of color in the aviation industry.

Among those who mentioned charisma, Dan Gallagher, the Pennsylvania boy who carried a briefcase like his father, looked up to Indiana Jones, for his "stoic character and interest in ancient history." Dan became a priest and classicist. Nathaniel Peterson, as a boy in Ohio, was enthralled with *Jaws*. "I appreciated the shark, as well as Spielberg's dramatic filmmaking." Nate became the TV host and YouTuber Coyote Peterson, making videos in which he allows himself to be stung by tarantulas, bullet ants, and executioner wasps. His channel, Brave Wilderness, has 20 million subscribers and 4.5 billion views.

The stories we inherit from our parents are part of our script; we write them from characters we had no choice in creating. The stories we compose about our role models are part of our scripture; we write them from characters we alone choose and from characteristics we alone elect to admire. When you're going through a workquake later in life, one of the most efficient ways to reconnect with your childhood dreams about work before they were corrupted by adult anxieties is to reconnect with your role models.

To diagnose *What is your what?* today, start with *What was your what?* back then.

Present: What's the Best Thing and Worst Thing about Your Work Today?

Then turn to *What is your what?* right now.

Dame Julie Andrews went through a lot of *whats* in her seventy-five years of work. She was a vaudevillian, a singer, a radio actor, stage actor, a television actor, a movie actor, and a writer; she won six Golden Globes, three Grammys, two Emmys, one Tony, and one Academy Award; she starred in some of Hollywood's most iconic films, including *The Sound of Music* and *Mary Poppins*.

In her seventies, Andrews began writing a two-volume autobiography. The first volume, *Home*, details her harrowing childhood involving war, poverty, drunkenness, even sexual advances from her stepfather, who twice tried to take her to bed. The second volume, *Home Work*, includes gut-wrenching descriptions of her self-doubts and depression; candid details of the drug problems of her second husband, the director Blake Edwards; and gossipy accounts of her most famous movies, including her being knocked to the ground nine times by a helicopter while filming the song "The Sound of Music."

At the end of *Home Work*, Andrews includes a brief epilogue. It begins with this thought: "I am often asked how I feel about the success I have enjoyed." But what is success? she asks. Is it the pleasure in doing the work, or the way the work is received?

Her answer: "The latter is ephemeral. The doing is everything."

For Julie Andrews, her *what* is *the work*.

What is your *what* right now? Not six years ago. Not six months ago. Today.

In 2001, Jane Dutton and Amy Wrzesniewski, two psychologists at the University of Michigan, published a milestone study that introduced the idea that became a foundation of narrative career construction. The idea was called *job crafting*. For too long, scholars focused almost exclusively on the passive, top-down model of a job, the authors wrote, in which tasks are assigned to a worker. Those scholars overlooked the worker's active, bottom-up role in choosing their own tasks and then arranging them into a meaningful narrative.

Job crafting is the process by which a worker takes the objective raw materials of a job and converts them into subjective psychological constructs that give the worker a sense of purpose. Line cooks view themselves as *masters of cuisine*, hairdressers as *purveyors of self-worth*.

Builders as *shelterers*.

These rhetorical flourishes, far from incidental, are core to a person's ability to define who they are and why their work matters. Those who job craft most effectively are much happier at work. Dutton and Wrzesniewski offered the memorable example of Candice Walker, a hospital cleaner who viewed her job emptying bed pans and disposing of needles not as dehumanizing but as *healing*, and who described her workplace not as a sick ward but as a *house of hope*.

Reflecting on their work decades later, the two researchers added an important amplification. As the pace of work has quickened and the ability of workers to assemble a collection of multiple jobs has grown, the new world of work has put "more and more responsibility on the individual" to craft their own stories. The workers who are most successful, Wrzesniewski said, are the ones who don't focus on the prestige of the firm or the status of the position, both of which "burn off pretty quickly," but on "the kind of work you'll be doing every day because the work itself is engaging and because you feel that work matters."

In other words, know *What is your what today?* because only that knowledge will sustain you in the future.

I asked people two questions to understand what attributes they most value in what they do. The first was, *What are the top three emotions you feel during work?*

Forty-five percent listed three positive emotions. Ariel Daunay, the body healer, said *empathy, peace*, and *gratitude*. Chely Wright, the country music singer, said *empathy, joy*, and *curiosity*. Derrick Ray, the Alaska deep-sea fisherman turned Hawaii coffee farmer, said *joy, appreciation*, and *bliss*.

Another 45 percent listed two positive emotions and one negative. Trevor Boffone, the TikTok Spanish teacher, said *enjoyment, annoyance*, and *creativity*. Sang Kim, the Goldman Sachs lawyer turned interior designer, said *panic, satisfaction*, and *pride*. Laura Spaulding, the crime scene cleanup specialist, said *excitement, exhaustion*, and *ambition*.

The final 10 percent gave two negative emotions and one positive. Courtland Savage, the founder of Fly for the Culture, said *stress, sad-*

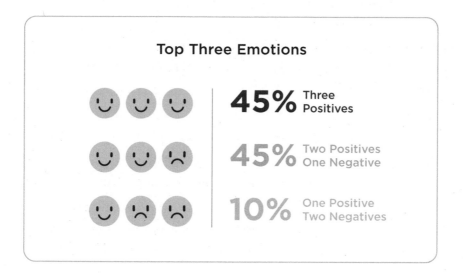

ness, and *joy*. Wendy Chisholm, the Microsoft executive, said *curiosity*, *frustration*, and *grief*.

The most important takeaway from these answers is that a majority of people mentioned at least one negative emotion. And these are people who love what they do! This finding is a reminder that experiencing some adverse feelings in your work is not enough of a reason to seek new work. Even the happiest people at work are unhappy with certain aspects of their work.

So what *does* constitute a reason to make a change?

The second question I asked offers some clues. That question was, *What's the best thing about your work today and what's the worst thing?*

The worst things people mentioned largely paralleled their negative emotions and were more or less what you'd expect. The top answers were *stress*, *dealing with difficult people*, *too much grunt work*, and *long hours*.

But the best things people mentioned were more enlightening. Ten percent said that the best thing about their work was the freedom.

Karen Noel, the Kansas native who left her thirty-year job as a bank manager to become a long-haul truck driver, said that what she liked best about her work was that she could set her own hours. "I can drive when I want to drive, eat when I want to eat, and sleep when I want to sleep. I could make $30,000 a month if I really wanted to." Nishita Kothary, an interventional radiologist at Stanford University Medical Center who's both a clinician and a professor, said that the best thing about her work was the flexibility in her schedule. "If my cases are done, I can go home. I don't have to be at work for work's sake. Plus, I tend to be fast, which means I can be with my family when I need."

Eighteen percent of people were like Julie Andrews: They valued the work itself. Nate Venturelli, the steelworker in Indiana who performed country music gigs on the weekend, said, "I would wake up and weld every day if I could. I've always been interested in welding, and I enjoy it. I realize not many people feel that way, but I do." Wynne Nowland, the Long Island insurance executive, said, "The best part is strategizing. Coming up with different techniques to propel the company forward, whether it's a new sales procedure we're instituting or looking for a strategic acquisition."

The vast majority, though—72 percent—said that what they liked best about their work was the people. Not the work, not the money, not the accolades.

The people.

But which people? For some it was their colleagues. Dominique Turrentine, a Bay Area native and LSU alumna who works as a program officer at the Chan Zuckerberg Initiative, said, "I get to work with some of the dopest people I've ever met, like people I consider family. As much as I complain about this place, they help me feel passionate about it."

WHAT IS YOUR WHAT?

Joey Clift, an aspiring comedian who went to Washington State University to become a weatherman because he "didn't see any Native American comedians on television," eventually cracked the comedy world. He landed eighty-two gigs in his first ten years, including Looney Tunes and Nickelodeon. (He also created the LA Underground Cat Network, a thirteen-thousand-member Facebook group for Los Angeles comedians to share pictures of their cats.) Today, Joey works at Netflix on "the first-ever animated TV show about Native American people, created by Native American people, in the one-hundred-and-fifty-year history of animation." The best thing about his work? "I love to make my colleagues laugh. There's something cool about being in a writers room, saying a dumb idea, and watching everybody get the joke."

But the single most popular quality people like in their work is the people whose lives they improve. *Fifty-two percent* of people mentioned this attribute as their favorite. Cassie Barrett was the executive assistant to a bank president in North Carolina when the death of her stepmother spurred her to follow her passion of becoming a green funeral director. She now heads operations at Carolina Memorial Sanctuary in Asheville. "What I like best is holding space for the families we serve. We meet people when they're in pain; our job is to reduce that pain. There's a Buddhist practice called *tonglen*, which means 'giving and taking.' We take people's suffering and give them love in return."

Alexandra Herold, a child of fashion entrepreneurs in New Jersey, lost her mother, Patti, to a brain tumor when she was a teenager. She also grew up close to her cousin Ricky, who used a wheelchair.

As a child, Alex felt plagued by insecurities because of dyslexia, ADHD, and an undiagnosed auditory processing disorder. "My mom really empowered me to embrace my disability, to self-advocate." When

Alex was transitioning to ninth grade, her middle school put all the students with disabilities on a bus and took them to the high school. "It was a terrible, terrible experience. Many of the students started crying because they didn't know they were different. Then once we arrived, all the high schoolers knew exactly who to pick on. I got back from that trip, walked into the principal's office, and said, 'Tell me you'll never do it again.'"

In college, Alex volunteered at an organization that matched disabled students with mentors and then went to work for them full time after graduating. She quit to follow her boyfriend to Denver and sank into depression. Alex was scrolling through Pinterest one day looking for a way to "manifest my future," when she came across a shirt with magnetic fasteners instead of buttons.

"Both my parents were salespeople. I see this shirt—it's ugly; it's boxy; it's poorly designed—and I think, *Holy shit! This is brilliant. It's a button-down shirt you don't have to button.*"

Alex immediately tracked down the woman who made it. Her name was Maura Horton, and her husband, a college football coach, was diagnosed with early onset Parkinson's and was humiliated he couldn't button his shirt in front of his players in the locker room. "I asked her if anyone had reached out to her about bringing companies like hers together."

When she said no, Alex said, "I will." Today her adaptive fashion online marketplace, Patti + Ricky, includes one hundred brands selling five thousand products ranging from unicorn eye patches to leopard-skin canes to camouflaged tracheotomy covers.

"I believe I was born to do what I'm doing," Alex said. "The best part of my work is when I speak with customers and help them find products that can change their lives."

What is her *what*?

"Bringing people together."

The common element in many of these answers is that helping others is the sleeper motivation of modern work. It's not a requirement to be happy, but if you're looking for the most popular *what*, it's the one on top.

Future: I Want to Do Work That _____

That brings us to the future and your answer to the question *What is your what?* going forward.

At this moment in my life, I want to do work that_____.

For Ninah Davis, the answer was independence. Ninah grew up in Chicago and was sixteen when her father had congestive heart failure. "In the Black home, when the dad isn't working, the first thought is, *Oh no, are we going to be homeless?*" So Ninah dropped out of high school, worked two jobs, and attended night classes. "I learned that work was not hard for me and that I could enjoy it. But I never want to be beholden to somebody else." Today she's an intuitive energy healer, an interfaith minister, and the creator of the personal development startup Natal+Home. "I want to do work that helps others be free."

For Ericka Rodriguez, the answer was purpose. Ericka, who is a third-generation descendant of California farm workers and whose childhood role model was the primatologist and animal activist Jane Goodall, worked in the legal marijuana business, sold time-shares, and ultimately concluded she preferred work that served her passion for veganism. "I read *The Artist's Way* by Julia Cameron, and it was life changing. I was always an animal lover, and I was shocked to discover that all the makeup I owned was tested on lab animals. The book encouraged me to start formulating my own natural lipstick, even though I have no background in chemistry."

With her fiancé, Ericka moved to Bali for a year, because "it's a big entrepreneurial hub," then to Bend, Oregon, "because it has a big mountain biking culture." The two lived in an Airbnb while Ericka launched Axiology, a "100 percent vegan, cruelty-free, affordable makeup line." In its first year, Axiology did $150,000 of sales. "I realized I wanted to do work that aligns with my values."

For Kelly Lively, the answer was pride. Kelly grew up in "a little cornfield in Iowa. There were two hundred people in my entire school, K through twelve." Her parents leased and managed service stations, with her father serving as mechanic and her mother running the office. "My mother was very much the dominant personality. It never occurred to me that there were *men things* and *women things* to do."

Kelly's parents moved to Idaho three weeks after she graduated from high school. "My sister and I bawled the entire way. She, because she was popular; me, because I didn't even know if Idaho had indoor plumbing." Kelly went to work at the local Ace Hardware, then at an auto parts store, before landing a job as a secretary at Idaho National Laboratory, the country's largest nuclear research facility.

"I worked with a bunch of engineers who were overhauling the refueling systems of nuclear submarine reactors. They would write step-by-step procedures, and I would type them up."

Kelly progressed through a series of jobs, each with greater security clearance, each with more responsibility. "I learned about quality assurance and dimensional lab inspection. I learned about magnetic particle testing and liquid penetrant testing." But she knew she was trapped. "I was making a glorious fifteen dollars an hour. That was good change back then, but I saw the writing on the wall. I needed to go to college." Kelly was married by then and eager to have children. "My academic clock and my biological clock rang at the same time." Over the next five years, she had two children while earning a degree in electrical engineering. She also faced a nonwork workquake.

"My marriage was not my happy place. My husband grew up in the South and had traditional values. How he ended up falling in love with a woman as independent as I am, I have no idea. I thought having children would help our marriage; it did just the opposite. It made me realize how much I valued myself. I had to make a choice between staying home to make him happy or going back to work and making myself proud."

Kelly chose the latter. As the manager of radioisotope power systems and the chief liaison with NASA for all space missions, Kelly became the highest-ranking woman in her office. For the launch of NASA's Perseverance land rover on a mission to Mars, Kelly was "the first woman and the only woman" chosen to escort two thermonuclear power generators from Idaho to Cape Canaveral.

"When my assignment was announced, I got a few phone calls. *How can a woman have the stamina to perform this mission? How can she travel alone with all these men?* That was ridiculous. Frankly, it made me even more determined to prove them wrong."

The generator arrived on time and unharmed.

"What I discovered about myself is that there always are going to be challenges, but I'm capable of meeting them. Especially as a woman, I may not always have the self-confidence. If anything, I have to put my competence over my confidence. But I've learned that at the end of the day, I care far less about what other people think and care far more about what makes me proud."

Independence. Purpose. Pride.

For Ninah, for Ericka, for Kelly—for most of us—*What is your what?* rarely comes down to what you do. More often it comes down to what you make of what you do. What words you assign to the numbers in your control. What story you tell about the actions you take that makes you proud of who you are.

CHAPTER 8

When Is Your When?

I'm at a Moment in My Life When _____

have been fishing commercially for seventeen years, and up until the summer of 1997, nobody cared."

That tantalizing sentence opens Linda Greenlaw's 1999 best-seller, *The Hungry Ocean.* Greenlaw, a Connecticut native who spent summers in Maine, paid her way through college by working on a swordfishing boat. After college, she went to work on the boat full time and was eventually named captain of the *Gloria Dawn*, making her the first and only female captain of a swordfishing vessel in the Americas.

"I never anticipated problems stemming from being female," Greenlaw writes, "and never encountered any."

The reason: fishing isn't a line of work defined by *who* or *what.*

It's a line of work defined by *when.*

"There exist no nine-to-five swordfishermen," she writes. "Twenty-hour days are the norm. . . . The game is never postponed due to darkness, and seldom delayed for weather." There are no weekends, no holidays, no sick days. "When the lines are cast from the dock, all time cards are considered punched 'in,' not to be punched 'out' for over seven hundred hours—seven hundred hours of physical labor, in poor conditions, that you might not be paid for." You might not be paid because when you leave shore, when you arrive at your destination, and when you cast your lines all determine how much you catch. No wonder, she writes, commercial fishing is widely considered "the most dangerous profession."

But as important as all those day-to-day *whens* are to that line of work—or to any line of work—each of us also faces a series of larger *whens* that shape our narratives about work—*when* we fall in love with a job, *when* we fall out of love, or *when* some perfect storm comes along and changes our lives forever.

On October 28, 1991, Linda Greenlaw was captaining the *Hannah Boden*, the sister vessel of a seventy-foot swordfishing boat named the *Andrea Gail*. That night, off the coast of the Grand Banks, a nor'easter absorbed the remnants of Hurricane Grace, creating ninety-mile-per-hour winds and hundred-foot waves. The *Andrea Gail* and all six of its crewmembers were lost. A journeyman tree climber and floundering freelance journalist named Sebastian Junger had just "whacked the back of my leg" with a chainsaw and was limping around Gloucester, Massachusetts, when the storm hit. Three years later, he submitted a fifteen-thousand-word piece on the events of that night to *Outside* magazine, which ran a shortened version under the headline "The Storm." That article became the 1997 bestseller *The Perfect Storm*, which in turn became the Hollywood blockbuster starring George Clooney and Mark Wahlberg.

Greenlaw was in many ways the star of Junger's book. She calls in Mayday for the *Andrea Gail*, and she reads the eulogy at the funeral; in the film she's portrayed by Mary Elizabeth Mastrantonio. Junger calls Greenlaw "one of the best captains, period, on the entire East Coast."

The book changed Greenlaw's life. First she was commissioned to write *The Hungry Ocean*; when it became a hit, she went on to write four more memoirs, four novels, and two cookbooks. In her forties she took in a troubled teen; in her fifties she got married for the first time; three separate times she retired from fishing, only to be called back. Today she runs lobster boats and leads moonlight tours.

"To survive on the water is to course correct," Greenlaw says. "You're going from point A to point B, you have a destination in mind, but tides, currents, and winds can upset your course, and you have to adjust. You still get to your destination, but perhaps not in the same way you had originally intended."

And not in the same time frame, either.

When is the forgotten element of most work stories.

Herminia Ibarra, a professor of organizational behavior at INSEAD, says that even after a generation in which changing jobs became the norm, workers still overly rely on the *linear plan-then-implement* model of seeking work. This outdated approach, in which we keep replacing one job with the next, "presupposes an existing, fully formed self that gets exchanged for a new and improved model." But our work selves are constantly changing, she says, in response to the world around us.

I would go even further: Our work selves are constantly changing not just in response to our environments but also in response to a host of internal clocks. Our biological clocks. Our psychological clocks. Our guilt about being absent parents. Our sense that our bodies will soon give out. Altogether our work lives are being heckled every day by a chorus of inner voices that speak to us in messages we can barely make out, saying, *Now is the right time*; *Now is the wrong time*; *How about next year?*; *Why not today?*

All of these clocks form the irregular ticktock of our work lives. They are the fickle timetables of *When is your when?* Sometimes they toll when you want. Sometimes they toll when you don't want.

Sometimes they toll all at once.

Which is exactly what happened to Alexander Vindman one July afternoon in the Situation Room at the White House.

Alex was born in Kyiv, Ukraine, when it was still part of the Soviet Union. He has a twin brother, Yevgeny, and an older brother. Their father, who is Jewish and a veteran of the Soviet Army, had a "plum job" with the city; their mother died of lymphoma when Alex and his twin brother were three. Alex's father emigrated with the three boys to the United States, where he remarried and settled the blended family in Borough Park, Brooklyn.

Alex was a science geek. He loved *Star Trek* and did well in school, but he didn't work hard. "My brother and I were kind of the black sheep in that regard." They followed in their father's and brother's footsteps and joined the military. "We heard all these stories about jumping out of planes and helicopters. It sounded like just the kind of activity we needed to get back on track. Also, we were immigrants and intuitively embraced the narrative of giving back."

Alex served in the ROTC, graduated from SUNY Binghamton, and was commissioned as a second lieutenant in the army. But at ranger school, he got injured and had to bow out of that elite corps. "It was a major setback. I really had to overcome the stigma."

Which he did. Alex served in an anti-armor platoon along the Korean DMZ and a Stryker brigade in Washington State; after passing ranger school on his second try, he led an infantry company in Iraq, where he was wounded by an improvised explosive device, earning a Purple Heart. At that point he became a foreign area officer and, with his wife, returned to Ukraine as an attaché. "There was something familiar about the country, but it wasn't really home. I'm American."

Alex found his calling as a national security analyst, along with the intellectual rigor he never felt earlier in his life. He earned a master's degree in Russian, Eastern European, and Central Asian studies at Harvard, served at the US embassy in Moscow, became a defense specialist for the chairman of the Joint Chiefs of Staff. Then he was assigned to the National Security Council in the White House. In that capacity, Alex coauthored the national military strategy toward Russia and was part of the US delegation at the inauguration of Ukraine's president, Volodymyr Zelensky, like him a Jew from Kyiv.

Did his work seem linear? I asked.

"There's a kind of templated career in the military, and I was always outside of that, so no, it never felt linear. It's like any other job. Details matter, performance matters, but timing is what matters most of all. You can be a rock star, but if your timing isn't right, then nothing happens. History makes heroes out of ordinary men."

And in the summer of 2019, history met Alexander Vindman.

Alex had been working in the White House compound in the same office that Henry Kissinger once occupied. A few months after he arrived, a series of questionable events began unfolding in Ukraine involving the West Wing, the State Department, and the president's closest advisers. The events culminated in a July 25 telephone call in which the American president asked his Ukrainian counterpart to investigate a domestic political rival.

"I knew immediately that if this became public that the president would be impeached. As a matter of fact, I looked around while still taking my copious notes to see if anybody else in the Situation Room registered the import of what was going on."

Afterward, Alex hurried to his twin brother's office, which was also in the White House. He closed the door and said, "Eugene, if what I am about to tell you ever becomes public, the president will be impeached."

Within days, the call did become public. The House of Representatives subpoenaed many of the personnel involved, including Alex. In his opening statement, he thanked his dad for bringing him to the United States. "I am grateful for my father's brave act of hope forty years ago and for the privilege of being an American citizen and public servant, where I can live free of fear for my and my family's safety. Dad, my sitting here today, in the US Capitol talking to our elected officials is proof that you made the right decision forty years ago to leave the Soviet Union and come here to the United States of America in search of a better life for our family." Alex relayed a story in which his father begged him not to rock the boat and asked why he wasn't afraid. Alex told him what he later told me was his motto.

"Here, right matters."

The president was impeached by the House but acquitted by the Senate. Three months later, Alex was fired from the White House. Five months after that, following "a campaign of bullying, intimidation, and retaliation," he was forced to retire from the army after twenty-one years of service. He joined a national security blog, enrolled in a PhD program at Johns Hopkins, and wrote a bestselling memoir. It was called *Here, Right Matters.*

What did he learn from this experience?

"The moment was much, much bigger than me. And in a way, I was willing to sacrifice everything that I had worked for for this moment.

I was a student of history, and I looked at this moment through a historical lens. I'm still young, but I knew this would likely be my mark. I was in the right place at the right time to defend the national security of the United States. In this case, not against an external adversary, but against an internal adversary. I didn't want to miss the moment."

We all have moments in our lives that are defined by this confluence of work, fate, and time.

Of *who*, *what*, and *when*.

To fully actualize those moments is to grapple with all three of those dimensions, including the one that most people appear to struggle with—timing. *Is now the right time for me to make this move? Is now the wrong time to pursue my idea? Should I push? Should I pause? Should I stay? Should I jump?*

Here are three questions to ask when you find yourself in that moment of *when*.

Past: When Does Your Work Story Start?

On Monday, January 27, 1986, I boarded Korean Air Lines Flight 007 from New York City to Seoul. I remember the flight number because the same plane had been shot down by the Soviet Union three years earlier. I remember the date because just as I landed in my ultimate destination, Osaka, Japan, to begin a semester-abroad program, the space shuttle *Challenger* exploded.

That evening a group of international students went out to dinner. I ordered soba noodles, which were served on top of a lacquer box. I carefully poured the au jus–style sauce over the noodles, which promptly leaked through the slats and dripped on everyone's laps. I had no idea you were supposed to dip the noodles into the sauce, not the other way around. When we departed, I left my credit card at the table. The owner ran down the street after me. My visit was off to an inauspicious start.

Four days later I moved in with my homestay family. The Nagatas lived in a modest home in a crowded Osaka suburb. Their family included a teenage daughter who spoke minimal English; a father who worked for a large industrial company; and a mother who is among the loveliest people I've ever met. Her name was Makiko, and she had a high-wattage smile, librarian glasses, and a giddy laugh. Like her husband, she didn't speak a word of English.

We sat down to a welcome feast that Makiko had prepared using a few inches of countertop, two gas burners, and a toaster oven. All that equipment, plus a small fridge and sink, fit behind a shower curtain. Even with those limitations, Makiko served ten dishes, including braised chicken, steamed vegetables, a sweet potato cake in the shape of Mount Fuji, and, her specialty, homemade, warm liver pie. In my family, I was known for eating anything—except liver.

I ate the pie.

Afterward, I went upstairs and lay down on my bed. It was short and the family had learned that I'm tall, so they had gone around to all the neighbors and collected microwave and TV boxes, which they covered with towels and appended to the end of the bed so my feet didn't stick out. I barely slept.

The next morning I learned my first lesson about life in Japan. Breakfast is leftovers from the night before. So on Sunday morning, I was served cold liver pie. That afternoon I took a pad of crinkly air mail paper and wrote my first letter home. *You're not going to believe what happened to me today.* I haven't stopped writing since.

My work story had begun.

When does your work story begin? When is the moment that the energy enters, the momentum builds, the meaning starts to assemble? Did it happen when you were a child? An adult? Are you still waiting for it to happen? Did it happen once a long time ago and you want it to happen again? Knowing when your story starts will help you tell a better story, because all good stories, on some level, involve a break in time. Just look at some of the most iconic first lines in history: They're all about moments when time starts over.

Orwell, *Nineteen Eighty-Four*: "It was a bright cold day in April, and the clocks were striking thirteen."

Plath, *The Bell Jar*: "It was a queer, sultry summer, the summer they electrocuted the Rosenbergs, and I didn't know what I was doing in New York."

Márquez, *One Hundred Years of Solitude*: "Many years later, as he faced the firing squad, Colonel Aureliano Buendía was to remember that distant afternoon when his father took him to discover ice."

The book of Genesis: "In the beginning God created the heavens and the earth."

What all of these openings have in common is that they involve a rearranging, a reinvention, a recognition that something is beginning anew.

A change in *when*.

I asked everyone when their work story started. A minority said when they were young. Chely Wright knew when she was three that she wanted to be a country music star; Lauren Nichols knew at nine that she wanted to enter public safety; Courtland Savage knew at ten that he wanted to be an aviator. All three fulfilled their dreams.

A majority said their story started in their adulting years, that long decade between late adolescence and early adulthood. Nishita Kothary decided to become a doctor during those years; Eric Vélez-Villar an FBI agent; Nate Venturelli a welder; Shellye Archambeau a corporate CEO.

But as popular as young adulthood is for starting work stories, almost everybody restarts their work story these days at some later point, as Chris Donovan did with shoes, Michael Smalls did with baskets, Cherie Scott did with sauces, and Beverly Jenkins did with writing.

Sara Sherr did the same with music. Sara grew up in Philadelphia in a nontraditional home. Her mother was an art teacher; her father quit advertising to play bass in a cover band. "My parents divorced when I was young, so in elementary school, I would hang out in bars until three in the morning with my dad." Her father eventually went bankrupt and turned to deejaying. "He remade himself again, and I admired that. I just accepted that work involved lots of change."

Sara tried molding herself to traditional jobs. She sold clothes at the Gap; she took a job in accounting at Urban Outfitters. "I heard it was a cool place to work, but I couldn't handle the morning hours." So she quit and returned to her nontraditional roots. Her work story restarted at thirty-seven when she opened a karaoke company, which allowed her to hang out in bars until three in the morning five nights a week. *Philadelphia* magazine named her Best Karaoke DJ in Philly.

Ashley Brundage also restarted her life in middle age. Ashley was raised in suburban comfort in Florida. "I knew I didn't operate like normal boys in my neighborhood, because I chose to act like Jennifer Grey in *Dirty Dancing*, not Patrick Swayze." Confused about her identity, Ashley focused single-mindedly on work. Ashley started behind the counter at Boston Market and got promoted three times in three years, rising from hourly worker to supervisor to managing her own store. In her fifth year Ashley was named general manager of the year for the entire company. "It was like tunnel vision to ignore what was happening." Ashley also got married, had two children, and bought two homes.

But after twelve years, the blinders no longer worked. "I reached a point where I couldn't hide any longer. I started seeing transgender people in society and on TV—Candis Cayne was the first recurring transgender character on network television—and I was like, *Whoa!*" Ashley sank into depression, torpedoed her jobs, lost her homes, and went bankrupt. She also decided to transition to presenting as a woman. "I thought, *If I'm going to start at the bottom again, I might as well be me.*"

Unlike Wynne Nowland, whose role as an insurance executive provided stability during her transition, Ashley had to rethink her work life from scratch. Despite having served as southeast regional director for Boston Market, Ashley was turned down for 101 entry-level jobs; two interviewers called the cops on her for being "a man in a dress." "Finally I decided to take control. I was a bit abrasive, to be honest. I'd walk into an interview and say, *Hi, my name is Ashley Brundage. You can call me Ms. Brundage or Ashley. And by the way, you see this big thing on my shoulder? It's a chip. I'm going to be coming into your organization to prove myself. But if you give me a shot, I'll be your entry into the $1.7 billion LGBTQ spending market.*"

Ashley was finally hired as a part-time teller at PNC Bank for nine dollars an hour. "In the restaurant business I started at four bucks an hour, so that was an improvement!" Within five years, she was a vice president of the entire $17 billion company and was inducted into the employee hall of fame. "The only way to succeed today is to expect the unexpected."

Which is exactly how Ashley restarted her work story when she was forty-one.

When the unexpected happens to you, start by asking, *Am I continuing a story that started long ago or starting a new story that begins right now?*

Present: Should You Stay or Should You Go?

Then turn to the present and ask, *Is now the right time for my next step or should I first plot, and plan?*

In 1951, the poet Langston Hughes, who had first come to prominence twenty-five years earlier, set out to create an unconventional masterwork called *Montage of a Dream Deferred.* Inspired by the rhythms of blues and jazz, the book-length poem explores the continuing experience of racial injustice that prevented many Americans from achieving the recognition they deserved—including him.

Today *Montage* is best known for a stand-alone poem called "Harlem (A Dream Deferred)." The work was inspired by a passage in Proverbs 13:12, "Hope deferred makes the heart sick," and in turn inspired Martin Luther King Jr.'s "I Have a Dream" speech. The poem begins with a question, "What happens to a dream deferred?" then asks, does it wither and fade? Does it turn sugary and sweet?

"Or does it explode?"

Three quarters of a century later, I found that question to be among the most haunting for those in a workquake. Should I act now on my dream, or should I defer?

Some years ago, I spent a morning with Professor Laura Carstensen at Stanford University. Carstensen studies how time affects our decisions. I was writing a book about happy families at that time and was interested in Carstensen's research showing that as people get older they pare back their relationships. They cast off casual friends and focus instead on those closest to them, especially their families.

But Carstensen's research extends to work as well. In a study called "Taking Time Seriously," Carstensen and two former students show that "as people move through life, they become increasingly aware that time is somehow 'running out.'" They have less patience for waiting; more urgency to act. "It becomes increasingly important to make the 'right' choice, not to waste time on gradually diminishing future payoffs." In other words, the longer the past becomes and the shorter the future becomes, the greater the pressure becomes on the present to make the right decision.

What creates that pressure is not aging, per se; it's the transitions that come with any age—ending a relationship, graduating from school, completing a medical treatment, leaving a job. The key to being emotionally fulfilled, Carstensen writes, is to *lean into that urgency*—to decide as if your clock is running out. If you do, you're more likely to choose what makes you happy.

I spent considerable time in my conversation trying to suss out exactly how people factor timing into their biggest work decisions. In the end, I found they do three things:

They read their gut.

They read the room.

They read the clock.

Let's review these one at a time.

The first of these time checks, *reading your gut*, means asking yourself a simple question. It's the same question that Brian Wecht asked when he left his job as a tenured theoretical physics professor at Queen Mary University in London to devote himself to his YouTube comedy band, Ninja Sex Party, and that Lisa Ludovici asked when she left her senior job in internet sales at Microsoft in New York City to become a medical hypnotist: *Which is greater, the fear of staying or the fear of leaving?*

Half the people who said that *when* was a primary motivation during their biggest workquake said they wanted to act *before it was too late.* Alton White, who walked away after twelve years from a secure job playing Mufasa on Broadway, said, "It was time to fly higher. I was afraid of learning lines; I was afraid of being on a movie set; I was afraid of losing my house. But these were all fears I wanted to conquer."

Tim Pierpont, who left his two-decade job in commercial real estate for his nerve-racking job running a painting startup, said he was motivated in part by seeing a colleague get sick. "He had worked in the same office from eighteen to sixty-four. One day the boss told him to go home early because he wasn't looking well. A year later he died from cancer. I didn't want to show up for another six years just because I had always showed up. I wanted to have more control over how I spent my life."

The second time check, *reading the room*, involves understanding the larger forces at play in the world. The people who do this successfully focus less on what's happening in their own heads and more on what's happening in the society around them. Alicia Rodis believes that her work as an intimacy coordinator would never have taken off without the exposé of Harvey Weinstein and the subsequent rise of #MeToo; Shardé Davis knows she would never have touched a nerve with her hashtag about discrimination in the ivory tower without the protests around Black Lives Matter.

Ben Conniff became interested in the boutique food business in high school while working the morning shift at Beach Donuts in Old Lyme, Connecticut. "Some kids would come in overnight and do the shaping and frying; I would come in around four in the morning and do the jelly, the frosting, and the powdered sugar." In college Ben bartended; after graduating he wrote about food and cocktails for *Playboy*; at twenty-four he answered an ad on Craigslist from an investment banker who was looking for a cofounder to open an artisanal lobster roll shack. "This was the period when sustainable food was just catching on. Our timing was perfect." Luke's Lobster went on to open thirty-plus franchises, ship sustainable seafood around the world, and generate $80 million a year in sales.

Nathaniel Peterson, the Ohio-born *Jaws* fan, was trying to get his animal television series off the ground just as the cable TV business was stalling and online streaming was taking off. Nate rebranded himself as Coyote Peterson after his role model, the Crocodile Hunter, Steve Irwin, but nobody was buying. "YouTube had just opened, but no one had monetized it yet. I went to a TV conference where all these companies announced their online services. I was like, *Holy cow, we've got to make a digital version.*" Discovery Digital was interested, but instead of offering Nate and his producer the half million dollars per episode they requested, the company offered $30,000 in total for twelve episodes. "We brought in fifty-two episodes with that money. Plus, we posted everything on our YouTube channel, Brave Wilderness." Within two years, their channel hit a million followers; eight years later it has twenty times that number. "*When* was critical in our story, because we launched at a time when YouTube was still in its infancy. Today, they've changed the algorithm and it's insanely difficult to build brands on that platform."

The final test, *reading the clock*, involves managing risk. Should you give yourself a deadline? Should you create a buffer zone that gives you a window of time to succeed or fail? Shelby Smith, the Iowa native who quit her job trading equity derivatives in Dublin to found the sustainable food startup Gym-N-Eat Crickets, set a benchmark. "If I don't make $10,000 in my first twelve months, I'm going to walk away." She achieved her goal. Jasminne Mendez was in her twenties, teaching theater in the Houston school system, when she came down with a chronic immune disease and had to step down from teaching. "I looked at my finances and said I have six months to try writing." She's since published two memoirs, three children's books, and a volume of poetry.

Sang Kim combined several of these time tricks when he quit his job as a contracts lawyer at Goldman Sachs to open an interior design firm. "I told myself, *One, you can't be unhappier than you are now. And two, I'll give myself three years. If I haven't made meaningful traction by then, I'll go back to law.*" Six years later, Sang Kim Designs LLC was still thriving.

No one I spoke to better illustrates the way that *whens*, both good and bad, shape our lives than Judith Heumann. Judy contracted polio in Brooklyn in 1949, seven years before the vaccine became available. At eighteen months she was put in an iron lung and outfitted with leg braces; she still became a quadriplegic. Her father, an architect, used money from the GI Bill to build a ramp onto their home.

In many ways, Judy was trapped by her times. She was denied access to kindergarten because she was deemed a "fire hazard;" in elementary school she was locked out of regular classes and confined to the basement with those with mental disabilities, even though she had no such learning issues; in high school she was told to forget college.

Judy instead enrolled at Brooklyn College, where she earned a degree in speech therapy. When she applied for a teaching job in New York City, however, she faced daunting challenges. Her friends had to carry first her, then her wheelchair, to the second floor to take the qualifying exam because the building was not accessible. Judy aced the test but was denied a job "because the Board of Education did not believe I could get my students out of the building in case of a fire." It was the same excuse she'd heard fifteen years earlier about why she couldn't enroll in kindergarten.

But here's where timing played to Judy's advantage. The ACLU turned down her case, saying the city was justified, but two independent lawyers agreed to help. At twenty-two, Judy filed a federal lawsuit against the City of New York. Invoking the country's most famous polio patient, the *New York Daily News* blared the headline YOU CAN BE PRESIDENT, NOT TEACHER, WITH POLIO; the article prompted the *Today* show to invite Judy to share her story.

Faced with a wave of publicity, the city settled. In 1970 Judy Heumann became the first teacher in a wheelchair hired in New York State. Overnight, she became a leading figure in the disability rights movement, leading efforts to shut down traffic in Manhattan, occupy the Federal Building in San Francisco for a month, and launch the independent living movement in California. After the Americans with Disabilities Act became law in 1990, Judy became the assistant secretary of education in the Clinton administration.

All this would not have happened, she believes, if it weren't for a confluence of timing. "My lawsuit was decided by the nation's first African American woman federal judge. My lawyers were trained in the civil rights movement. A lot of my fellow activists were veterans who lost limbs in the Second World War. All these factors created momentum, and I was just carried along by the moment."

The notion of being carried along by the moment may be the best way to characterize so many answers I heard to the question of *Should I stay or should I jump?* If your gut says yes, the room says yes, and the clock says yes, who are you to say no?

Future: I'm at a Moment in My Life When _____

The final step to deciding *When is your when?* is to put the earlier two questions together—*When does your work story start?* and *Should you stay or should you go?*—and complete this statement:

I'm at a moment in my life when _____.

Before you do, two reminders.

First, your answer is not forever. If the peril of the nonlinear work life is that we face existential moments like these more frequently than we'd like, the advantage of the nonlinear work life is that no answer lasts forever. Odds are, you'll face another defining moment in the not-too-distant future. When there is no path, there's far less consequence for stepping off the path.

Second, you'll almost surely look back on your decision fondly. I asked everyone to think back on their biggest workquake and answer this question: *Do you wish you had been more wary of risk, more embracing of risk, or did you handle the risk about right?* Only 9 percent said they wished they'd been more wary of risk. The rest split evenly between saying they got the balance right and wishing they'd been more embracing of risk. Psychologists have suggested a number of reasons why we remember our decisions favorably, from selective forgetting to rationalization. Whatever the reason, these tendencies are your friend. Even if you take the riskier choice and fall short, you're still likely to be grateful that you made that choice to begin with.

Some people take the risk because the rest of their life seems stable. Wei-Tai Kwok said that he could leave his job running an ad agency for an unknown future fighting climate change precisely because he was feeling secure. "I was already very successful on the outside. My family was healthy and happy. Everything seemed perfect. Until I saw that darned movie and realized that in a broader sense everything was *not perfect*. I was at a moment when I realized I was in a bubble and had to change."

Others take the risk precisely because their lives are not yet stable and thus failure seems less consequential. Deniese Davis is a second-generation Las Vegan who made promo tapes for her high school dance team and moved to Brooklyn to attend college and try to get into television. While interning at *The View*, she had a meeting with Barbara Walters, who told her, "As a woman, you'll always be overlooked, so you can't be second-guessed. You have to learn everything—how to shoot, how to edit, how to write." Deniese took that advice. She moved to Hollywood, attended film school, and instead of trying to work herself up as an assistant, took any freelance assignment she could get.

When Issa Rae, the rising actor and writer, was looking for a producer for a new YouTube series, she offered Deniese a pay cut to take the job; Deniese didn't hesitate. "If I hadn't listened to Barbara Walters, if I hadn't started at the bottom, I would never have been prepared. I was at a moment in my life when I finally understood that in order to be successful you have to be willing to go backwards as well as forward." Deniese and Issa went on to produce more than sixty hours of award-winning television, including two series for HBO.

Still more people take the risk because they know it's essential for their survival. Susan Venturelli, the Indiana native whom we met earlier as having a side job selling brownies and a care job tending her grandson, always dreamed of being a mom. After high school, she taught aerobics, hawked Mary Kay cosmetics, and then got a job as a security guard at a steel mill. She also married at twenty, had two children, and then divorced.

"Then my mother called one afternoon. 'Something happened with Dad. He fell out of bed, and I can't revive him.'"

Susan hopped in her car and sped toward her parents' house. "This cop pulled up next to me at a stoplight. 'Ma'am, you got to slow down.' 'Something's wrong with my dad,' I said. 'I've got to save him.' He turned on his lights and followed me. Just when I got to the house, the paramedics were bringing Dad down the stairs. I knew he was gone."

Her father was declared dead at the hospital.

"My dad was everything to our family. He was our rock, our stability. I knew in that moment that I had to change my life. I had to assume his role; I had to take more responsibility for my mom; I had to raise my children. I wasn't going to rely on any man. If someone in our family needed protection, I had to provide it."

That evening Susan logged on to the Blueline website, which lists jobs in policing. With her background in security, she was easily accepted into the academy. She was hired by her hometown police department in Thorntown, Indiana, then transferred to Amtrak, where she stayed for the next fifteen years.

"No one else believed I could do it, but I was at a moment in my life when I knew I had to be strong."

We all reach moments in our lives when time seems to stop. When the wind switches direction. When our heart skips a beat. We can succumb to these moments and remain stuck in place. Or, as Linda Green-law says, as Judy Heumann showed, as Susan Venturelli proved, we can tack. We can head in a different direction. We can make a difficult choice. We can course correct.

We can transform a moment when our story seems to stop into a moment when our story starts again.

CHAPTER 9

Where Is Your Where?

I Want to Be in a Place That _____

Sandra Cisneros loves houses. Born in Chicago to Chicano parents, Cisneros, the author of eight books of fiction and poetry, and the winner of the American Book Award, the MacArthur fellowship, and the National Medal of Arts, grew up splitting her time between Mexico and the United States. In her writing, she tries to bridge that divide by leaving a trail of love letters to the many homes where she's lived.

Her autobiographical collection of essays opens with a piece called "Hydra House," about a hideaway on a Greek island where she lived in her twenties. The collection ends with "A Borrowed House," about her first crush. "My first crush was over a book, and not just any book, but a book about a house." The name of that book, *The Little House*; the name of Cisneros's autobiography, *A House of My Own*.

In an introduction to her most famous work, Cisneros describes the Chicago house where she lived as a teenager and another where she returned after graduate school. There, she summons the courage to tell her unsupportive father that she wants a house of her own. A writer needs "quiet, privacy, and long stretches of solitude to think," she declares. "The father decided too much college and too many gringo friends had ruined her."

In the house she eventually settles in, Cisneros writes in the kitchen, "the only room with a heater." There she begins her book, which is not a novel, she insists, but "a jar of buttons." The book will go on to sell six million copies and be translated into twenty languages. It will be required reading in classrooms around the world. And before she writes a word of it, Cisneros already knows its title.

The House on Mango Street.

You can't write a story without a house to set it in. Setting is everything. Yet, when I asked people to rank their top influences in their work stories, *where* came in last. Perhaps that slight is the legacy of a time when caring about where you worked was considered a luxury. *You're lucky to have a job. Go where they tell you!* Or perhaps it's a deeper problem with storytelling itself.

The Pulitzer Prize–winning author and lifelong Mississippian Eudora Welty complained about the disrespect given to setting in a famous speech at Duke University in 1955 called "Place in Fiction." Place is "one of the lesser angels" of storytelling, she declared; it "gazes benignly enough from off to one side," while "character, plot, symbolic meaning, and so on are doing a good deal of wing-beating."

But don't take this lowlier angel for granted, Welty pleaded. All good stories are "bound up in the local"; all good stories are "bound up in place."

All good stories have a *where.*

Welty's admonition certainly applies to work stories. The American work narrative has always had a strong connection to place: the factory floor, the cubicle, the C-suite. The American Dream has always been deeply infused with physicality: the house, the yard, the garage, the picket fence. Even the American success story has always enjoyed a rich association with what the popular nineteenth-century Baptist firebrand Russell Conwell called *acres of diamonds.*

For some, those acres are metaphorical.

For others, they're real.

Carolina Guillen Rodriguez was the daughter of Mexican farm workers who emigrated to California's Salinas Valley in the 1940s. "My earliest recollection of working was when I was seven years old picking carrots in the field. I was paid twenty-five cents an hour. The winters were OK, but the summers were over a hundred degrees. I thought, *I can't cry because if I do, it will only get hotter.*"

Carolina's mother was the hardest-working woman her daughter ever saw. "She'd get up at four in the morning to make tortillas for everyone to eat in the fields for lunch." Her father, though, was drawn to drink. "After work, he'd walk over to the local bar with his buddies and spend whatever money he made."

The family was paralyzed by his habits. "My mother begged my father to buy her a house, but he would say, 'No, we're going back to Mexico.' I was always very respectful toward him. But one day, when I was fifteen, the roles got reversed. I don't know what possessed me, but I scolded my father like I was the parent and he was the child. *We need to buy a house! Seven of us are living in this tiny, five-bed, five-hundred-square-foot rental.* My mother was expecting another child at that time, but no one would rent us a bigger house because our family was too large."

Carolina's father just stared at her. "I thought he was going to hit me. Then he turned around and walked away. The next day he came to me, 'Carola, get dressed. We're going to look for a house.'"

The two of them drove around the community. "We spotted all the FOR SALE signs, and if the homes looked vacant, we'd peep through windows. *No, this one's too small; no, that one we don't like.* Once I knocked on a door and the family said, 'You'll have to talk to a Realtor.' I didn't know what that meant."

Finally, Carolina and her father drove onto a tree-lined street and saw a house that had "great curb appeal."

"We called the Realtor; the next day he picked us up in this big, black Cadillac. We lived in the poorest part of town; my father thought it was a heist! He sat in the front seat, my mom and I in the back. We looked at the house, which was a three bedroom, one bathroom, for $13,000. We all fell in love with that house. I had to do the translating because my parents didn't speak English. My mother cried at the closing. She called that house Paradise."

Carolina was smitten with real estate, but as a girl in a traditional family, that dream was out of the question. "My parents were very, very strict. I had to be home every night. I knew there was no way I was going to a four-year college."

Instead she attended a local business college and majored in bookkeeping. She got a job at a book publisher, then a beer distributor, then a frozen food plant. She also got married and had a child. "I stayed home for a month on maternity leave, then shocked my husband by saying I wanted to stay home full time. We had already closed on our own house by then; we had bare furnishings. I told my husband that if we paid off our MasterCard, which was eighty dollars, we wouldn't have any bills."

Her husband, an ironworker, reluctantly agreed.

Carolina stayed home for the next five years and had two more children. "I was a penny-pincher. I wouldn't drive anywhere. I would drop off our payments at the utility company to save on stamps." When her youngest child entered second grade, she started part-time book-keeping at their school.

But all this time Carolina was nursing her childhood dream. "I kept telling my husband, 'Ever since I was a little girl, I wanted to be a Realtor.' He kept giving me all kinds of excuses. Finally, when my youngest son was in seventh grade, I said to myself, *They're teenagers. They don't want their mother around.* My husband tried to stop me, but I said, *Nothing on earth is going to stop me now.*"

Carolina earned her license. She was hired by Century 21. Like her mother, Carolina got up at four every morning to make lunches for her family, then headed off to work. For her specialty, she chose entry-level homes like the "Paradise" she grew up in. "I met this Realtor who said she was so frustrated that a buyer didn't want to spend more than $135,000. I said, 'I'll find her a house for less!' I started going to the worst neighborhoods, knocking on doors. I approached this gang of boys and asked them where their mamas lived; I didn't stop until I found a seller."

Carolina, who went by her maiden name Guillen professionally, did face discrimination. "I took this listing from a white lady. She told me, 'The only thing I'm asking is, whatever you do, don't sell it to a Mexican.' I said, 'I just want you to know, my full name is Carolina Guillen Rodriguez. I am Mexican.' I ripped up the listing and dropped it on her feet."

But Carolina's ghost job was not race; it was the secret she kept from everybody. "My biggest regret in life, which I still have night-mares about at least once a week, is that I never got a college degree. It just bothers me so much. When I write emails, I have to really check my sentence structure. I always feel so intimidated by people I work with; I had no choice but to run circles around them."

Which is exactly what she did. In her first year, Carolina closed twenty-five sales. In her fifth year, Carolina started buying investment properties using debt, beginning with three duplexes for $43,000. "I was so scared." In her seventh year, the girl who once didn't know what a Realtor did was named Realtor of the Year in Ventura County. She became president of the National Association of Hispanic Real Estate Professionals. "My motto was 'Don't just sell, give back.'"

Today, Carolina manages 2,700 rental units and has 14 employees; she owns a number of commercial properties and multiple homes. Those three duplexes she paid $43,000 for? They're now worth more than a million dollars. When I asked her what places she likes to be in, she said, "Any place surrounded by family."

What places do you like to be in? Which environments make you feel most whole? Where is the ideal setting for your work story?

These three questions will help you discover your answer to *Where is your where?*

Past: Where Did You Most Want to Be as a Child?

In his 1984 book *The Role of Place in Literature*, the literary critic Leonard Lutwack makes the somewhat unexpected point that place doesn't really matter in literature. Instead, what matters is what a place says about the people in it. Setting is "intimately related to character," he writes. "It functions as the detailed and continuous environment in which character is formed and to which character reacts over a long period of time."

The same is true for the role of place in our work stories. Just as *who* locates your story in the context of all the people in your life, *what* in the context of all you do in your life, and *when* in the context of all the clocks in your life, *where* locates your story in the context of all the places in your life. That shaping begins in childhood, which is why the first question to ask when trying to discern *Where is your where?* is *What places did you most want to be in as a child?*

As with role models, what matters about these favorite places is less the setting and more the meaning you assigned to that setting. Someone who liked to be onstage, versus someone who liked to be on the ballfield, versus someone who liked to be in the library, versus someone who liked to be under the hood of a car are all saying something different about their internal scripture. And the goal is to identify the setting of that scripture. Determining what type of sandbox you liked to play in when you were young will help you determine what type of sandbox you want to play in now.

I asked everyone, *What environments were you most drawn to as a child?* The answers fit neatly along two axes—home versus away from home, and indoor versus outdoor—so I coded them twice. A quarter of people liked being at home (kitchen, bedroom, garden, garage) while three quarters liked being away from home (gym, theater, museum, church). Just over half preferred outdoor environments (rivers, forests, cemeteries), while just under half preferred indoor environments (honky-tonks, restaurants, locker rooms).

In eight of ten cases, one of the environments people mentioned as being meaningful in their childhood directly related to work they

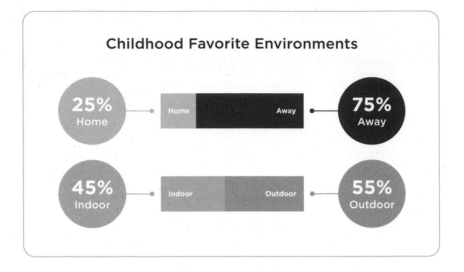

Childhood Favorite Environments

25% Home — Home | Away — 75% Away

45% Indoor — Indoor | Outdoor — 55% Outdoor

were doing as an adult. This finding suggests that place may actually be more important in work stories than it is in fictional stories.

Among home lovers, Cindy Edwards grew up in rural Georgia loving gardening and sewing. "I can't believe I'm telling you this, but in the sorority house, when everybody was going out, I would be needlepointing." After raising two children, she opened a skin care line using natural ingredients from her garden.

Sang Kim, a first-generation Korean American from Queens, said the environment he was most drawn to was the environment he most lacked. "As part of the whole immigrant story, I didn't have my own room until I was in high school. I always shared a bedroom with my sisters—and a bathroom. In a sense, that was OK. I liked being indoors." After fulfilling his parents' dream of becoming a lawyer, Sang left his well-paying job on Wall Street to fulfill his own dream: redecorating other people's apartments, starting with, you guessed it, their bedrooms and bathrooms.

Among away lovers, Divya Anantharaman, as a girl in Miami, loved the library and the natural history museum. "If I had to pick one, I'd say the natural history museum edged out the library. I've still never seen a live zebra in its habitat, but I've seen it and many other iconic animals through taxidermy." Divya started Gotham Taxidermy.

Anooj Bhandari, as a boy in Cleveland, liked social spaces. "I was definitely extroverted; I very much loved performing and being onstage." He grew up to become an actor, a community organizer, and a member of the Neo-Futurists theater troupe.

Among outdoors lovers, Larry Callies, who grew up on a Black-owned cattle farm in Texas and then became a civil servant, said, "I wanted to be on a horse." Following three decades as a postman, Larry opened the Black Cowboy Museum in Rosenberg, Texas.

Derrick Ray, as a boy in Oregon, hated school and loved sports and the outdoors. "I had an English class in high school where if you read four books and did a book report on each, you'd get an A; three books, a B; two books, a C; one book, a D. I got a D. I was like, *Hey, I got PE! Let's go lift some weights.* I took every cooking class I could; I took woodshop and metal shop." Derrick grew up to become a legendary Bering Strait king crab fisherman, with a starring role—as a villain!—on *Deadliest Catch.*

Among indoors lovers, Colin Bedell, the Long Island native who moved to North Carolina as a boy, said, "I've loved urban spaces. Things that are fast moving, high intensity, like the great experiment of civilization that is New York City." His urban astrology brand is called Queer Cosmos.

Shellye Archambeau said the places that she was most drawn to as a child were any places with other people. "I always wanted to belong, so I joined everything. I was a Girl Scout; I was involved in church. In high school, I was a member of the French club, the American Field

Service, the National Honor Society. I really wanted to learn about leadership." She went on to hold leadership positions at IBM and Blockbuster, serve as the CEO of MetricStream and as a board member of Verizon and Nordstrom, and write a book called *Unapologetically Ambitious.*

What all these stories demonstrate is that our forgotten childhood inclinations toward place cast a far longer shadow on our adult inclinations toward work than we realize. If you want to know where you should be when you're older, start by remembering where you wanted to be when you were younger.

Present: Where Do You Want to Be Now?

The next question in pursuit of *Where is your where?* is *Where do you want to be now?* This question is probably the one that's been most upended by events of recent years. Through the confluence of flex work, borderless work, Slack, Zoom, higher rents, higher inflation, the Great Resignation, and the Great Relocation, the centuries-old consensus that the only way to *do work* is to be *at work* has come under serious threat.

In what seemed like overnight, *where* went from being the variable where employers had most of the power to one where employees have a lot more power.

Again, a few statistics make the point.

Before the pandemic, 4 percent of Americans worked exclusively from home; at the height of the pandemic, the number reached 43 percent. Among white-collar workers, the numbers were even higher. Before COVID, just 6 percent of white-collar employees worked exclusively from home; during COVID, the number topped 65 percent. After COVID, twenty-three million Americans said they planned to relocate to a new city now that remote work had gained acceptance.

A big lesson in the global experiment of working from anywhere is that a lot of people don't like working in the office—at least not all the time. Future Forum surveyed ten thousand knowledge workers and found that only 17 percent wanted to return to the office full time, 20 percent wanted to work remotely full time, and two thirds wanted a hybrid. Those numbers were even higher among women and people of color, who were far more likely than their white male colleagues to see working remotely as beneficial to their lives. The reason, Future Forum explained: women and minority workers face a host of additional challenges in the workplace, from code switching to microaggressions.

Being in the office is not the only part of work that's been threatened by change; workplace culture has been, too. The father-and-son researchers Donald and Charles Sull published a study in *MIT Sloan Management Review* in which they analyzed thirty-four million Glassdoor reviews of employees who left their companies in the 2020s. The number one reason: toxic work culture. The Sulls identified five elements of toxicity. The first was *noninclusive*; workers felt unwelcome because of their gender, race, sexual orientation, or disability. The second was *feeling disrespected*; workers felt as if they were being treated like cattle. These workplace challenges were ten times more predictive of quitting than compensation.

What all of these data suggest is that the greater emphasis on meaning at work is beginning to rewrite the rules of *where* we work.

Place is becoming more important in our work stories.

In some ways, this change should not surprise us. Widespread physical relocation has followed every collective workquake in American history, from the Great Migration to the Great Depression to the Great Recession. Economic crises often result in *wherelessness*. In America, "none of us seems to know who he is or where he's going," Ralph Ellison wrote in an epilogue to *Invisible Man*. "Perhaps to lose a sense of *where* you are implies the danger of losing a sense of *who* you are."

I asked everyone in my interviews, *Did you go through a physical change as a result of your biggest workquake—a new office, a new company, a new city?* Ninety-one percent said yes, one of the highest percentages of any question I asked. Those physical changes included a new workplace, a new home, a new travel schedule. Many of these changes were neither anticipated nor welcome. But they're a reminder that if you do change your work, you'll likely change your surroundings, too, so you better consider that variable.

Among those who changed workplaces, Michael Smalls, after he left his job at a South Carolina rug plant to make sweetgrass baskets, faced enormous physical challenges. First, he had to battle alligators and rattlesnakes as he hunted for raw materials; next, he had to battle his own body while weaving the baskets. "I'm doing what I'm passionate about, but with that passion comes sitting down for hours. My doctor tells me, 'Michael, you have to get up every couple of hours for circulation.' But sometimes I get too focused on the work. My hands are OK, but my shoulder, my hip, and my back all hurt."

Meroë Park, when she left the CIA for the civilian world, was shocked by the changes. "In my first job, I had a little office with a window. It was nice, but if anybody had seen my previous office, they would have laughed out loud. I had a suite and a staff of eight." The biggest change, though, was the lack of secrecy. "I'd look over and see my phone on my desk and think, *Oh my God, I committed a national security breach!* I can't tell you how many times I took a piece of paper out of the office and had a moment of panic. *Oh no. It's classified!* When you live in a world for twenty-seven years, even the smallest changes can feel life changing."

Among those who changed residences, Rishi Chidananda, when he walked away from his investment banking office in Cleveland for an ashram in Germany, renounced far more than air-conditioning and catered lunches. "I gave up all my possessions. I took a vow of poverty and celibacy. I no longer ate meat; I no longer drank alcohol; I no longer did drugs. But I found the energy peaceful. The whole point of going to a place like that is to apply what you learn to the rest of your life." After seven years, Rishi relocated to New York City, where he lived in a bare room and taught meditation.

Jordan Reeves, an Alabama theater geek raised in a conservative family, was still closeted when his acting teacher at the University of Alabama at Birmingham shared his own coming-out story. "I started sweating; my heart was beating fast. I can pinpoint his story as saving my life. Afterward, I went up to him. 'I gotta tell you. I'm a homosexual, too.'" The two became friends and when Jordan graduated, the teacher told him, "You need to leave Alabama." Jordan moved to Queens, worked at a Christmas tree factory, and then got a job curating educational conferences at TED.

"Once I was in New York, my whole life changed. I could fill out my body; I could grow out my hair; I could even walk down the street and put my wrist in the air in a way that I would have died rather than do at home." After four years, Jordan left TED to start VideoOut, an organization that amplifies LGBTQ+ narratives.

The final way changing work led to a changing sense of place was the amount of travel involved. Judy Cockerton, when she sold her toy stores and started her foster care community on the far side of

Massachusetts, went through five cars. Karen Noel, when she stopped being a bank manager in Kansas to become a long-haul trucker alongside her husband, had to adjust to new habits. "Living on the road is very different. I usually sleep when my husband drives and vice versa. Food is probably the hardest thing. I put a small fridge in the back, and before I leave home, I try to stock up on fruits and vegetables." The one advantage? "At truck stops, there are usually a hundred men waiting for the bathroom and only one woman."

But the most poignant example I heard of how the places we choose to work reflect the values we hold most dear was Cathy Heying, the social worker who started the car repair shop. Cathy had always been motivated by place. After growing up in Iowa, she moved to Appalachia to volunteer with a charity, then relocated to Minneapolis and worked in community improvement. When Cathy started Lift Garage, she set up shop in the heart of the neediest neighborhood. Seven years later, that neighborhood became the epicenter of global attention. A few blocks away was the site where George Floyd was murdered. Within hours, protests filled the streets; on night three, protestors set fire to the Minneapolis Police Department's Third Precinct headquarters, which is just steps from Lift Garage.

Cathy hurried to the facility.

"Protestors were approaching our building with baseball bats and flamethrowers. This one group of young men was getting close. I was far back and didn't want to yell at them, because I didn't want to escalate. But I was worried they were going to break our windows. As they approached the front, I called out, 'May I help you?' One of them looked at me. 'Is this your building?' He couldn't have been more than seventeen. 'Oh, yes,' I said. Then he shouted to his buddies. 'Wait, wait,

wait! There's a peace sign in this window, we can't break it.' Then he said, 'Sorry, ma'am,' and ran off."

A thousand businesses were destroyed that night. Lift Garage was not one of them.

"I had a roof inspector out the next week because the winds were blowing cinders everywhere," Cathy said. "There wasn't an ounce of damage to our building."

Where you work matters. Where you work gives you meaning. Where you work makes a statement about who you are. But all of those qualities are fluid. When weighing where you want to work now, don't forget that where you want to work in the future might be completely different, and pick a place that at least is telling the kind of story you can be proud of.

Future: I Want to Be in a Place Where _____

Which brings us to the final step of knowing *Where is your where?* Putting what you've learned about your sense of location into a declaration of the kind of location you want to be in.

I want to be in a place where _____ .

For some that place is where they can set a good example. Benjamin Chancey, the wind turbine repairman in Houston, grew up on a honeybee farm in East Texas. "At times that was a cool life; my father was actually the president of the national beekeepers association. But there were dark times, too, like when there was a honey spill and money would literally flow out the door." Ben's favorite places were outdoors. "I loved being on a six-wheeler, following trails, building a treehouse." But when Ben's parents divorced, he moved to the city with his mother and ended up in a string of indoor jobs—bartending, managing a Verizon store, building a windshield repair business.

When the COVID-19 quarantine torpedoed his business, Ben plunged into depression. He told his wife and two sons he wanted to return to his love of the outdoors. "Turns out my phone was listening all along." It sent him a targeted Facebook ad for the Northwest Renewable Energy Institute in Vancouver, Washington. "I clicked on the link and saw a guy hanging off a blade two hundred feet in the air. The scene reminded me of my dad—of the type of dad I wanted to be. I was in a place where I wanted my boys to see me excited to go to work again." After earning his certification, Ben was again doing projects outdoors.

For some that place is what's best for their family—and they adapt. Jodi Mansbach spent much of her life putting other people's dreams before her own. Her father put himself through college, became an accountant, and ran a family tire business in New Jersey. Jodi pushed herself to live up to his exacting standards. She was the first female valedictorian in her high school's one-hundred-fifty-year history; she went to the Ivy League; she landed a coveted internship on Wall Street.

She quit after two days. "I already had this vision that this was not my identity."

Her first job out of college was at the Department of Education, but again she left before her two-year commitment was up. She returned to her first love, art history, earned a master's degree, and went to work for Acoustiguide, the Chicago company that designs interactive guides for art museums. "I enjoyed the work, but it didn't feel like my forever role. Then it hit me: *I'm a mom of two children traveling three weeks a month.*"

Again she prioritized someone else's needs. Jodi and her husband, Ross, decided to relocate to Atlanta "because of its kinder, gentler life-style." At the closing of their new home, the owner said, "By the way, I was the editor of the neighborhood association newsletter, and I left the archives in the upstairs bedroom. Would you mind taking them back to the president?" Ross said, "Oh, Jodi would be really good with helping with that."

"So the next thing I know," Jodi said, "I'm in charge of all the communication for the neighborhood."

And she loved it. She started meeting people, getting involved in the city, working with elected officials. "And it all just kind of clicked. All the stuff I liked—art, history, built environments—came together." She wanted to make a change but was afraid to tell her father. "When I did, my mom said, 'Your dad started something new when he was forty!'" Jodi earned a second master's degree in urban planning, worked at various firms, and then started a company called Living Playgrounds, which designs custom-made children's spaces.

"I was finally in a place in my life where I was willing to create my own narrative. Not my father's narrative, my husband's narrative, or my children's narrative. Mine."

For others that place is wherever they can be alone. As a child in Philadelphia, Charlie Santore stuttered, which led to anxiety, stress, and rebellion. "I never got along well with others. I guess you could say I had an authority problem." When Charlie was nine, his grandfather gave him a safe. "It was a brand-new, closed-vault safe. I kept toys in it." The next year, Charlie's uncle made him a birthday card. *Beware, Charlie. Guard your safe! The New York safecracking gang is coming down to burglarize you.*

"What I'm getting at," Charlie said, "is that there's always been a subtext in my life. I've been fascinated with collecting objects that are symbolic of keeping things locked away. I tend to be very secretive. Even my parents don't know me well."

Charlie drifted through early adulthood. He painted houses, gambled, moved to LA, and became a struggling character actor. "I was just emotionally crushed." One day he went to an auction house to make a few bucks on an old item and stood in line next to a locksmith. "I'd never met a locksmith, but I told him I'd always been interested in safes. It was the first time I ever felt genuinely enthused about something involving work." Charlie called the guy the next day and by the following week had his first gig.

Today, Charlie is LA's leading safecracker, not in the criminal sense, but in the somebody-gets-locked-out-of-their-vault sense. He does twenty jobs a week; he has a collection of blueprints, plans, and schematics going back to the 1930s; and he's got a garage full of cystoscopes, borescopes, and fiber-optic light sources that "would rival most hospitals."

And he has a 100 percent success rate.

"My father always said find something you love, and you'll never work a day in your life. It sounds trite, but when you're living it, it's true. I find myself on my knees in front of a diabolical lockout, and I just laugh. I'm laughing because I know I'm going to be there for hours, I know we're going to have to call riggers just to move the safe a few inches, but I also know that when that door swings open, it's better than sex.

"My only regret," Charlie continued, "is that I didn't start this work twenty years earlier. But after so many years of running from myself, I guess I finally realized that I couldn't be myself until I was working in a place all by myself."

What all these stories share is what all good stories share: an arc. A journey from a place where we feel uncomfortable to a place where we feel like ourselves.

A journey home.

In 1990, Rudine Sims Bishop, a professor of children's literature at Ohio State, wrote a much-quoted essay called "Mirrors, Windows, and Sliding Glass Doors." The best children's stories, she wrote, combine all three of these elements. They're windows into a world we might never have known; they're mirrors that allow us to see ourselves in a new light; they're sliding glass doors that invite us to enter a new realm.

The best work stories, I've come to believe, combine all three of these elements. They're mirrors that allow us to look back at where we came from, they're windows that allow us to appreciate where we are, and they're sliding glass doors that allow us to transport ourselves into new plateaus where we long to go.

Place may be the lowliest angel of storytelling, but perhaps it's the angel we most need to heed in order to reach our loftiest selves.

CHAPTER 10

Why Is Your Why?

My Purpose Right Now Is _____

n 1872, Hans Christian Andersen, the nearly seventy-year-old, moody Danish writer of novels, poems, and travelogues, published his most personal story. It was called "Auntie Toothache" and is considered the last of his 156 fairy tales, an unrivaled collection that includes "The Little Mermaid," "The Emperor's New Clothes," "The Ugly Duckling," and "Thumbelina."

In the story, a young boy, who's clearly a stand-in for Andersen, describes a beloved auntie who spoils him with sweets. She also tells him repeatedly that he has a way with words. "You're a poet! Perhaps the greatest we have." When the boy leaves home and describes to her his new lodgings, she raves, "You're a poet! Just write down your story, and you'll be just as good as Dickens."

Each of us is born with a gift, the boy muses, but that gift comes with a burden. In his case, that burden is that he suffers from toothaches. They "squashed and crushed me," he says.

"I know what that's like," Auntie says, for she, too, suffers from toothaches.

One evening, during a terrible snowstorm, the boy escorts Auntie home from the theater and is forced to bring her back to his boarding-house. That night, as the boy tries to sleep, his teeth flare. "It was as if a red-hot awl went through my cheekbone." As he squirms, the boy is visited in a dream by a ghastly, ghostly woman, whom he calls Auntie Toothache.

You have "an excellent set of teeth" for a poet, she assures. "A key-board of pain."

"Every great poet has a great toothache."

I love this line. I encountered it when I first began the Work Story Project, and it quickly became a kind of Rosetta stone, the key that helped me unlock the question that people said was the most valuable they asked in a workquake: *Why is your why?*

What is your underlying motivation? What's the obsession you've been wrestling with since childhood? The problem you've been trying to solve? The dilemma you've been trying to resolve? "Every good writer or filmmaker," Bruce Springsteen once said, "has something eating at them that they can't quite get off their back."

What's eating at you?

What's your toothache?

Mary Robinson knew exactly what her toothache was, though it took her half of her life to finally connect it to her work. Mary was adopted as a newborn into a family that had already adopted an older boy. "I had wonderful, wonderful parents, and a wonderful, wonderful childhood—until my dad got sick with cancer when I was twelve. Then, everything changed."

Mary's mother was a stay-at-home mom; her father, a chemical engineer, had just left his job to branch out on his own. "That meant my dad had no health insurance. Overnight we were wiped out financially. We lived in this lovely town of Madison, New Jersey, where the pharmacy kept providing the medication my dad needed and the electric company kept the lights on, even though we could afford neither. People we didn't know would drop off envelopes of cash so we could buy groceries."

Two years into her father's illness, Mary's mother called the children into the bedroom. "It will take a miracle for Daddy to come home from the hospital."

"In those days, kids weren't encouraged to go to the hospital," Mary said, "so I had no idea how sick he was. I thought, *OK, we'll get a miracle!*"

A few weeks later, Mary was filling out a get-well card for her dad at a friend's house when her friend's mom shouted upstairs. "'Your mom called. She's on her way to pick you up.' I got in the car, and my mother said, 'Mary, Daddy has died.' I just started to cry."

Mary had never been to a burial. "I walked into the funeral home, saw my dad in the casket, and just backed out of the room. Like I had been pushed back by the energy." Her friends came to the service, but Mary was inconsolable. "I gave the funeral director the finger. I thought, *You don't give a shit, but you're acting like you do. So, fuck you.*"

She skipped the wake and wept in her room.

In the months that followed, Mary spiraled downward. With her mother scrambling to earn a living in real estate, Mary started skipping school, she quit the track team, her grades plummeted. "All through high school, I felt uncomfortable with my peers. All through college, I isolated myself and became quite depressed. I developed bulimia and became promiscuous."

The one thing that kept Mary going was her fascination with human psychology. "I always loved the human drama that happens in airports—the hellos and goodbyes." So she followed a boyfriend to Florida, went to work at an airline, and got engaged. A year later, she canceled the wedding and quit the airline. She slumped back to New Jersey and went to work at Prudential.

"I did well in that job; I got promoted; I had benefits and a nice office. But I wasn't happy, and I couldn't figure out why."

The why was that she didn't know her *why*.

"I kept thinking back on my childhood," Mary said. "My parents were all about service—volunteering, giving to charity. I remembered that when my dad was sick, I volunteered as a candy striper at the hospital so I could sneak in and see him."

Mary started volunteering at hospice. "I would go into people's homes and provide respite for caretakers, then I'd talk to the person who was dying. I did it specifically because I never had the chance to talk with my dad when he was dying."

Her story was so moving to her employer that she won a $50,000 grant for her hospice through Prudential's employee giving program, then was recruited to run the division that gives out those grants. "A few months later, a woman approached me at church and asked what I did. When I told her I gave out community grants for Prudential, she said, 'Do you know about Rainbows? We'd love to apply.'"

Rainbows for All Children is an international nonprofit that provides grief services for children who lost a loved one. "I attended the meeting, and my heart melted," Mary said. She started volunteering; within months she joined the local board; within a year she was in a workquake.

"I was driving into Newark every day after work. I would go to Sacred Heart cathedral, sit in the chapel, and do centering prayer. Afterward, I'd go to mass. On Ash Wednesday, the sermon was from Matthew: *When you give to the needy, don't let your left hand know what your right hand is doing, so that your giving may be in secret.* I kept thinking, *What we do at Prudential is the exact opposite. When we do good, we let everybody know.*"

So after thirteen years, Mary quit the company. She sold her house to reduce expenses. She freelanced as a florist and an event planner. And a year later, when the job of executive director of Rainbows New Jersey opened up, Mary applied for the job. Under her leadership, the chapter quickly became the most successful in the country. Four years later, itching to have more impact, she left to start her own organization to build resilience among families suffering from grief. Seven years after that, she launched an even more ambitious initiative, Imagine: A Center for Coping with Loss, which provides free, year-round counseling to more than five hundred bereaved children, teens, and families.

The child who never properly grieved now provides grief services for hundreds of children.

Mary Robinson had found her *why.*

"I actually found it in my childhood bedroom," she said. "It was while I was still at Prudential. One day I was having a difficult conversation with my mom—we were going through a challenging time in our relationship—and I went upstairs to cry. By the bed, I found this book I had bought and forgotten about. It said, *We can't heal from the wounds of our parents unless we forgive them.*

"That's when I realized my *why,*" she continued. "I wanted to work for an organization that was about changing lives not charging profits. I wanted to say to any child in pain what I wish someone had said to me: *Mary, you had the best dad for fourteen years. Many people don't get that. He gave you his love; he gave you his values. You're going to be*

OK. *Your whole life is ahead of you, and your dad will be by your side the whole way. Don't forget to grieve. But don't forget to live, either."*

What is your *why*?

What is the message you need to hear?

The wound you need to heal?

The call you need to heed?

The following three questions will help you find out.

Past: What Was Your Toothache as a Child?

Some years before starting this project, I wrote a book about Adam and Eve. I got to visit some of the world's more remote places—from the confluence of the Tigris and the Euphrates in Iraq to the Galápagos in Ecuador—and study some of the world's more enduring works of art—from the Sistine Chapel to *Frankenstein*. One of those works of art was *Paradise Lost*.

In book 2, Satan convenes a council of fallen angels to discuss whether to wage a counteroffensive against heaven. One angel, Moloch, says yes, they should stage a frontal assault, "turning our tortures into horrid arms." Another angel, Mammon, says no, goodness can prevail in even the darkest places. We should find strength in our own hurts; we should "seek our own good from ourselves." He then utters one of the more quoted lines in the ten-thousand-line poem.

"Our torments also may in length of time | Become our Elements...."

A question for all of us at some point in our lives is, *Do we do what our lesser angels want and turn our tortures into horrid arms, or do we do what our better angels want and turn our torments into our essential elements?*

Andersen provided his answer in "Auntie Toothache," explaining, "I have to make something of the torments that are inflicted on me." Freud offered his answer in the form of narrative therapy, saying that the act of self-examination turns our *external pains* into *internal strengths.* Alfred Adler suggested his answer in holistic psychotherapy, stating that our goal should be to turn our *felt minus* into our *perceived plus.*

Our job as tellers of our own work stories is to identify the painful patterns we keep repeating, then unrepeat them. An effective first step is to ask yourself, *What was your toothache as a child?*

If, as I believe, any question is only as good as the answer it elicits, this question may be the most effective I've asked in three decades of posing questions professionally. The answers were simply breathtaking. If you could ask yourself only one question in your workquake, I recommend this one.

The answers fell into five categories: *injustice, helplessness, escape, identity,* and *money.* Nearly half the answers were in the top category—*injustice*—while only 3 percent were in the bottom category—*money.* These numbers provide more evidence that (a) doing work that is personally meaningful is not some passing fancy but a conviction that many people settle on when they're young, and (b) the American success story is becoming less focused on accumulating wealth as the leading metric of accomplishment and more focused on caring for oneself and for others.

Let's look more closely at people's answers. One in six said their toothache was *escape*—escaping their homes, escaping discrimination,

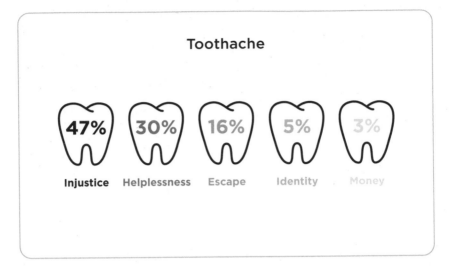

escaping poverty. Laura Spaulding said her toothache was fleeing her toxic family in Florida. "I was compelled to just get out of that environment. It was terribly negative and extremely depressing." After being run out of the military, Laura became a police officer, returned to Florida, and opened Spaulding Decon to help other families clean up their toxic homes.

Kirby Metoxen was the first member of his family not born on the Oneida Reservation in Wisconsin. Using a VA loan, Kirby's parents purchased a home in Milwaukee, where his father worked as an autobody mechanic for twenty-five years. "I didn't want to be like my father—that was my toothache. And I ended up being like my father. I ended up drinking beer and being an abuser." Today Kirby lives on the reservation, where he serves on the tribal council and works as a youth alcoholism counselor.

One in three people said their toothache was *helplessness*. They wanted to take control of their lives, assert their autonomy, fulfill their destiny. Alton White said he felt suffocated as a child in Cincinnati. "I am a survivor of constant bullying, of abuse, and of rape. I was a very shy kid, too, and never thought I would find the courage to perform in front of anybody." Alton went on to perform in front of millions with roles in *The Lion King* and *Miss Saigon* on Broadway and on *Law & Order* and *Bull* on television.

Larry Quinlan was raised in the Caribbean with the expectation that he would take over his father's gas stations, poultry farm, or real estate business. "My toothache was that it quickly became apparent to me that I didn't want to work in my father's businesses. I liked to fix them. I would go into his office, see all the typing and retyping, and think, *This is very untidy. There must be a better way.* Once I took a rudimentary computer and hacked together a system to make files more accessible. Over time, that interest became the itch I needed to scratch: *How can I use technology to avoid drudgery?*" Larry earned an MBA from Baruch College in New York City and spent thirty years at Deloitte, the last eleven as global chief information officer for the 350,000-employee firm.

By far the biggest category was *injustice*, with one in two mentioning this pain as their primary toothache. They craved helping others, improving society, making the world a better place. Brian O'Loughlin was born to Irish immigrants who worked their way into the middle class. His father was a psychologist; his mother was a risk assessment analyst at J.P. Morgan; they dreamed that their son would follow them into a white-collar profession. But Brian had other ideas. "As a kid, I spent time in Harlem and the South Bronx, places where you see the worst of humanity. I was able to articulate early on that I wanted to leave every room I entered a little bit cleaner and earth a little bit better."

Brian became an emergency nurse for North Shore University Hospital on Long Island, a helicopter rescue specialist with the Combat Aviation Brigade of the army's First Armored Division, and a law enforcement officer with the Nevada State Police.

Ken Tang escaped Vietnam at age six with his mother, blind father, and two younger siblings. Their refugee boat was robbed by pirates and abandoned for a week in the South China Sea. After being rescued by the US Navy, the Tangs were resettled in Glendale, Arizona, where Ken said his toothache was feeling left alone. "I wanted to have someone take care of me, because my mom was always working and my dad needed someone to take care of him. I'm the one who had to help my siblings in elementary school do their homework because my parents weren't able to."

Ken became an elementary school teacher.

"My parents were against this idea. We had all these arguments, because, *If you're Asian, you're supposed to be a doctor or a lawyer.* They thought being a teacher was a kind of failure. But I really wanted to be a teacher so I could be the kind of adult in my students' lives that I'd lacked as a child."

But Ken's toothache wasn't cured by his time in the classroom. After twenty-three years in the school system of Alhambra, California, he felt called to run for the board of education. Before he even announced his candidacy, he received some unexpected support.

"Some former students reached out to me. They said, 'Mr. Tang, we heard you were interested in running for school board. We remember in your class how you used to say that you wanted to be a voice for your students. Well, we want to be your voice. We want to knock on doors for you.'"

Ken Tang won his race by thirty thousand votes, garnering 60 percent of the electorate. He was the first Vietnamese immigrant elected to any office in the city of Alhambra, California.

There's a drama in these stories. And a poetry. Many of them feel like fairy tales themselves. The idea that our childhood pains might be salved, even indirectly, through our adult lives is an idea so old-fashioned that it seems utterly removed from the modern discourse about work, obsessed as it is with aptitudes, assessments, productivities, and efficiencies. If you want to find meaning at work, however, a simple step is to reconnect with this mythic quality of healing.

Find the balm to your toothache.

Find your *why*.

Present: What Kinds of Stories Do You Like?

A big reason we sometimes forget our *why* is that we forget that we're actually telling a story about who we are through our decisions about what we do. That story, at its heart, involves a tension. It's the tension between the narrative we inherit about what it means to be successful and the narrative we write about what it means to be successful.

That earlier story is what I've been referring to in this book as a *script*. Coined by Princeton professor Silvan Tomkins in the 1950s, *script theory* suggests that we all have mental constructs that shape our lives. A *restaurant script*, for example, guides us in how to act when we go out to eat—we find a table, place our order, eat our food, pay our bill, etc. No one ever teaches us this script; it's imprinted onto us by our upbringing and experiences.

A *work script* performs a similar role. It shapes our decisions about *what* we want to do, *where* we want to do it, *when* we want to do it, and so on. Again, rarely does someone explicitly convey that script; it's handed down to us through generations of expectations and guideposts.

As valuable as that script can be, it also has consequences. As the Canadian psychiatrist Eric Berne observed, scripts usually end up restricting us because they "inhibit spontaneity and limit flexibility." We're so busy trying to live up to the script we've been given that we don't recognize when we've actually outgrown it.

What I've been calling in this book our *work scripture* is our reaction to that script. It's the personal story that each of us writes that both includes the expectations that we absorb from our upbringings, and then layers on top of them a host of individual ingredients that we adopt from our role models, learn from our environments, glean from our toothaches, and so on.

While our *script* is unchanging, our *scripture* is ever changing.

Our script is what we *should* do; our scripture is what we *want* to do.

Perhaps the primary reason to ask yourself the six Kipling questions is to separate your scripture from your script. It's to isolate *who* you want to be as opposed to who those around you want you to be, *what* you want to do as opposed to what others want you to do, and on down the line.

When it comes to the *why* in that story, a great way to identify what kind of story you'd like to tell is to ask yourself what kind of story you like to consume. These stories can be from books, movies, television, YouTube, TikTok, manga, or wherever. Someone who binges *This Old House* versus someone who binges *Star Trek* versus someone who binges *Law & Order* versus someone who binges *Bridgerton* are all saying something different about their internal scripture. The same goes for someone who gorges on travel videos versus Civil War videos versus cooking videos versus investment videos.

I asked everyone the open-ended question, *What types of stories do you like?* This question is a *why* question because the answers capture the prisms through which we view the world. The stories we consume become the templates for the stories we tell.

My answer to this question, for example, would be nine-hundred-page biographies of consequential lives (William James, Vincent van Gogh), novels by new voices (Chimamanda Ngozi Adichie, Tommy Orange), and hardship memoirs. My wife, Linda, meanwhile, who works with high-growth entrepreneurs and high-net-worth investors, enjoys high-stakes TV dramas like *Succession* and *Game of Thrones*, juicy tell-alls about boardroom intrigue (Uber, WeWork), and prestige fiction. As you can see, we have entirely different taste in stories that reflect our different work lives.

The answers I heard reflect a similar diversity. The top four categories were *wisdom stories*, *heroic stories*, *life stories*, and *suspense stories*.

Among those who said *suspense stories*, Isiah Warner, the LSU chemistry professor, said he likes "intriguing mysteries. It's the same element I like in chemistry—trying to figure out solutions to difficult problems, like being a detective." Daphne Jones, the tech CEO from Chicago, said, "I like espionage movies—the FBI, the CIA, James Bond. Stories that involve money, spies, enemies of the state. Maybe it's because I've been a woman in corporate America—you never know who you can trust, there's some collateral damage along the way, but the good guy always wins."

Among those who said *life stories*, Jodi Mansbach, the art historian turned urban developer in Atlanta, said, "I like memoirs written

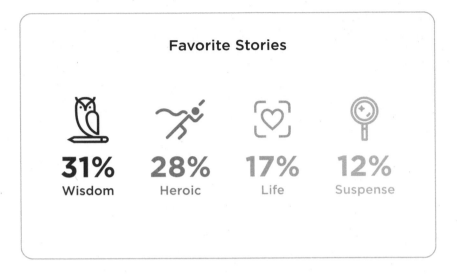

by strong women—Madeleine Albright, Katharine Graham, Michelle Obama." Aaron Krause, the Philadelphia-area inventor and entrepreneur behind Scrub Daddy, said he enjoys listening to audiobooks of inventors and entrepreneurs. "I like biographies—Benjamin Franklin was way ahead of his time, as was Phil Knight, who created Nike. My God, there were points in *Shoe Dog* where he was talking directly to me."

Jasminne Mendez, the Houston schoolteacher who came down with a chronic illness and became a full-time writer, said, "I like stories that delve into real human experience. I was drawn to memoir for a long time, like Jeannette Walls's *The Glass Castle*. But now I like children's literature because there's an honest simplicity when writing for that audience. I really love *The Moon Within*, by Aida Salazar, about the ancestral ritual that Mexican girls go through when they have their first periods." Jasminne started writing poetry but now concentrates on YA.

Many of the stories people are drawn to fit the classic hero's journey of triumphing over adversity; they're *heroic stories.* Joey Clift, the

Hollywood comedy writer, said, "Growing up in a low-income household that was split by divorce, I was definitely beaten up a ton. So I'm always excited about stories from the perspective of the bullied, the marginalized, the underdogs who earn their day in the sun."

Wendy Chisholm, who grew up feeling emotionally abused and went on to run AI for Accessibility for Microsoft, said her favorite story was *The Trumpet of the Swan* by E. B. White. "It's one of those cool, almost divine, works of art. The main character, Louis, based on Louis Armstrong, is a trumpeter swan who doesn't have a voice. So his father steals a trumpet so the instrument can be his voice. For me, the story highlighted one of the blessings of my upbringing, which is that I really had to fight for my health and for my agency. That inspired me to fight to make it easier for other people to get the same kind of agency."

The largest category was people who said they like *wisdom stories*, stories that teach them lessons about life. Cathy Heying, the social worker and founder of Lift Garage, said, "I like redemption stories, but not too cheesy. I prefer stories that are funny and dark. *Harold and Maude* is my all-time favorite movie, for example. I have a tattoo on my arm of the two of them—the young man who rejects his upbringing then falls in love with a seventy-nine-year-old Holocaust survivor who teaches him how to live."

Ben Conniff, the teenage doughnut maker turned foodie, cofounded Luke's Lobster in his twenties and helped lead it through stratospheric expansion. But when the company experienced growing pains, Ben, whose true love was food, not supply chains and debt vehicles, was slowly pushed out by his cofounder. Heartbroken, he left New York City for Maine and turned to building a sustainable seafood ecosystem. "I like funny-sad stories," he said. "They don't have to have a happy ending, but they have to have a beautiful ending, like *Brideshead Revisited*, every Vonnegut novel, or *It's a Wonderful Life*. These stories remind you that in general you don't get everything you want out of life."

Teju Ravilochan was born in Ohio to hard-charging parents who pushed him to attend medical school like his neurosurgeon father. But Teju was more interested in alleviating suffering and asked his parents if there was a "medical school of poverty." Teju grew up to become cofounder and CEO of Uncharted, a nonprofit that raised over $150 million to help scale social-impact startups. "I like stories that involve kindness, where the characters are wrestling with how to be good. *Beloved* is a good example, as is *Anna Karenina*.

"But the best example is Moses," he continued. "He learns that he's not the prince of Egypt, as he wanted to be; but he's not a slave, either, as he should be. He has to find the faith and courage to do the right thing when everyone around him is scared and worried. Then he has to write an entirely new kind of story. Of course, that's the story we're all telling today."

The stories we consume are not just recreation. They're actually a form of re-creation, helping us to create new molds into which we pour the details of our own, ever-changing lives. These molds, in turn, begin to mold our actions.

In 2012, Geoff Kaufman of Dartmouth College and Lisa Libby of Ohio State published a study showing that the more we relate to our favorite stories the more we adopt the worldview of their characters. Through a process they call *experience-taking*, we assume the identity of those characters, adopting their thoughts and actions. We enter our heroes' lives as if they were our own lives, simulating their decision-making and moral outlook. The more we untangle why they do what they do, the closer we come to untangling why we do what we do.

To unpack your *why*, try unpacking the *why* in the stories you love.

Future: My Purpose Right Now Is ————

Once you've identified the *why* of your childhood and the *why* of your favorite stories today, you're ready to home in on the *why* you want to embrace going forward.

My purpose right now is ——————.

Kirsten Green, the criminology professor in Alabama who became a doula after the daughter of a relative became pregnant, said her purpose was helping others. "I now have the chance to make another kind of impact. The maternal mortality rate in my community is through the roof. If I can help change that number in any form, if I can make sure that all the people using my services go home with a healthy baby, that will be meaningful. My purpose right now is to help other families navigate the kinds of waters my family had to navigate."

Mary Scullion, the Sister of Mercy who started a homeless initiative in Philadelphia, quickly found herself in a legal showdown with the city, which tried to shut down one of her shelters after neighbors complained it was lowering their property values. Mayor Ed Rendell called Mary "Philadelphia's Joan of Arc," "because so many people want to burn her at the stake."

But Mary, who spends her one day off a week living among the homeless, fought back. "I believe the people living on the streets are the prophets of today. They're telling us that something is radically wrong with our society. Everybody told me we would lose that lawsuit. *Move on, Mary.* But my purpose was to adhere as much as possible to my dignity, and it was through God's grace that we were able to win the case and show that everyone has the right to live wherever they want."

Perhaps the most remarkable story I heard of purpose prevailing over adversity came from Richard Miles Jr. Richard grew up in a "spiritually guided household" in Dallas. His single mother was a schoolteacher who married a pastor when Richard was five. As a boy, Richard was allowed to listen only to gospel music; as a teenager, he was allowed to skip church only for a job. So at fifteen, he inflated his age and started washing dishes at a hamburger joint.

Richard enrolled at Texas State Technical College to study plastics. He earned good grades and rented an apartment with a friend. "I was beginning to fly on my own," he said.

Two weeks after Richard's nineteenth birthday, a friend offered to drive him to his girlfriend's house one night. The friends stopped at a 7-Eleven; Richard paid his buddy five bucks to thank him and then set out on foot to his girlfriend's. Within seconds, helicopters swarmed, police cars screeched, and cops threw Richard to the ground. They read him his rights and shoved him into the back of a cruiser. En route to the precinct, cops stopped at a Texaco. "I'm looking around; I see police lights and ambulances; there's obviously been a crime. The officers put some stuff on my hands and drove me to the station."

Richard spent the next seventeen months in jail awaiting trial. His attorney explained that a dispute at the Texaco had left one man dead and another wounded. "The shooter was described as being six-two or six-four, dark complected, wearing a white shirt and shorts," Richard said. "I'm five-seven, light-skinned, and was wearing a white shirt and pants."

But that stuff the officers placed on Richard's hands? It was gun residue.

Despite having an airtight alibi, having none of the qualities of the shooter, and having nine of ten witnesses say he wasn't the shooter, Richard was convicted of first-degree murder. When the prosecutor was asked why Richard's skin tone was so much lighter than the alleged shooter, he said, "He faded while in jail."

"May 15, 1994, is the day that Richard Ray Miles Jr. died," Richard said. "They took my clothes, my name, my freedom, and my identity. All they gave me was a number: 728716."

But they didn't take away his character. Richard spent his first five years in prison picking cotton, yams, and blueberries. "There was a strong slavery vibe," he said. Through good conduct, Richard eventually landed a job at the infirmary and started taking college courses. But the most profound thing that happened occurred on day one. Richard was sitting in the barbershop sharing his story. Afterward, an inmate approached him. "Look, you might think everyone in here says they're innocent, but they don't. Guilty people don't want to go back into the system. If you really are innocent, I'm going to introduce you to Centurion Ministries, the only innocence organization that does non-DNA cases."

Richard began a dialogue with the group, who set off doing their painstaking work. Thirteen years later, Richard was lying in his cell one day when the mail carrier delivered a large box. "I jumped out of bed. Centurion had purchased the transcripts and police records from my trial. My family had requested them right after I was convicted, but they couldn't afford the fee."

Their cost: $3,000.

Their contents: "The first piece of paper I read was about a phone call that a witness made to the Dallas Police, long before I went to trial, telling them who the murderer was. The moment I read that paper I knew it was a Brady violation. The police had withheld this evidence. Fifteen months later, I walked out of jail. My case is the fastest in history that Centurion ever resolved."

But now what? Richard Miles was thirty-four years old. No one would hire him, rent to him, or date him. "I had to move in with my mom." Two more years passed before the state offered him a financial settlement. Instead of spending the money, though, Richard used it to start a nonprofit, Miles of Freedom.

"Our mission is to provide holistic services for individuals and families who are rebuilding their lives after incarceration." In its first decade, Miles of Freedom helped equip and employ more than two thousand former inmates. During that time, Richard also got married and had a child. He got a side job teaching Sunday school at his church. And in 2021, the state of Texas passed the Richard Miles Act, which requires law enforcement to provide a written statement that every piece of evidence has been handed over to defendants.

"Joseph is a biblical story where a gentleman was wrongly incarcerated for twelve years," Richard told me. "When he gets out of prison, Joseph doesn't just save himself; his saves the entire nation. That's self-sacrifice. My purpose now is not to help myself; it's to turn what happened to me into a tool to help others."

Joseph. Moses. Matthew.

The Trumpet of the Swan. Harold and Maude. It's a Wonderful Life.

Auntie Toothache.

When scripting the stories of our lives, we turn to the greatest stories ever told. In their morals, we find our truth. In their characters, we find our heart.

In their wisdom, we find our *why*.

CHAPTER 11

How Is Your How?

The Best Advice I Have for
Myself Right Now Is _____

had another grandfather, too, besides the one I worked alongside every Saturday, though I never knew him. Benjamin Samuel Abeshouse was born in New Haven, Connecticut, on February 7, 1901. The youngest of nine born to farmers who fled religious persecution in Lithuania, Bucky, as he was called, was the only member of his generation to attend college. He graduated from Yale at a time when Jews were not allowed to live on campus, and then enrolled at the Yale medical school. He married Carrie Kehrmann, moved to Baltimore, and went on to have a distinguished work life as a urologist, pioneering research into renal dyes and kidney dialysis.

Bucky died of a heart attack at age sixty, three years before I was born; the first two initials of my name, Bruce Stephen, pay homage to his.

But Bucky's life turned out to foretell mine in a more meaningful way. He had a robust side job as a writer. He penned academic articles on everything from infertility to testicles to "inflammation of the bladder due to the presence of a pencil." He contributed an introduction to a widely read 1936 sex guide. And he wrote a book of popular history, *Troubled Waters*, that explores the genital and urinary diseases of famous men, including Isaac Newton, Ben Franklin, and Woodrow Wilson. His description of Napoleon begins, "The body was almost hairless, the genitalia small."

Bucky's most consuming writing project, though, appears to have been something of a ghost job. Bucky lost his father, Abraham, when he was two; he spent most evenings of his adult life sitting alone in his den, scouring books, journals, and magazines, amassing the world's largest collection of epitaphs. Filling five volumes and 1,500 pages, the collection now resides in the Smithsonian Institution. Confronting my own mortality after being diagnosed with cancer in my forties, I went on crutches to the National Museum of American History and read every page.

What struck me most was my grandfather's obsessive interest in the words people chose to be remembered by. Some epitaphs weren't the deceased's choice at all; they were causes of death: poisonings, railroad accidents, bee stings, hangings. Some were words at the expense of the departed: "Here lies the body of young Miss Charlotte, / Born a virgin, dies a harlot."

But by far the largest number were carefully chosen expressions of eternal wisdom:

> *Don't grieve, for what we love comes around in another form*
> *Hitch your wagon to a star*
> *Go traveler, and, if you can, imitate one who with his utmost strength*
>   *protected liberty*
> *There are always flowers for those who want to see them*
> *Love is enough*

Was my grandfather quietly grieving his own lost childhood? Was he searching for the wisdom he never heard from his own father?

We're all searching for something. That eternal longing helps explain why advice is the lingua franca of the modern world. We are awash in guidance. Advice stalks us before we're born: *What to Expect When You're Expecting.* It trails us after we die: *famous last words.* And it dominates most days in between. Our loved ones offer us advice; our colleagues offer us advice; our devices offer us advice. Entire industries are devoted to financial advice, dieting advice, dating advice, parenting advice. Advice is among the most popular type of newspaper article, social media post, and YouTube video. This book is full of advice.

But the central piece of advice in this book is not to listen to all of that other advice. It's to seek your own counsel, consult your own past, write your own story.

Follow your own advice.

It's to decide for yourself—and only for yourself—*How is your how?*

How is the most practical of the six Kipling questions. It's how you make it happen. How you get from here to there. How you maneuver from *once upon a time* to *happily ever after.* Prosecutors must prove three things in order to convict someone of a crime: *opportunity*—that's the *when* question; *motive*—that's the *why* question; and *means*—that's the *how* question.

How is the means to the end.

How is often the first question people ask in a workquake. *How do I get a job? How do I preserve my income? How do I ensure that those around me still see me as a success?* But if you ask *how* too early, you'll find yourself trapped. The reason: You'll likely succeed! You'll find a job. You'll preserve your income. You'll persuade those around you that you're still a success. But you won't necessarily be fulfilled because you won't have taken the time to identify what actually makes you fulfilled. That absence of self-reflection is a main reason that up to 70 percent of people regret quitting a job. Soon enough, they're back where they started, asking the wrong questions and finding the wrong answers.

I put *how* last because that's where it belongs. Only after we do the internal work of the meaning audit—exploring *who, what, when, where,* and *why*—are we ready for the practical work of *how*. Only after we settle on what story we want to tell are we truly ready to start telling it.

Only after deciding what advice we need to hear are we ready to start giving ourselves that advice.

Robin Arzón didn't need any advice; she always knew exactly what she wanted—or at least she thought she did.

Robin grew up in Philadelphia. Her mother was a Cuban refugee who taught herself English by watching PBS and put herself through medical school; her father was a Puerto Rican émigré who sidestepped pressure to become a tradesman and became a law professor instead. "The idea of writing your own story, not taking no for an answer, betting on yourself—that's what I learned from them. That they sometimes missed my play or my mom didn't bake cookies—she feels guilt, but I didn't care."

As a girl, Robin loved watching her dad grade exams. "I used to sit on his stack of blue books and wonder, *How can someone fill up one of these with ideas?* I loved argument, so I joined the debate team in high school." She also cleaned floors in a butcher shop, "which was as grimy a job as you could get," and made her eager to work in a corporate environment.

"I thought, *OK, law school it's going to be.*"

Robin attended NYU, then law school at Villanova, and soon got her wish—a coveted job as a corporate litigator on Park Avenue. Her story was the classic immigrant American Dream. Only her story wasn't done.

In Robin's junior year in college, she was in a bar in the East Village when a gunman carrying three pistols and a sword took forty guests hostage, randomly shooting a few. After dousing everyone with kerosene, the shooter grabbed Robin by the hair, held a lighter to her head, and used her as a human shield. The standoff continued until two patrons tackled the assailant from behind, allowing police to enter the bar and subdue him.

"That incident spurred me to start running," Robin said. "I literally had to run the trauma out of my body." Having never been an athlete, Robin became a superathlete. Over the next decade, she ran 10Ks, then marathons, then ultramarathons; she ran a one-hundred-mile race from Key Largo to Key West and once ran five marathons in five days to raise money for multiple sclerosis.

"It was grueling. I was billing eighty hours a week during the day and running twenty hours a week at night. A bunch of us would show up at 10:00 p.m. on a Wednesday and just run bridges. There were artists, musicians, drug dealers; I was the only one with a corporate job." Robin began training some of those runners and building a reputation as a coach. "I'd show up at races; there'd be a bunch of forty-year-old men in short shorts, and here I was in lipstick, gold necklaces, and earrings. There was swagger with my sweat."

Finally, the firm sat her down: "Do you want to become a partner or a fitness guru?"

"I chose the latter."

But how could she make her choice a reality? How could she make the giant leap from corporate litigator to—well, she didn't know exactly?

Here's how.

How number one: set aside time. "I began blocking out ten minutes a day—eight forty-five every morning. My executive assistant and teammates had no idea what I was doing. But in those ten minutes I sent emails; I made informational interview requests; I googled *What do sports editors do?* I literally had no idea."

How number two: set aside money. "I started saving money. I was living in a walk-up apartment, no luxuries. I didn't travel. I was planning financially long before I was planning intellectually."

How number three: social media. "I started a Tumblr for my marathon training; it was an online scrapbook, but it helped me hone my storytelling."

How number four: a sabbatical. "I eventually took a three-month leave of absence and really ramped up my training and my posting."

How number five: the big leap. "Finally, two years in, the London Olympics were approaching, and I thought, *I have to be there!* So I quit. I bought a plane ticket that cost more than my rent; I stayed on a friend's couch; and I hustled. I met PR agents and athletes; I met the CEO of Nike. 'Wow, you have great style,' he said. 'You should start a blog.' 'I already have one!' I said. 'Here's my card.'"

How number six: a vision board. "I got hired as a social media coordinator for Nike Women. I opened my own website, Shut Up and Run: For Athletes Who Think Medals Are the Highest Form of Bling. I got certified as a yoga instructor, then a running coach, then a fitness trainer. And just because I was bored, I started a vision board using cutout images from magazines. It was a way of manifesting who I was and where I wanted to go."

How number seven: the cold call that changed her life. "One of the companies on my board was Apple; I knew I was interested in disruptive technology. Then I read an article about a man named John Foley who was opening a company that offered online spinning classes. I sent him an email. 'I want to work with you.' Two days later I had an audition at Peloton."

Two months later she had a job. Two years later she became the vice president of fitness. Three years after that the company went public. The following year, when the pandemic supercharged stay-at-home fitness, Robin became a global phenomenon, with a million Instagram followers, two bestselling books, and a brand as a brash, inclusive spokesperson for the power of personal transformation.

As she says in her rides, "Chin up. Crown on. If you give up now, what was it all for?"

"To me, the mind of an athlete is all about story. Like this morning, when I had a barbell on my back that weighs more than my body, when I'm nine months pregnant, when I'm finishing a book, my story starts always with my body as the embodiment of confidence and ends with my mind asking what my mother always told me to ask: *Why not me?* The best advice I give to myself is the best advice I give to my riders: *Do epic shit.*"

Four years.

Seven *hows*.

One reminder: doing epic shit requires lots of fits and starts.

Here are three questions to help you determine what advice you need to get that shit done.

Past: What's the Best Advice
You Ever Received about Work?

Near the end of the 1939 film *The Wizard of Oz*, a giant pink gumball descends on the Emerald City, and Glinda, the good witch, emerges in full, poufed regalia. Wearing a baby-pink taffeta gown and a birthday cake–size crown, Glinda sashays over to Dorothy and the motley crew she's collected along the Yellow Brick Road. Dorothy curtsies and pleads, "Oh, will you help me?"

"You don't need to be helped any longer," Glinda says. "You've always had the power to go back to Kansas."

"I have?"

The Scarecrow, who allegedly lacks a brain, asks the eminently sensible question: "Then why didn't you tell her before?"

Glinda responds with a piece of wisdom that echoes back to Delphi and echoes forward to Yoda: "She wouldn't have believed me. She had to learn it for herself."

As much as we love advice, we often don't need it. The answer already lies within us.

I asked everyone a number of questions about the *how* of how they navigated their biggest workquake. The first questions focused on advice. *Was there someone who gave you advice during this period that was helpful? If so, who was it and what did they say?*

The answer to that first part was yes, 83 percent received advice they found helpful. No surprise. People like advice! Indeed, many of the people who hadn't sought input from others said they wished they had. Their advice to themselves: *Seek advice from others.*

As to whose advice people found most helpful, here the answers contained a surprise. Colleagues were by far the most popular advice givers: one in three participants gave this answer. The second most popular group was professionals—therapists, life coaches, religious leaders, teachers. The third most popular group was friends, with family clocking in a distant fourth. A mere one in six people said that they received helpful advice from a family member during their biggest work crisis, which, I dare say, is far fewer than the number of people who actually sought that advice, or received it unsolicited. Family members either give bad advice or go unremembered for the good advice they give.

As to what advice people found most helpful, these answers were even more revealing. The top two categories, each with 37 percent, were *affirmation* (*You're on the right track! I believe in you!*) and *go for it* (*Make the leap! Take the risk!*). The next two categories, each with 11 percent, were *reframing* (*Maybe you should look at the problem this way*) and *a helpful tip* (*I think you should do this one specific thing*). To tally those numbers up: three quarters of people said that the advice they found most constructive was to continue in the direction they were already heading. They didn't need a punch to the gut; they needed a pat on the back.

They needed to hear, *Trust thyself.*

Among the people who said they heard affirmation, Issa Spatrisano, the refugee coordinator in Alaska, said she felt crippling self-doubt before taking on the role of statewide chief, so she called her mentor and former colleague. "Karen, how do I do this? I'm in way over my head. I have no idea how to manage a multimillion-dollar budget." Karen told her, "Managing a million dollars is the same as managing a hundred dollars. Stop worrying. The staff already respects you because you've spent years earning their respect. Just be you."

Dominique Turrentine, who left a stable job at the Hewlett Foundation for a provisional role at the Chan Zuckerberg Initiative, felt the experiment was backfiring, so she called her old boss. "I can be very intense and frenetic, and he knew exactly what to say. 'I think you're doing well. It may not pan out exactly how you want, but if you shoot for the moon, at least you'll end up among the stars. If not, they're not the only game in town.'" Dominique earned a permanent position as manager of strategic initiatives.

Among those who said the best advice they got was to go for it was Chris Donovan. When he was considering leaving his long-standing job at the phone company to become a women's shoe designer, he went to the Massachusetts Small Business Development Center. The adviser he was assigned to was a former CEO and business school professor who later in life became a professional mentor. "He was my greatest cheerleader. He gave me lots of practical tips and tricks, but the most valuable advice he gave me was, 'Shoot, then aim. You don't have to know exactly what you're doing. You'll figure it out.'"

Deniese Davis, the Las Vegas native who moved to New York to pursue television and then to Los Angeles to attend film school, was fretting over whether to take the traditional, but slow, path of working her way up in Hollywood by starting as an assistant or to continue the path she was on of seeking subsistence jobs producing YouTube videos. "In college I had an unpaid summer internship with a woman named Connie Orlando who was an EVP at Black Entertainment Television. At our final meeting, she gave me her card and said, 'You're going to need me someday. Reach out.'"

Deniese kept the card.

"I emailed her, 'Hey, I don't know if you remember me, I was an intern with you years ago. Here's a photo of me. I'm about to graduate from film school and am looking for mentors.'" Connie invited her to a meeting. "I was so nervous, I started rambling. I told her I wanted to be a producer; I talked about my ambitions—and she interrupted me. 'Stop telling people you want to be a producer; start telling people you are a producer. You're already doing the work; own it.'" Two weeks later Deniese met the rising superstar Issa Rae, and her life as a producer took off.

One of the more moving advice stories I heard came from Alicia Rodis, the actor turned bartender turned intimacy coordinator. When Alicia was in her twenties, her acting dried up as her drinking ramped up. "I felt like I was in free fall. Finally, I crashed to the rocks." At twenty-nine, she turned to AA. Five years later, when she found herself in the maelstrom of #MeToo and the birth of intimacy training in Hollywood, Alicia drew on an unlikely source to help get her through her work storm: her AA sponsor.

"He always told me, 'When you don't know what to do, do the next right action.' So many times in those early months, things were happening so fast that I just wanted them to stop. That's when I remembered his advice: *It's not about you. It's about something larger than you. Whenever you don't know how to respond, be humble, look at what's in front of you, and just do the next right action.*" Alicia became the industry leader in an industry that was just being born.

We all want advice; we all need advice. As I learned in my first round of interviews, seeking wisdom from others is an essential part of any life transition. But as I learned in this round, much of that wisdom merely reinforces instincts we already have. So the next time you're inclined to seek direction from others, by all means do it. But when you don't have the opportunity or the time to reach out to someone else, start by determining what direction you're already headed in.

Then keep walking.

Present: How Do You Give Yourself Permission to Change?

Lots of people quit their jobs. But few have done so in quite so colorful a way as the postmaster of the University of Mississippi in 1924. Born in New Albany in 1897, the oldest son of a railroad family, he joined the Royal Canadian Air Force, matriculated at Ole Miss, and then dropped out after three semesters and, through a patron, was hired to run the post office. He was epically bad at his job. He opened when he wanted to, closed when he wanted to, played cards, drank, tossed circulars in the trash, threw bulletins in the corner, and was generally considered, even by his patron, as "the damndest postmaster the world has ever seen."

"Let us imagine," Eudora Welty wrote, "that here and now, we're all in the old university post office and living in the '20's. We've come up to the stamp window to buy a two-cent stamp, but we see nobody there." We knock and pound, she continued; we harangue and holler. Finally, he appears. "We interrupted him. . . . When he should have been putting up the mail and selling stamps at the window up front, he was out of sight in the back writing lyric poems."

The situation got so bad that a postal service inspector was sent to investigate. Sensing his demise was near, the postmaster submitted the following letter:

As long as I live under the capitalistic system, I expect to have my life influenced by the demands of moneyed people. But I will be damned if I propose to be at the beck and call of every itinerant scoundrel who has two cents to invest in a postage stamp.

This, sir, is my resignation.

The letter was signed: *William Faulkner.*

Sixty-three years later—nearly half a century after he won the Nobel Prize for Literature and a quarter century after he died—the failed postmaster of zip code 38677 was honored by his former employer with a commemorative stamp. Its amount: twenty-two cents.

How do you get from where you are now to where you want to be? You can try the Faulkner approach, or you can be more adroit.

I asked everyone two questions to tease out what steps they found most constructive. The first question was practical: *Of the hundred things you did during your transitions, which single one was the most valuable?* The top three categories involved *people, planning,* and *personal development.*

On the people front, Andrew Gauthier, after abandoning his dream of being an indie filmmaker and turning instead to digital media, embraced a strategy my wife has long trumpeted for entrepreneurs: stalking. He followed industry leaders on social media, where he discovered that *BuzzFeed* was opening a video arm. He landed an interview, sent in a budget, and waited. "Then I learned on Twitter that the editor in chief was going to be on a panel at the 92nd Street Y. So I put on a blazer, went to the venue, and lingered outside the theater door until he came out. 'Oh, wow. You're here!' I said, as if I had planned to go all along." Andrew landed the job of head of the new department.

Meroë Park knew when she ended three decades at the CIA that she didn't want to follow the traditional revolving door of becoming a defense contractor or lobbyist. "I needed to build out my network, so I made the goal of having three breakfasts, coffees, or meetings every day. I literally ate and drank my way through learning about different sectors. Turns out there are a lot of Starbucks! Also turns out people really enjoy telling you why they like their jobs or don't like their jobs. And since these meetings were just informational—I wasn't asking them for anything—I was able to learn so much."

By the end, Meroë had completed two hundred fifty conversations. "I made a giant family tree that showed each person, what they did, and who they connected me to. Since every person said, *Keep in touch*, I'd check in from time to time." Six months into her journey, one of the people she met early on had a job opening. Meroë became the executive vice president of the Partnership for Public Service; two years later she became the deputy secretary and chief operating officer of the Smithsonian.

On the planning front, Curtis Basina, after deciding to sell his gas station and open a distillery, traveled to Washington State to take a course from a master distiller, Rusty Figgins. "After the first class, he pulled me aside. 'Curt, you're from Wisconsin. You guys are the dairy state. Look into making spirits from whey.' I said, 'Whoa, that wasn't necessarily my first choice, but I accept your challenge.'" Copper Crow Distillery now sells vodka made from wheat, rum made from cane, and gin and vodka made from whey, "an eco-conscious, sustainable by-product of the Wisconsin cheese industry."

Tim Pierpont, when he left his banking job in the Bay Area to open Pierpont Painting, made two business plans. "The first contained all the customary metrics—strategy, marketing, budget. The second was an emotional business plan: *What are the good outcomes? What are the bad outcomes? What happens if the business succeeds? What happens if it doesn't succeed?* So much of starting a new venture is the fear of the unknown. Being specific allowed me to reduce those anxieties."

On the personal development front, Lauren Nichols, when she came down with long COVID and decided to supplement her main job as a defense analyst with a side job as a medium, had to boost her self-confidence. "I called it my awakening. First, I had to let my guard down and learn to be vulnerable. Next, I needed to be OK with failure and rejection. Finally, I had to learn to be vocal. It's one thing to write in a journal that I wanted to use my gift; it's something else to let the whole world know." With clients growing more comfortable having consultations over Zoom, her business soared.

Leah Smart, the LinkedIn sales executive who wanted to pivot to employee well-being, visualized her quest. "I made a pie chart on Excel called 'What I Would Be Doing in My Life If I Were Doing What I Really Wanted.' The slices were *writing, podcasting, coaching*, and *speaking*. I gave percentages to each one. Every time I faced a decision—*Do I go to this conference? Do I seek out this opportunity*—I would check the chart and see if it got me closer to my ultimate goal." Once, using this method, she attended a conference she otherwise would have skipped; LinkedIn's VP of learning was on a panel. "I sat in the front row, went up to him afterward, and introduced myself. 'I've heard about you,' he responded." He asked her to write her ideal job description and two weeks later offered her a position on his team. Instead of leaving the company, she was able to redefine her role within it.

The second question I asked homed in even more on the emotional aspects of how people navigated their transition. The question was, *How did you give yourself permission to make a change?*

The most popular answer was to draw strength from the past—*I've done this before; I can do it again.* Nygil Likely, the student affairs dean in Michigan who felt called into ministry, drew on the messages of confidence he received from his creator. "When I listened to the pastor at my church preach from Jeremiah, I heard the message that even with all my brokenness, I was still being called to help shape and mold people. God reminded me that I have always struggled with *Am I good enough to be doing this work?* and he always showed me: *You will bring forth what I want you to bring.*"

The next most popular answer was to draw confidence from the present—*I'm doing well now; I can build on that momentum.* Daphne Jones, the tech executive who walked away from prestige jobs at IBM and Johnson & Johnson because she thought she could do better over the long run, said, "I do things that are risky. I'm a boxer. I'm a scuba diver. I drive a Porsche 911. Leaving my husband was not traditional, but I was the one in power. Leaving IBM was not traditional, but I was not getting what I wanted. I was not always this confident of a person, but I became this confident of a person. I evolved from someone who used to ask permission into someone who gives myself permission." After a stint at a pharmaceutical company, Daphne was recruited to lead GE Healthcare Global Services, a $13 billion division.

The third most popular answer was to draw inspiration from the future—*It's not going to get easier; I might as well act now.* Sonali Dev, the tech journalist who got inspired to write women's fiction after her husband accidentally brought home a romance novel, was frustrated by her inability to sell her first book. "I had been sending query letter after query letter and received fifty rejections. Finally, I went to a convention of the Romance Writers of America. I identified my dream publisher and went to a session run by one of its editors. You basically have a roomful of hungry authors all trying to sell their books.

"By this point I was pretty cynical, but also pretty confident," Sonali continued. "The guy said, 'We're always looking for something different.' My eyes rolled, and I raised my hand. 'When you say *different* what would you think if someone came to you with a Bollywood romance?'

"'I'd think that'd be great,' he said.

"'Well, would you be willing to look at one after this meeting?'

"By now, there was complete silence in the room. Every woman was looking at me like, *How the hell is it OK for you to do this?* I was so nervous I sweat through my clothes. I had to change before going to see him."

In their meeting, the editor asked to see the manuscript but warned her not to send it before she was completely happy with it. Six months later, she sent the book. Two days later, he responded. Sonali was too nervous to open the email. Finally she asked her husband to do it for her.

It said, "When's a good time to call?"

"I'm sobbing," Sonali said. "I'm lying on the kitchen floor crying for a good fifteen minutes."

The following year, Kensington published Sonali's first novel, *A Bollywood Affair*. NPR named it a best book of the year. She's since published nine more.

"All because I was a badass in that meeting."

All because she gave herself permission to be a badass.

Because giving yourself permission might be the hardest part of *how*.

Future: The Best Advice I Have for Myself Right Now Is _____

The final question of *How is your how?*—indeed, the final entry of all the Kipling questions we've been asking—is in many ways the question we began with: Because the answer you've been looking for is already inside you, what is the answer? How would you complete this sentence?

The best advice I have for myself right now is _____.

For Ebony Peay Ramirez, the answer was to take the plunge. After working as an executive assistant at Goldman Sachs and Oculus, then as a consultant for Facebook and Apple, Ebony was debating between getting an MBA or joining a team starting a venture capital fund. "I cold-called a number of women entrepreneurs for input. One of them ran a billion-dollar company. 'Don't go back to school if you don't want to,' she said. 'It won't teach you what you need to know. The space is very welcoming.' Her advice to me was that there's a kind of sisterhood in the tech world and that I should embrace it. So I channeled that advice and told myself, *Dive in.*"

For Colin Bedell, the advice was to take ownership of his life. Colin is the Long Island native who walked away from studying prelaw after being confronted by his brother; five years later, when faced with another inflection point after losing his job in the fashion world and considering starting an astrology brand, Colin hosted a candle-lighting ceremony with a friend. "I told her—and the god of my understanding—that I wanted to be an astrologer, I wanted to write books, I wanted to have a life with meaning. Basically the ritual was my way of putting my intentions into the world." Six months later, on the day Colin's unemployment ran out, an editor at Cleis Press read an interview Colin did with *Refinery29* and offered him a book contract.

But the most universal self-advice comes from Aaron Quinn. Aaron was born to union loyalists in Wisconsin who relocated to Oakland. Aaron's father was a firefighter, his mother a schoolteacher. As a boy, Aaron battled dyslexia and barely spoke before he was six; he didn't learn to read until he was twelve. "People could never understand what I was saying, so I constantly had to reframe things. That may be why I ended up so interested in storytelling."

Aaron worked as a swim coach after high school and considered applying to the fire department academy. His father thought it was a bad idea. Aaron was too young, had limited life experience, and was unlikely to be admitted. He recommended Aaron go see the local fire chief for advice.

"The chief sat me down and said, 'Listen, the written test is pass-fail; the physical test is pass-fail; the psychological test is pass-fail. The whole weight of your score is how you do in the interview. If you want to succeed, take a piece of paper, write out all the relationships in your life and what you learned from them. Write out all your life experiences and what they taught you. Write out your hard times and how they made you stronger. Be honest, be heartfelt, be sincere. They want to hear your story.'"

Aaron did as he was told.

"I walked into the interview. All the questions were situational— *What would you do if this happened or that happened?*—except the first question, which was, *Why do you want to be a firefighter?*" This question is the one Aaron had been preparing for.

"I've lived my entire life in Oakland," he told them. "I grew up here. I shop here. I have friends here. I think it's important to work in a place that you know—and that knows you. Firefighting in essence is a very simple craft; the art is how you interact with the community and how you work to make that community better. I want to be a servant leader."

Afterward, the interviewer came up to him. "You had us after that first answer."

Twenty years later, Aaron still works fifty-six hours a week as a firefighter for the City of Oakland; he volunteers an additional ten hours a week training recruits; he then spends another six hours a week making inspirational videos that he posts on his Instagram page, @live.serve.thrive. His mission: offer similar life-changing advice to the one he received.

"What I like to tell people is what the chief told me: Anybody can do their job. Not anybody can tell their story. But in the end, it's your story that gives you depth; it gives you empathy; it gives you compassion. In the most painful moments of my life, like when I watched people die in my arms, I went back to those words I wrote on that page. And I remind myself: When I'm not conscious of my story, I spiral out of control. When I'm in touch with my story, I spiral upward."

When you've learned how to tell your story, you've learned the most important *how* of all.

The New Rules of Success

The American Dream Is Dead,
Long Live the American Dreams

Aldo Leopold once called himself "the poster boy of the American Dream."

"I was born in 1887 in Burlington, Iowa, to German immigrants," he wrote. "I spent my days being a model student and exploring the grasslands and bluffs surrounding Burlington. I loved floating down the Mississippi River to get to the woods that were on the other side." Leopold likened himself to a modern-day Tom Sawyer, "without the truancy or the silver tongue. Or the lying, or the moneymaking schemes. OK, so I wasn't exactly Tom Sawyer; I was Tom Sawyer's well-behaved and studious cousin."

Burlington, Iowa, in the 1880s was one of many midwestern border cities located at the far western edge of the eastern United States and the far eastern edge of the western frontier. Leopold's father had been a traveling salesman who turned to making oak desks; his mother was a socialite who loved opera. When their first son was born, they commemorated the occasion by planting a red oak.

Perhaps it was this life on the margins that led Leopold, who studied forestry at Yale and became the first US official to manage the Grand Canyon, to identify one of the more inventive ideas about life on the margins of the environment. In his trailblazing 1930 book, *Game Management*, which earned him the nickname the father of wildlife conservation, Leopold introduced the term *edge effect*.

Edges are places where two ecological systems converge: land and water, wood and plain, desert and marshland. What Leopold called the *edge effect* is the vitality that erupts in those marginal regions. Imagine, for example, a forest meeting a pasture: the forest is home to, say, five hundred species, the pasture to a different five hundred; another five hundred require both. That formula means that in the fifty yards on either side of the edge, an area called the *ecotone*, three times as many species live as in either individual zone.

"Game is a phenomenon of *edges*," Leopold writes. "Every grouse hunter knows this when he selects the edge of a woods, with its grape tangles, haw-bushes, and little grassy bays, as the likely place to look for birds." Predators know it, too, which is why they also flock to edges.

Edges are more alive.

Fifty years later after Leopold introduced the edge effect, the Kentucky-born poet and activist Gloria Watkins, better known by her pen name bell hooks, built on his idea in her writings about marginalized communities. "To be in the margin is to be part of the whole but outside the main body," she wrote. Anyone who grows up "on the edge" she said, develops "a particular way of seeing." They understand the edge, but they also understand the center. They understand, above all, that our society will never realize its full potential until the margins have migrated to the heart.

Until we've *centered the edge*.

The New American Dream

As long as there's been an America, there's been a dream of America. "America is a poem in our eyes," Emerson wrote. But there's been an *American Dream* only since 1931. That was the year when former Wall Street financier turned historian James Truslow Adams published his book *The Epic of America*, which popularized the phrase. The Pulitzer Prize–winning Adams actually wanted to name his book *The American Dream*, but he was rebuffed by his publisher.

"America," Adams wrote, is "that dream of a land in which life should be better and richer and fuller for every man, with opportunity for each according to his ability or achievement."

Depression-era Americans lapped up the term, even though Adams himself expressed ambivalence about it. The blue-blooded New Englander said Americans were too prone to self-congratulation and too fixated on money. In our "struggle to 'make a living,'" he wrote, "we forgot to *live*."

Others went even further. Langston Hughes, in his 1951 poem "Children's Rhymes," harshly criticized the American Dream. What's written down for white people, isn't for Black people at all.

Liberty And Justice—
Huh—For All.

No less of an American dreamer than astronaut Buzz Aldrin, the second person to walk on the moon, added his critique, too. "I think the American Dream used to be achieving one's goals in your field of choice—and from that, all other things would follow. Now, I think the dream has morphed into the pursuit of money: Accumulate enough of it, and the rest will follow." Comedian George Carlin also piled on. "It's called the American Dream because you have to be asleep to believe it."

The definition of the American Dream has fluctuated widely over the decades. Today, it contains four primary ingredients: *Up!* America is the land of aspiration, ascension, ambition. *Me!* America is the land of freedom, opportunity, individualism. *Mine!* America is the land of prosperity, affluence, abundance. *Win!* America is the land of achievement, victory, success.

The critique of the American Dream has also grown sharper. *Up?* Not everyone aspires to climb higher all the time. *Me?* Not everyone insists on always putting themselves first. *Mine?* Not everyone measures success by materialism. *Win?* Not everyone has access to the playing field to begin with.

Every year brings new data showing that the zip code you're born into and the circumstances you grow up in all limit your ability to achieve your potential. No wonder polls show that only half of Gen X and half of Gen Z believe they can attain the American Dream; among millennials, the number is even lower.

Is the American Dream even relevant anymore? More to the point, does it play any meaningful role in how we think about work?

I decided to ask everyone in my study. The first question I posed was, *What does your story say about the American Dream?* The second, *Complete this sentence: We should _____ the American Dream.*

The answers to the second question were resounding. Only 8 percent said we should kill the American Dream; it's outlived its purpose and outgrown its usefulness. Thirty-two percent said we should celebrate the American Dream; it's alive and well and deserves to be heralded. But a strong majority—60 percent—said we should update the American Dream; the idea needs to be revised for the twenty-first century to be more inclusive, more communal, less acquisitive, and less careerist.

The overwhelming message: we need an American Dream that reflects today's American dreamers.

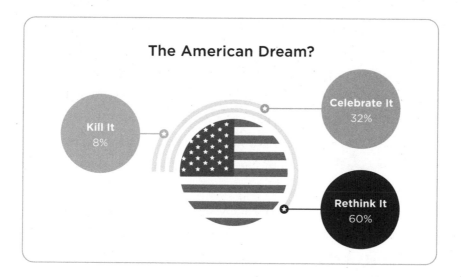

Let's look at the feelings reflected in these responses. Those who want to retire the American Dream use phrases like *kill it, annihilate it, bury it.* Daniel Minter, the painter from Maine, said, "I would be happy to just let it go and not even think about it anymore. It caused so much pain, why would we want to keep it? There are so many more ideas out there we can embrace; we don't have to keep dragging this idea around just because it has the word American in front of it."

Anooj Bhandari, the prison reformer and actor, said, "What I'm challenged by with the American Dream is that I want to say that it's not real. It's oppressive. But the main problem is even bigger: The phrase itself suggests that there's a universal definition of success. Whereas each of us really needs to listen to our bodies to decide what success means to us. I would rather we set aside the American Dream and make space for something new."

The third of people who favor celebrating the American Dream use phrases like *believe in, take pride in, be thankful for, never give up on.* Troy Taylor, the aerospace engineer, said, "Nobody's looking to immigrate to the United States so they can pick tomatoes for the next three generations. The people who come here say, *I'll pick tomatoes so that my kids can go to school and become the next doctor, lawyer, or scientist.* That to me is the American story. And if that's the story you want, America is the best place to make that happen."

Deniese Davis, the Hollywood producer, said, "Statistically speaking, I'm the least likely to succeed. I'm a minority woman from Las Vegas; I had a single mother; I didn't go to the right schools; I had no nepotism whatsoever. But those obstacles fueled me. What I found is that if you work hard, have a passion that drives you, and focus on what's meaningful to you, you can reach your dreams."

But the biggest energy was among the final group, the nearly two thirds of people who say it's time to rethink the American Dream. They use phrases like *redefine, reimagine, redesign, reboot.* Robin Arzón, the Peloton executive, said, "I absolutely believe that the American Dream is still possible. But I believe that because we have so many people, at various levels of success, who are working to dismantle systems that arbitrarily or intentionally subject some communities. Now that we have a lot more people with power who are willing to have uncomfortable conversations, I see a commitment to making sure everyone is getting a chance. What should be done with the American Dream? I say upgrade it."

Teju Ravilochan, the social entrepreneur, said, "I think the American Dream as most people use it is a myth. The idea that you can come here and create any life you want and that the individual is the primary agent. I think about my parents. They were allowed to take only $200 out of India. One way of telling their story is, *Even from those humble beginnings, they found a way to create a beautiful life.* But in fact, what's beautiful about their story is all the people who supported them along the way. When they arrived in Cleveland, my uncle came to stay with me while my dad looked for work. My dad couldn't find a job until someone made a phone call and he got his first position.

"It's that complexity that I'd like to see in the American Dream," Teju continued. "Right now, I'm working with people who are homeless, who are jobless, who are food insecure. The story of pulling yourself up by your bootstraps is so ingrained in them that asking for help is shameful. There's an internalized oppression they feel against relying on others. In American culture, we say, *If you succeed, it's on you; but if you fail, it's also on you.* But that's not true. All of these outcomes are on all of us. I'd like to see an American Dream where you pull yourself up not by your bootstraps, but by your community, your friends, and your neighbors."

The Four Rules of Success

In 1808, the Italian inventor Pellegrino Turri set out to help his blind childhood friend, Contessa Carolina Fantoni, communicate with the outside world. A prodigious letter writer, the contessa found it discomfiting to have to dictate her innermost thoughts to a scribe. Turri's solution was to build her a machine that used mechanical keys to imprint letters on paper so she could write her letters herself. That device is widely considered to be the first manual typewriter. It's also one of the earliest examples of how a solution intended to benefit a small community actually benefits the larger community.

Other examples include the flexible drinking straw, which inventor Joseph Friedman patented in the 1930s after watching his young daughter struggle to drink a milkshake at a soda fountain and wrapping dental floss around the shaft to create corrugations; and email, which internet visionary Vint Cerf helped popularize in the 1980s after using it to communicate with his wife, because both have hearing loss. And the Aeron chair, which designers Bill Stumpf and Don Chadwick introduced in the 1990s using a webbed material originally intended to protect older people from bedsores.

Perhaps the best example of centering the edge, which no fewer than three people cited in our conversations, is curb cuts. For the four thousand years that sidewalks have existed, they had no ramps, making them perilous for those who are disabled. In 1962, Ed Roberts, a California polio survivor who used an iron lung to breathe and attended high school over the telephone, was accepted to the University of California, Berkeley. Unaware of his disability at the time of his acceptance, the university rescinded his admission on the grounds that his iron lung would not fit in a dorm room. Roberts appealed the ruling and won.

Once on campus, Roberts and other disabled students formed an advocacy group; after graduating, he, along with Judy Heumann, helped found the Center for Independent Living. Their first success: persuading the city of Berkeley in 1971 to install curb cuts on all sidewalks. These ramps, designed to help those in wheelchairs, ended up helping people with walkers, mothers with strollers, toddlers with scooters, movers with dollies, and anybody pulling a little extra weight on a busy day.

By centering the edge, everyone's life was improved.

By listening to those on the margins, everyone benefited.

The same is happening with work today. As more women, more younger workers, and more diverse workers flood into the workplace, not only are the rules of work changing; the essential nature of success is changing. We don't have to create new standards of success; they're already being created in real time. All that remains is to codify them.

I'd like to propose such a code. The new definition of success contains four rules:

1. Success Is Not Climbing; Success Is Digging

The first new rule of success is that you won't find fulfillment by following someone else's script; you'll find it only by following your own scripture. You won't find it by claiming the largest office, securing the best view, or reaching the highest rung of the ladder; you'll find it only by tapping into your toothaches, excavating your memories, and unearthing your dreams.

Success is not climbing; success is digging.

Karléh Wilson, the daughter of a struggling jazz musician in Louisiana, earned a shot put scholarship to Yale and went to work in what she thought was the meaningful field of nonprofit housing, only to quit and pursue something more meaningful: becoming a jazz musician like her father. "It was scary to me watching my dad struggle growing up. He wanted me to go to college, get a great career, and make a bunch of money. No one in our family had ever done that. But as soon as I started, I thought, *Is this how people live? You work hard and nothing changes.* The answer, it turns out, was inside me all along. I may not be doing what my dad thought he wanted me to do, but I'm doing something better: what I want to be doing."

Kirsten Green, the Alabama criminologist who helped her relative's daughter give birth, said, "When that daughter first suggested I become a doula, I was standing at the kitchen sink getting ready to bake. I do my best thinking when I'm using my hands. And everything just started making sense. I said, *Kirsten, this is where you began. Biology was your first love. You went to college to become a doctor.* We're taught as children that success is the house with the white picket fence, 2.5 kids, and the dog. No. Success is what makes Kirsten happy, which in my case meant going back to where I started."

Michael Running Wolf, the computer scientist at Amazon who started Indigenous in AI, said, "I grew up without running water or electricity, with grandparents who spoke only tribal languages. I longed for escape. But the older I get, the more I've longed to go back to my roots and protect those vanishing cultures. Five years ago, I would have said that success was making a big paycheck, having a fancy car. Now, success is more personal for me. How do we sustainably carry our people's knowledge into the future? How do I protect what I didn't appreciate when I was young?"

2. Success Is Not Individual; Success Is Collective

The second new rule of success is that no one succeeds alone. No frustration with the American success narrative comes through more clearly in conversations with today's workers than its overreliance on self-reliance. Emerson elevated self-reliance to the pinnacle of American identity; Toni Morrison attacked his sacred cow head-on. "When you kill the ancestor, you kill yourself," she wrote. "Nice things don't happen to the totally self-reliant."

Success is not I; success is we.

Success is not individual; success is collective.

Beverly Jenkins, the romance novelist, said, "Success in America is achievable, but it depends on how much community you have in your life. America was built on the backs of people who look like me. Our ancestors had to be so clever and creative just for me to be able to do my job. I ain't gotta go into the fields every day; I ain't gotta go to the steel mills. But if they hadn't, I wouldn't be here. I look at the people whose shoulders I stand on and try to do the same thing for the people coming up behind me, because that's the only way America gets stronger."

Ken Tang, the schoolteacher and board of education member, said, "Success is not about individual achievement, because success is never something you achieve by yourself. Anyone who's done anything in life, there's someone who pushed them, who inspired them, who gave them confidence. The Garvey School District gave me the chance to be a teacher; the Alhambra community gave me the chance to be a school board member; the California Teachers Association gave me the chance to be part of their leadership. Every success story is a shared story."

Joey Clift, the comedy writer, said, "I think that for any marginalized group, it's very important to help one another. I'm the type of person who when I'm being interviewed for a job, I'll say, 'Hey, if you're looking for other writers, here's some Native names.' I'll actively pitch people for jobs that I'm up for. Because there's never been a Native person on *SNL*; there's never been a Native comedian on a Netflix special. Don't get me wrong. I'd love that opportunity. But I'd be just as stoked if another, crazy-funny Native comedian got it, because once they do, it does immense good for Native representation. I didn't have heroes growing up, and it's super important to me that the next generation does."

3. Success Is Not Means; Success Is Meaning

The third new rule of success harks back to the formula we started with:

$$WORK = NUMBERS + WORDS$$

For too long, success was calculated almost entirely by the first variable. The more money you made, the more successful you were.

Today, a rival interpretation has taken hold. Success is a function of words. It's about the meaning you assign to success. And each person gets to decide that meaning for themselves.

For many, the meaning still comes largely from money, and that's OK. Depending on your personal history, money can represent security, freedom, self-confidence, or the ability to support your family. The difference between that past and today is that money is no longer the only metric by which meaning is calculated. For an equally large number of people, meaning is found through service, creativity, self-expression, or giving back.

In the world of work today, the role of numbers has decreased; the role of words has increased.

Success is not means; success is meaning.

Ben Conniff, the cofounder of Luke's Lobster who left to build a sustainable seafood community in Maine, said, "You wouldn't think it from 99 percent of the businesses out there, but there's a role in business for people like me. People who put purpose over profit. I hope to show with our success that if you run your business exclusively to maximize profits, you won't be as successful financially or spiritually. Especially as younger generations come into more purchasing power, people will realize that there's value in values."

Harmit Malik, the biogeneticist and sci-fi novelist, said, "I don't have the aspiration to start a huge company and make a ton of money. It upsets a lot of people when I say this, but I'm very happy with the life I have. I can be a mentor; I can spend time with my special-needs son; I can write fiction. I know friends who've made the opposite choice. They're making three times what I am, but they have three times the responsibility—and ten times less fun. We've become trapped by getting on an escalator and rising far beyond where we're comfortable. I'm perfectly happy to step off that escalator."

Eric Vélez-Villar, the former FBI intelligence chief who left Disney to deal with his childhood trauma, said, "The traditional definition of success was all about how much money you made. Now, the definition is to achieve the things that mean the most to you. Right now, I'm focused on being a successful father and a successful son. And those things are more important to me than being a successful CEO. I feel there are a lot of people out there like me who have achieved a high level of success, but who are weighed down by personal struggles. If I could say anything to them, it would be, *All those prizes mean nothing if deep down you feel shame. You'll never feel more successful than the day you start doing the right thing.*"

4. Success Is Not Status; Success Is Story

The final new rule of success may be the most consequential: Success is not fixed; it's always moving. Success is not a destination; it's a narration. Orson Welles famously said, "If you want a happy ending, that depends on where you stop your story." Success is not the pot of gold; it's the downpours and rainbows that got you there, along with the sunshine and mud puddles that follow.

Success is not status; success is a story.

Jasminne Mendez, the schoolteacher who came down with a chronic illness then became a writer, said, "My story shows that success is not perfect; it's fluid. In fact, even when it appears perfect, something comes along and you have to start all over. I thought I had a dream life. I was a full-time teacher; I had a fiancé; we owned a town house. Then I got a rare chronic illness and *boom!* I had to give myself a serious sit-down. It wasn't, *Girl, what are you going to do?* It was, *Girl, you need a new story.* I'm grateful that in this country at least we've normalized starting over."

Ninah Davis, who dropped out of high school when her father got sick and went on to become an energy healer and interfaith minister, said, "Success is what you dream, not what someone tells you to dream. My story has violence, it has trauma. Nobody wants that to be their story. But we have to learn to tell those stories—and to hear them—in order for all of us to succeed. After all, we don't just dream for ourselves; we dream for one another."

Issa Spatrisano, the Alaska refugee coordinator, said, "I grew up in a family that believed in storytelling. But what I've learned from the refugees I work with is that there's not a single way to tell a story. There are unlimited ways. The problem with the story we've been telling in this country is that it's too focused on meeting certain qualifications. The American story shouldn't be about the house I own, or the car I drive, or the money I make; it should be about the ability of all of us to tell our individual stories and the ability of the rest of us to hear those stories in a spirit of welcome and understanding."

The Six Answers

Faith Ringgold certainly had a story to tell—all she needed was someone to goad her into telling it.

Born in New York City in 1930, Ringgold earned two degrees from City College, entered and exited a challenging marriage, and started painting vibrant, searing works infused with imagery from her own life. Frustrated that she was not being taken seriously by her icons, Maya Angelou and Toni Morrison, Ringgold complained to a friend, the attorney Florynce Kennedy. "They don't even know we exist," Ringgold said. "You ask them about artists, they go to Van Gogh or Picasso."

Kennedy's response: "Write about your own damned self."

So Ringgold did. She went on to write three children's books and a memoir, illustrate fourteen more books, and master a form of narrative quilt making that earned her a place in the Metropolitan Museum of Art, MoMA, the Guggenheim, and every other major institution in the United States.

Speaking of that conversation decades later, Ringgold said, "At the time I thought it was mean of her to say that. . . . But, you know, she was right. I had no control over what other people thought—or did—about my career. So I began writing my story. I became a primary source about my own damned self."

You're now at the point when you're ready to become a primary source about your own damned self. Fortunately, you have a rough draft in front of you. The Kipling questions we've been reviewing involve plenty of looking backward; now the payoff arrives in that the answers point you toward the future.

Your rough draft is the first draft of the next chapter of your work story.

> *In going through this transition, I've realized that I want to be the kind of person who _____. I want to do work that _____. I'm at a moment in my life when _____. I want to be in a place that _____. My purpose right now is _____. The best advice I have for myself right now is _____.*

If you want, you can also layer in some of your answers from the other questions:

> *The upsides about work I learned from my parents were _____. The downsides were _____. My waymaker right now is _____. My role models growing up were _____. The qualities I admired in them were _____. The best thing about my work today is _____. The worst thing is _____. My work story starts when _____. My view on whether I should stay or go is_____. The places I wanted to be when I was young were _____. The place I want to be today is _____. My toothache as a child was _____. The kinds of stories I like are _____. The best piece of work advice I ever received was _____. The best thing I can do to find work right now is _____.*

Your answers to these questions need not be fixed. This rough draft is not locked. Your work story is not being typeset, bound in leather, and enshrined in the Library of Congress. You can change it anytime, for any reason, by any means.

Your work story is always a work in progress.

Above all, it's a story that need not conform to anyone's expectation and almost assuredly won't align to any preexisting shape. It's not meant to be every story.

It's simply meant to be your story.

The Gift of the Wrong Decision

My father's story ended the week that I started writing this book. For the last eight years of his life, I emailed him a question every Monday morning. *How did you spend your summers as a boy? Who was your first boss? What was your greatest accomplishment?* My father was suffering from Parkinson's at the time and could barely move his fingers. But he answered those questions, one after the other, until, just weeks before he died, he completed a sixty-five-thousand-word memoir—one question, one answer, one life-affirming story at a time.

Flying home for his funeral, I found myself reflecting on some of his most iconic sayings, many of which involved work.

> *You know it's a good deal if neither side is entirely happy.*
> *Dress for the job you want, not the job you have.*
> *Be a team player.*

As he vowed in his college thesis, my father passed up the opportunity to follow his classmates into top jobs in industry or finance in

New York; he didn't even stay in the Northeast, he later wrote, because "the folks who lived there were too pushy and acquisitive for me." Instead, he returned home to work with his father in Savannah, because it was "a good place to raise kids." My mother, who grew up in the Northeast, resented that decision for many years. One of the biggest gifts my father gave was not forcing me to make the same choice.

He let me make my own decisions—good *and* bad.

The night of my father's funeral I went to his office in downtown Savannah, the same one I drove to every Saturday of my childhood. The vault door was open. Inside, in the clangy top drawer of a filing cabinet, I found the overstuffed file with my name on it that he had created more than fifty years earlier. Tucked away amid the photographs and report cards were two collections of poems. The first poem I read was called "T.V."

T.V. IS VERY SPECIAL,
IT MEANS SO MUCH TO ME,
AND IF I COULDN'T WATCH THE TUBE,
I DON'T KNOW WHERE I'D BE.

I JUST TURN ON MY T.V.
AND LET IT DO THE WORK,
SINCE I DON'T REALLY DO MUCH,
MY MOM THINKS I'M A JERK.

So, Mr. and Mrs. Feiler, at least we know he won't become a writer!
One poem, though, did jump out at me. Made when I was ten, it was written in blue ink around the edges of the paper.

A line is so very special. It can do most anything.
It could be a corner. Or form into a ring.

A line could be quite wavy, I added. *Or could be quite straight. It could*
form a zigzag. Or even separate.

A line is very weird. It's as sly as a fox, and when the ends are joined.
It becomes a box.

By the end of the poem, the line had reached the beginning and formed a closed container.

Even as a boy I seemed to long for a life that was undulating and nonconforming—and fearful of one that would trap me in a box.

If working on this book taught me anything, it's that I'm not alone in that fear. In one of my last conversations, I was speaking with Leah Smart. Leah is the Oakland native who after graduating from Cal Poly in San Luis Obispo, went to a job fair and got hired in sales at LinkedIn. She bounced from office to office, left for a real estate startup, and then returned to LinkedIn, where she started a podcast and reinvented herself as a life coach. As a millennial woman in tech who'd been through ten workquakes in ten years, Leah described herself as "one of the *one and onlys.*"

Except, these days, no one is a one of many.

Everyone is a *one and only.*

And we achieve that distinction because at one time or another, each of us does what Leah did, what I did, what even my father did: we make a decision that seems, on the surface, to be wrongheaded. It defies logic; it bucks convention; it upsets the plan.

Even worse, each of these decisions disappoints . . . somebody.

The banker who disappoints his neighbors by becoming a painter.

The lawyer who disappoints her bosses by becoming a trainer.

The immigrant who disappoints his parents by becoming a teacher.

The comic who disappoints her critics by becoming a pundit.

The spy who disappoints her colleagues by becoming a bureaucrat.

The nun who disappoints her mayor by becoming an activist.

The bookkeeper who disappoints her husband by becoming a broker.

Each of these people, at a defining moment in their work lives, made a choice that seemed by all measures to be the wrong choice.

Only it turned out to be the right choice.

If there's a universal message in these stories, it's that there is no universal story anymore. With no single job that will make you happy, you are free to accept whatever job you want. With no single path that will lead to your dreams, you are free to follow whatever dream you wish. With no single career that will define you forever, you are free to create your own *uncareer*.

The lesson of the Work Story Project is that there is power in the unright choice.

There is pride in the unseized compromise.

There is beauty in the unaccepted trade-off.

Every search for meaningful work seems to contain at least one such uncustomary twist.

The tragedy in these stories is that our unconventional decisions often cause pain to someone in our lives—a loved one, a colleague, a boss. The glory in these stories is that our unnormal choices are becoming so common that they're fast becoming the norm.

We are centering the edge. We are rewriting the narrative. We are converting our ghosts into ancestors. We are turning our toothaches into poetry.

We are forging new rules for success in America.

Write your own damned story.

If not you, who?

If not now, when?

ACKNOWLEDGMENTS

"Find a group of people who challenge and inspire you," the comedian and actress Amy Poehler once said. "Spend a lot of time with them, and it will change your life." I am deeply grateful to the 155 people who spent a lot of time with me, challenged and inspired me, and in the process changed my life. The stories gathered here are their stories, in their own words. Because this book is based on the premise that we all have work stories that define and shape us, I purposefully did not check the stories I heard against accounts of colleagues, bosses, partners, family members, or loved ones. Others may have recollections that differ, but I was focused on the views of the people I was in conversation with. Thank you for trusting me with your memories and your dreams.

Most of the people I met for this book I identified and tracked down myself, but I would like to thank a number of people who served as introducers, including Max Stier, Andy Levine, and Sabrina Bleich.

I was uplifted and enhanced by the remarkable team around me who helped code these stories, identify patterns, build analytical models, and run statistical comparisons. I am honored to pay tribute to the superb work of Lucy Ackman, Spencer Feinstein, Jack Robeson, Lina Tate, Tiber Worth, and Andie Youniss. Special thanks to the incomparable Elda Monterosso, who worked with me on my last two projects, and to Lauren Bittrich. And a hearty welcome to Mike Yoon, the wonderful designer who brought our data to life.

A nod to my own team that keeps me going, including Ben Sherwood, Joshua Ramo, Jeff Shumlin, Lauren Schneider, Sunny Bates, Jennifer Aaker, Leslie Blodgett, Campbell Brown, and so many more. And to the sharp eyes and warm hearts of Craig Jacobson, Mahdi Salehi, Alan Berger, Bruce Vinokur, and Katie Maloney.

I have been fortunate to have David Black by my side for nearly thirty years of friendship, debate, and a shared passion for storytelling. For nearly ten years now, Scott Moyers has been my advocate, interlocutor, co-conspirator, cheerleader, and unflagging presence who always insists, above all, that we hold ourselves to the highest standards of integrity, ideas, and good writing. Under Ann Godoff's leadership, the entire team at Penguin Press has reimagined and published my work with the utmost care and commitment. Thank you to Matt Boyd, Sarah Hutson, Danielle Plafsky, Megan Buiocchi. And a special salute to Mia Council and the unflagging Helen Rouner. Also, my deepest gratitude to Karen Mayer.

I'm an ABC for a reason—family is extremely important to me. I am blessed to have two thoughtful, lively, and loving ones—the Rottenbergs and the Feilers. We've all endured a few trying years and feel closer than ever. My brother, Andrew Feiler, continues to be the keenest reader and sharpest eye and makes every draft better.

Linda Rottenberg has done more to reimagine work for more people in more places—especially in the more than forty countries where her organization, Endeavor, has helped find meaningful work for tens of millions of people—than anyone I know. A profound gift of this project has been the ongoing conversation we've been able to have and the deep wisdom she has gleaned from her own work that has in turn deepened mine.

The work involved in this book coincided with years in which our daughters had their own first workquakes, and this book appears in the world just as they begin to venture forth into it. Tybee and Eden: As someone who once comforted your toothaches, I hope above all that you tap into any lingering pains from those or any other aspects of your childhood, take the upsides and downsides you learned from us, and listen to your yearnings wherever they come from as you find work that brings you meaning, purpose, and joy. And I also wish for you, as your parents both had, a never-ending stream of inspirational teachers, mentors, role models, and others who point you down a new path just as another seems to close. The reward is worth the search.

One of those role models for me was a man who had deep seas of pain and turned them into oceans of beauty that touched millions around the world. I treasure the roads that Pat Conroy helped make seem possible for me and the shared walks we were able to enjoy toward the end of his remarkable life. For the indelible work he made—and the constellations of work he inspired—this book is dedicated to him.

FURTHER READING

In the many years I worked on this project, I read hundreds of books and more than five hundred academic studies. Any source I relied heavily on is mentioned in Sources. Instead of listing everything I consulted, I've opted to highlight selected recommended books for those interested in particular themes explored in the book.

History of Career

Mark Savickas has produced an extraordinary output of ideas and practical advice. I especially recommend his *Career Counseling and Career Construction Counseling Manual*. For more academic theory, I benefited from *Career Counseling*, edited by Mary McMahon and Wendy Patton.

History of Success

The literature of success is particularly rich. I thoroughly enjoyed *Self-Help Messiah* by Steven Watts, along with Richard Huber's *The American Idea of Success*.

History of Work

Because this space is so large, I'm happy to endorse works that I believe are universally helpful. These include Robert Kanigel, *The One Best Way*; Robert Putnam, *Bowling Alone*; Nikil Saval, *Cubed*; Jamie McCallum, *Worked Over*.

Psychology of Work

Bullshit Jobs, David Graeber; *The Corrosion of Character*, Richard Sennett; *Range*, David Epstein.

Nonfiction about Work

The Personality Brokers, Merve Emre; *Nomadland*, Jessica Bruder; *Six Degrees*, Duncan Watts.

Memoirs about Work

The Hungry Ocean, Linda Greenlaw; *Lab Girl*, Hope Jahren; *Minor Feelings*, Cathy Park Hong; *The Beauty in Breaking*, Michele Harper; *Old in Art School*, Nell Painter.

Fiction about Work

Behold the Dreamers, Imbolo Mbue; *On Earth We're Briefly Gorgeous*, Ocean Vuong; *Homeland Elegies*, Ayad Akhtar; *Transcendent Kingdom*, Yaa Gyasi.

SOURCES

The bulk of this book is comprised of work stories I collected, along with data that I gleaned from those conversations. I also draw on the wide literature of narrative psychology, positive psychology, applied neuroscience, sociology, anthropology, economics, and other contemporary social sciences, along with history, philosophy, literature, and art history. In this chapter-by-chapter accounting, I offer sources for all the quotations and academic references included in the book.

Epigraphs

Mary Oliver, "The Summer Day," from her 1990 collection, *House of Light*. Brian Eno, from Basic Income UK meetup, London, December 2015, available at YouTube, "Brian Eno Message—Don't Get a Job."

Introduction: The Work Story Project

The Bureau of Labor Statistics (BLS) monthly report of quit rates appears at bls.gov/news.release/jolts.t04.htm. For more on the history of narrative psychology, see my previous book, *Life Is in the Transitions*. The word *workquake* has appeared periodically over the years, including in Steve Cadigan's 2022 book *Workquake*, which credits my use of the term *lifequake* with inspiring his adoption.

The BLS data on most popular jobs is at bls.gov/emp/tables/emp-by-detailed -occupation.htm. Here's my bingo card:

LIFE	CREATIVE	INDUSTRIAL	KNOWLEDGE	WORLD
HEALTH Doctors, Nurses, Technicians, Pharmacists, Veterinarians, Physical Therapists	**ARTS** Visual Artists, Illustrators, Graphic Design, Interior Design, Museums, Galleries	**MANUFACTURING** Industrial Production, Engineers, Factory Operators, Assembly Line Workers	**BUSINESS** Founders, Managers, Assistants, Accountants, HR, Lawyers, Consultants, Customer Service	**AGRICULTURE** Farming, Food Production, Horticulture, Animal Production
WELLNESS Religion, Spirituality, Fitness, Nutrition, Mental Health, Sobriety	**ENTERTAINMENT** Film, Television, Music, Theater, Dance	**TRANSPORTATION** Automobiles, Railroads, Airlines, Public Transportation, Infrastructure, Taxis, Rideshares	**TECHNOLOGY** Hardware, Software, Internet, Digital Technology, Big Data, Cybersecurity	**ENERGY** Oil + Gas, Coal, Wind, Solar, Electric, Nuclear, Mining
FAMILY Child Care, Elder Care, Pet Care, Laundry, Social Work	**MEDIA** Publishing, Journalism, Social Media, Video Games, Marketing, PR, Influencers	**DISTRIBUTION** Wholesalers, Warehousing, Trucking, Shipping, Postal Service, Teamsters	**FINANCE** Banking, Insurance, Wall Street, Fintech, Economists, Taxes	**ENVIRONMENT** Forestry, Oceans and Rivers, Mountains, Parks, Zoos, Hunting, Conservation
EDUCATION Professors, Teachers, Administrators, Librarians, Graduate Students	**FASHION + BEAUTY** Apparel, Shoes, Jewelry, Hair, Skin, Makeup, Nails	**CONSTRUCTION** Builders, Carpenters, Plumbers, Electricians, Architects, Real Estate, Furniture, Flooring	**SCIENCE** Biologists, Chemists, Physicists, Geologists, Space Program	**FIRST RESPONDERS** Police, Fire, EMT, Military, Security, Corrections
LEISURE Sports, Hiking, Gaming, Summer Camps, Amusement Parks, Sex Workers	**FOOD + BEVERAGE** Chefs, Servers, Bartenders, Butchers, Bakers, Baristas	**MAINTENANCE** Custodians, Superintendents, Housekeepers, Pest Control, Window Cleaners	**NONPROFITS** Government, Foundations, Social Entrepreneurship, Social Justice, Philanthropy	**TRAVEL** Hotels, Resorts, Cruises, Conventions

The demographics of my participants were as follows: 50 percent women, 46 percent men, 4 percent nonbinary; 22 percent boomers, 37 percent Gen X, 41 percent millennials; 52 percent had income between zero and $99,000; 27 percent between $100,000 and $199,000; 20 percent over $200,000; 43 percent white, 27 percent Black, 13 percent Asian American, 11 percent Latinx, 6 percent Indigenous; 15 percent identified as having a minority religion; 14 percent as LGBTQ+, 12 percent as having a disability.

"Minority workers have become the majority of new hires": *Washington Post,* "For the First Time, Most New Working-Age Hires in the U.S. Are People of Color," September 9, 2019. "Women now hold": *Time,* "Women Are Now the

Majority of the U.S. Workforce," January 16, 2020. See also, "Women of Working Age," U.S. Department of Labor, Data and Statistics, dol.gov.

1. Lie #1: You Have a Career

"95 percent of human history" from Joyce Appleby, *The Relentless Revolution*, p. 5. "Other ancient cultures" from Andrea Komolsky, *Work*, p. 8. "English word *office*" from Nikil Saval, *Cubed*, p. 13. "Ability to define" from Peter Bernstein, *Against the Odds*, p. 2. "Led by numbers" from Bernstein, *Against the Odds*, pp. 23–25. "Agricultural productivity" from Appleby, *The Relentless Revolution*, p. 79. "Rise of literacy" from Appleby, *The Relentless Revolution*, p. 90.

For more on the origins of *career*, see *Online Etymology Dictionary*. "Factories quadrupled" from Robert Putnam, *Bowling Alone*, pp. 368–70. My description of Frederick Winslow Taylor and management science relies on Robert Kanigel's *The One Best Way*. "Those patents" from Putnam, *Bowling Alone*, p. 368. "Population of urban areas" from Putnam, *Bowling Alone*, p. 370. "Tenements" from Brian Hutchison, Spencer Niles, Jerry Trusty, "The Evolution of Career Counseling in Schools," in *Career Development in the Schools*, edited by Grafton Eliason and John Patrick.

My account of Frank Parsons and the rise of career counseling draws from Arthur Mann's "Frank Parsons," in *The Mississippi Valley Historical Review*, vol. 37, no. 3; Mark Savickas, "Helping People Choose Jobs," in *International Handbook of Career Guidance*, edited by James Athanasou and Raoul Van Esbroeck; Mark Savickas, "Constructivist Counseling for Career Indecision," *The Career Development Quarterly*, vol. 43, no. 4; as well as Parsons's own book, *Choosing a Vocation*.

For "Da Vinci," see Robbie Gonzalez, *Gizmodo*, February 7, 2015. "Worked in agriculture" from Donald Fisk, "American Labor in the 20th Century," BLS, January 30, 2003. "The word *economy*" from Rutger Bregman, *Utopia for Realists*, pp. 111–12. "Term *white collar*" from Saval, *Cubed*, p. 7. "Phrase *knowledge workers*" from Saval, *Cubed*, p. 196. For more on personality tests, see Margaret Nauta, "The Development, Evolution, and Status of Holland's Theory of Vocational Personalities," *Journal of Counseling Psychology*, vol. 57, no. 1. "A third of corporations" from Saval, *Cubed*, p. 165; "employees' wives" from Saval, *Cubed*, p. 171.

"Pattern of work" from Monique Valcour, Lotte Bailyn, Maria Alejandra Quijada, "Customized Careers," in *Handbook of Career Studies*, edited by Hugh Gunz and Maury Peiperl. My history of the résumé, including the quotations, the journalistic references, and the advice manuals comes from the extraordinary work of Sam Hoffman DeKay in his unpublished PhD thesis, "The Historical Evolution of a Written Genre," Fordham University, 2003. "Factory workers" from Charles Heckscher, *White Collar Blues*, p. 3. "White-collar workers" from Savil, *Cubed*, p. 240.

"A little over one hundred fifty years" from Guido Caldarelli, Michele Catanzaro, *Networks*, p. 53. "Satellite in the sky" from Harry Baker, "How Many Satellites Orbit Earth?" *Live Science*, November 14, 2021. "Terabits" from "Internet Speed Record Shattered," *New Atlas*, August 20, 2020. "Grand narratives" from Umberto Eco, *Chronicles of a Liquid Society*, p. 1.

2. Lie #2: You Have a Path

For more on my data about *lifequakes* see my book *Life Is in the Transitions*, pp. 75–95. BLS data on job changes can be found at bls.gov/news.release/nlsoy .nr0.htm. "Follow your bliss" appears in Joseph Campbell with Bill Moyers, *The Power of Myth*. "Butterfly effect" first appears in Edward Lorenz, "Predictability: Does the Flap of a Butterfly's Wings in Brazil Set Off a Tornado in Texas?" presented before the American Association for the Advancement of Science, December 29, 1972. Jeff Goldblum *Butterfly Effect* scene appears on YouTube as "Jurassic Park (1993)—Chaos Theory Scene (2/10)."

"32 percent lower" from Jing Hu, Jacob Hirsh, "Accepting Lower Salaries for Meaningful Work," *Frontiers in Psychology*, September 2017. "Nine out of ten" from Shawn Achor, Andrew Reece, Gabriella Rosen Kellerman, Alexi Robichaux, "9 Out of 10 People Are Willing to Earn Less Money to Do More-Meaningful Work," *Harvard Business Review*, November 2018.

3. Lie #3: You Have a Job

For more on Richard Scarry, see richardscarry.com, famousauthors.com. "Raised their own food" from John McPhee, *The Crofter and the Laird*, p. 38. "Only since the nineteenth century" from Anatoly Liberman, "The Word 'Job' and Its Low-Class Kin," *The Oxford Etymologist*, December 13, 2017. "Keynes," "Shaw," and "Asimov" from Bregman, *Utopia for Realists*, pp. 128, 130, 185.

For detailed statistics on American working hours, see Jamie McCallum, *Worked Over*, pp. 4–25, along with Putnam, *Bowling Alone*, pp. 61–87. "Work performed for money" is discussed in David Graeber's *Bullshit Jobs*, p. 193ff. For "Even by this definition," see *The Random House Dictionary of the English Language*, 2nd ed., unabridged. For "Feminist scholars," see Mariarosa Dalla Costa, Selma James, *The Power of Women and the Subversion of the Community*.

"Work performed on a fixed schedule" from Hudson Sessions, "Comforted by Role of Community or Refreshed by Role Variety," unpublished PhD thesis, Arizona State University, 2019, p. 13. "Jobless jobs" from Mark Savickas, "New Questions for Vocational Psychology," *Journal of Career Assessment*, vol. 19, no. 3. For "Half of us," see "Only 47% of Working Age Americans Have Full Time Jobs," *Business Insider*, January 24, 2011.

For "moonlighting," see *Online Etymology Dictionary* and Andrew Gibson, *The Strong Spirit*, p. 227. For "side hustle," see "The Origins of 'Side-Hustle,'" meriam-webster.com, September 2022. "Employees happier" from Sessions, "Comforted by Role of Community," p. 16; "entrepreneurship," from Sessions, "Comforted by Role of Community," p. 15.

"Hope job" first appears in Kathleen Kuehn, Thomas Corrigan, "Hope Labor," in *The Political Economy of Communication*, vol. 1, no. 1. Her bio appears on kmkuehn.com, as does her description of the origin of the term "Hope Labor as, well, hope labor."

"Primary breadwinners" from "More than Half of Women Are Primary Breadwinners," *Dallas Business Journals*, December 17, 2018. "Parts of parenting" from "8 Facts About American Dads," Pew Research Center, June 12, 2019. "Thirty million Americans" from "Caregiver Statistics," caregiver.org/resource.

"Negative, untelegenic" from Cathy Park Hong, *Minor Feelings*, p. 55. "American optimism" from Hong, *Minor Feelings*, p. 56. "Prove myself" from Hong, *Minor Feelings*, p. 9. "Reality is distinct" from Hong, *Minor Feelings*, p. 18. "Remain silent" from Audre Lorde, *Sister Outsider*, p. 41. For "Brewster," see Harold Sack, "David Brewster and the Invention of the Kaleidoscope," *SciHi Blog*, July 10, 2021.

4. We All Need Another Hero

My review of the history of success draws from a wonderful collection of books, including Richard Huber, *The American Idea of Success*; Steven Watts, *Self-Help Messiah*; Peter Lyon, *Success Story*; and Gary Scharnhorst, Jack Bales, *The Lost Life of Horatio Alger, Jr.* "Best clothes" from Benjamin Franklin, *The Autobiography of Benjamin Franklin*, p. 25. "Dominant visual" from Harold Bloom, *The American Dream*, p. 27; "rags to riches" from Bloom, *The American Dream*, p. 23.

"Timeless" from Daniel Rodgers, *The Work Ethic in Industrial America*, p. ix; "leisure" from Rodgers, *Work Ethic*, p. 7. "Made a fortune" from Huber, *American Idea of Success*, p. 15. "Industrious" is available at d.lib.rochester.edu/cinderella /text/alger-ragged-dick-plot-summary. "Collectively selling" from Scharnhorst, Bales, *Lost Life*, p. 149; "so 'excited'" from Scharnhorst, Bales, *Lost Life*, p. 77. "Abominable" and "wish him" from Scharnhorst, Bales, *Lost Life*, p. 2.

"Change the thought" from Rodgers, *Work Ethic*, p. 38. "Most popular" from Huber, *American Idea of Success,* p. 164. "Sit down" from Watts, *Self-Help Messiah*, p. 48. "No faith" from Watts, *Self-Help Messiah*, p. 6. "Harmonic" from Watts, *Self-Help Messiah*, p. 50. "Shout" and "Really feel" from Watts, *Self-Help Messiah*, p. 51.

For more on David Jepsen, "Career as story," see *Ten Ideas That Changed Career Development*, edited by Mark Savickas. All quotes from Savickas come from my conversation with him, January 2022.

5. The Meaning Audit

"Very conservative" from Maggie Bullock, "The Changeling," *Elle*, June 23, 2009. "Really frustrated" from Lauren Tegtmeyer, "Jessica Alba Shares How She Handles the Big Parenting Conversations," March 24, 2021. For the story of Alba's business, I relied on Derek Blasberg, "How Jessica Alba Built a Billion-Dollar Business Empire," *Vanity Fair*, December 1, 2015. "Hospitalized several times" from Jessica Alba, *The Honest Life*, p. xiv. "AMERICA'S RICHEST" from "Jessica Alba," *Forbes*, December 12, 2016. "Understand yourself" from David Artavia,

"Jessica Alba Regrets Not Starting Therapy Earlier in Life," Yahoo!, February 7, 2022.

"Narrative of ascent" from Robert Stepto, *From Behind the Veil*, p. 164. Seamus Heaney, "Digging" in *Death of a Naturalist*.

I discuss the original research behind the ABCs of Meaning in *Life Is in the Transitions*, pp. 104–5.

"Present-oriented" from Roy Baumeister, Kathleen Vohs, Jennifer Aaker, Emily Garbinsky, "Some Key Differences Between a Happy Life and a Meaningful Life" in *The Journal of Positive Psychology*, vol. 8, no. 6, p. 510. "Elephant's Child" from Rudyard Kipling, *Just So Stories*. "Invent" from Ryan Babineaux, *Fail Fast, Fail Often*, p. 106.

6. Who Is Your Who?

"It's me" from Isaac Butler, "The Blurred Boundaries of Memoir and Fiction in *Homeland Elegies*," *Slate*, December 7, 2020. "Loved by her" from Ayad Akhtar, *Homeland Elegies*, p. 216. "Ourselves as individuals" from Duncan Watts, *Six Degrees*, p. 217. For more on Chekhov's gun, see Donald Rayfield, *Anton Chekhov*. "Ghosts into ancestors" from Stephen Mitchell, "From Ghosts to Ancestors" in *Psychoanalytic Dialogues*, vol. 8, no. 6, p. 825.

7. What Is Your What?

My father's thesis is unpublished but remains in our family's archives. "Cheaper in Beaufort" from Matt Schudel, *The Washington Post*, March 6, 2016. My account of Merton draws from Gerald Horton, "Robert K. Merton," in *Proceedings of the American Philosophical Society*, vol. 148, no. 4. "Partial" from Robert Merton, *Social Theory and Social Structure*. "Ephemeral" from Julie Andrews, *Home Work*, p. 315.

"House of hope" from Amy Wrzesniewski, Jane Dutton, "Crafting a Job," in *The Academy of Management Review*, vol. 26, no. 2. "Burn off" from "Crafting Your Job into a Calling," president.yale.edu/president/yale-talk/crafting-your-job-calling.

8. When Is Your When?

"Fishing commercially" from Linda Greenlaw, *The Hungry Ocean*, p. xi. "Female captain" from Greenlaw, *The Hungry Ocean*, p. 58. "Nine-to-five" from Greenlaw, *The Hungry Ocean*, p. 15. "Whacked" and this account draw on Elizabeth Hightower Allen's "The Story Behind 'The Perfect Storm,'" in outsideonline.com, October 27, 2021. "Course correct" from Janet Ungless's "Becoming a Mother at 46," *Prevention*, May 20, 2013.

"Presupposes" from Herminia Ibarra, *Working Identity*, p. 33. For more on my time in Japan, see my book *Learning to Bow*. Those first lines come from George Orwell, *1984*; Sylvia Plath, *The Bell Jar*; Gabriel García Márquez, *One Hundred Years of Solitude*; *The Hebrew Bible*, New International Version.

Langston Hughes, "Harlem," in *The Collected Poems of Langston Hughes*. "People appear" from Laura Carstensen, Derek Isaacowitz, Susan Charles, "Taking Time Seriously," in *The American Psychologist*, vol. 54, no. 3. For more on Wecht and Ludovici, see my book *Life Is in the Transitions*.

9. Where Is Your Where?

"First crush" from Sandra Cisneros, *A House of My Own*, p. 341. "Quiet, privacy" from Sandra Cisneros, *The House on Mango Street*, 25th anniversary edition. Eudora Welty, "Place in Fiction" is available at xroads.virginia.edu/~DRBR/welty.txt. I also relied on Reynolds Price, "One Writer's Place in Fiction," *New York Times*, July 27, 2001.

"Character, plot" from Leonard Lutwack, *The Role of Place in Literature*, p. 17. "4 percent" from Emma Goldberg, "A Two-Year, 50-Million-Person Experiment in Changing How We Work," *New York Times*, March 10, 2022. "Twenty-three million" from Jane Lanhee Lee, "Up to 23 Million People in U.S. Could Move Thanks to Remote Work," Reuters, October 29, 2020. "17 percent" from "Inflexible Return-to-Office Policies Are Hammering Employee Experience Scores," Future Forum, April 2022. "Thirty-four million" from Donald Sull, Charles Sull, and Ben Zweig, "Toxic Culture Is Driving the Great Resignation," *MIT Sloan Management Review*, January 11, 2022.

"None of us" from Ralph Ellison, *Invisible Man*, p. 577.

10. Why Is Your Why?

"Auntie Toothache" appears in *The Stories of Hans Christian Andersen*, selected and translated by Diana Crone Frank and Jeffrey Frank, p. 269ff. "Good Writers" appears in "Springsteen: Silence Is Unpatriotic," *60 Minutes*, October 4, 2007.

My book on Adam and Eve is called *The First Love Story*. "Turning our tortures" from John Milton, *Paradise Lost*, Book II, line 274. "Make something" from a letter Andersen wrote to Henriette Collin, June 1870, in Frank and Frank, *Stories of Hans Christian Andersen*, p. 269.

For more on script theory, see Silvan Tomkins, *Affect Imagery Consciousness*, vol. 4. "Inhibit spontaneity" from Richard Gordon Erskine, "Script Cure," *Transactional Analysis Journal*, April 1990, p. 102.

11. How Is Your How?

For more on the life of Benjamin Samuel Abeshouse, see my book *The Council of Dads*, p. 132ff. "Help me" clip from *The Wizard of Oz* can be found at youtube.com/watch?v=ZrotkcWJFwo. My account of William Faulkner, failed postmaster, draws on Emily Temple's "William Faulkner Was Really Bad at Being a Postman," *Lit Hub*, September 25, 2018; and "William Faulkner Resigns from the Post Office Job with a Spectacular Letter," *Open Culture*, March 26, 2015, which contains the Welty quote.

Conclusion: The New Rules of Success

The life of Aldo Leonard, including his creation of the phrase *edge effect*, is covered in Fred Guthery, Ralph Bingham, "On Leopold's Principle of the Edge," in *Wildlife Society Bulletin*, vol. 20, no. 3; Tristan Gooley, *The Nature Instinct*, p. 85; and Bill Cronon, "Why Edge Effects," in *Edge Effects*, October 9, 2014. "To be in the margin" from bell hooks, *Feminist Theory*, p. ix.

"Poem in our eyes" from Eddie Glaude, *Begin Again*, p. 38. "Dream of a land" from Matthew Wills, "James Truslow Adams," *JSTOR Daily*, May 18, 2015. "America" from James Truslow Adams, *The Epic of America*, p. 404; "In our 'struggle,'" Adams, *The Epic of America*, p. 406. "Liberty And Justice" from Bloom, *The*

American Dream, p. 38. "I think" from "Buzz Aldrin on The American Dream," *Forbes*, March 22, 2007. "It's called" from "George Carlin—The American Dream," YouTube, April 26, 2009. "Zip code" from Stephen Dubner, "Is the American Dream Really Dead?" *Freakonomics*, January 18, 2017. "No wonder" comes from a YouGov poll in July 2020.

"Turri" from "Typewriters Were Originally Created to Help the Blind," Dictionary.com, April 29, 2011. "Friedman" from Kat Eschner, "Why You Should Appreciate the Invention of the Bendy Straw," *Smithsonian*, September 28, 2017. "Cerf" from "Vint Cerf—Co-creator of the Internet and Email," *Ability Magazine*, April 2020. "Roberts" from Joan Leon's "Ed Roberts," *Britannica*, November 6, 2014.

"Kill the ancestor" from Bloom, *The American Dream*, p. 211. "Happy ending" from Jonathan Rosenbaum's "Afterword to *The Big Brass Ring*, A Screenplay by Orson Welles," December 17, 2021, jonathanrosenbaum.net. "Damned self" from Geoff Gehman, "Faith Ringgold Stays True to Her Roots and Herself," *The Morning Call*, March 6, 2005.

For more information about doing a Life Story Project with a loved one similar to the one I did with my dad that inspired this project, please visit storyworth.com/lifestoryproject.

To contact me directly; to learn more about my TED course on mastering life transitions, speaking, or my newsletter; or to share your story, please visit brucefeiler.com.

INDEX

Aaker, Jennifer, 152

AARP, 115

ABCs of meaning, 146–49

Abeshouse, Abraham, 264–65

Abeshouse, Benjamin Samuel
"Bucky," 263–65

Achor, Shawn, 79

ACLU, 217

Acoustiguide, 238

Adams, James Truslow, 285

Adler, Alfred, 249

advice, 265, 266
best for oneself right now,
280–82
best received, 270–74

Aeron chair, 290

African Americans, *see* Black people

age, 213

agency, in ABCs of meaning, 146–49

agricultural economy, 35–37, 40, 41,
47, 58, 82

AI (artificial intelligence), 73, 95,
257, 292

Akhtar, Ayad, 157–58

Alaska, 38–49

Alba, Jessica, 133–35

Aldrin, Buzz, 285–86

Alger, Horatio, 22, 118–19

Ali, Muhammad, 187

Amazon, 95, 292

American Dream, 1–3, 7, 16, 19, 22,
112, 119, 224–25, 267, 283,
285–89
see also success stories

American Idea of Success, The
(Huber), 117

Americans with Disabilities Act, 217

American University, 80, 172

Amtrak, 220

Anantharaman, Divya, 79, 230–31

Andersen, Hans Christian,
243–44, 249

Andrea Gail, 202
Andrews, Julie, 190–91, 194
Angelou, Maya, 297
Apple, 269, 280
Appleby, Joyce, 35
Arab-American Comedy Festival, 53
Arabs Gone Wild, 52
archaeology, 140
   personal, 137–43, 149, 153
Archambeau, Shellye, 173, 210,
   231–32
Arnaz, Desi, 51
Artist's Way, The (Cameron), 197
Arzón, Robin, 266–69, 288
ascent, narratives of, 135–36, 142
Asimov, Isaac, 83
Atomic Energy Commission, 32
"Auntie Toothache" (Andersen),
   243–44, 249
Austen, Jane, 189
authenticity, 187–88
Autobiography of a Yogi (Yogananda),
   76–77
automobile repair, 67–68, 236
Axiology, 198

Bach, Julian, 185–86
Ball, Lucille, 51
Bank of America, 63, 138
Barrett, Cassie, 195
Basina, Curtis, 166, 276
basket making, 127–28, 234
Baumeister, Roy, 152–53
Bedell, Colin, 173–74, 231, 280–81

Bee Movie, 57
Bell Jar, The (Plath), 209
belonging, in ABCs of meaning,
   146–49
Berne, Eric, 254
Bernstein, Peter, 36
Bhandari, Anooj, 92–93, 231,
   287–88
Bishop, Rudine Sims, 241
Black Cowboy Museum, 231
Black History Month, 182
Black Lives Matter, 169, 214
Black people, 23, 24, 31–33
   buffalo soldiers, 182
   literacy narratives of, 135–36
   novelists, 183–84
   pilots, 189
   racism and, 32, 104–5, 169, 214
   women, 23, 24, 105, 168–69,
   183–84
Bleich, Sabrina, 141–42
bliss, following, 62–65
Bloom, Harold, 111–12
Boardwalk Empire, 122
Boffone, Trevor, 19–22, 24, 192
Bolles, Richard Nelson, 23, 50
Bollywood Affair, A (Dev), 279
boomers, 60
Borum Chattoo, Caty, 79–80,
   172–73
Boston Market, 211
Bradley & Parker, 176
Brave Wilderness, 189, 215
Brewster, David, 106–7

Bridgewater, Marcus, 100, 165
Brown, Tony, 102
Brundage, Ashley, 210–12
buffalo soldiers, 182
Burnett, Carol, 187
butterflies (unanticipated changes),
    66–70, 76
butterfly effect, 68
BuzzFeed, 74, 163, 275

Cadry, Jeff, 166
Caldwell, Tye, 175–76
Callies, Larry, 231
Cameron, James, 133
Cameron, Julia, 197
Campbell, Joseph, 62
capitalism, 36–37, 41
career, 25, 31–55
    counseling for, 43, 125, 130, 131
    as path, 25, 48, 57–80
    résumés and, 44, 47, 49–50,
        54, 152
    use of word, 40–41, 54
    see also jobs; work
care of someone else, 25, 97–100
Carlin, George, 286
Carnegie, Dale, 22, 23, 124–25
Carolina Memorial Sanctuary, 195
car repair, 67–68, 236
Carstensen, Laura, 213
cause, in ABCs of meaning,
    146–49
Cayne, Candis, 211
Center for Independent Living, 290

Center for Media & Social Impact,
    79–80, 172
centering the edge, 284, 290, 291
Centurion Ministries, 261
Century 21, 227
CEOs, 173, 210, 232, 295
Cerf, Vint, 290
CertaPro, 139
Chadwick, Don, 290
Challenger, 207
Chancey, Benjamin, 69, 237–38
Chan Zuckerberg Initiative,
    194, 272
Chapelle, Dave, 52
character, 188
    personality and, 122–23
    success and, 113–19, 131
charisma, 188, 189
Chekhov, Anton, 162
Chidananda, Rishi, 75–77, 235
childhood, 26, 70–71, 162
    favorite places in, 228–32
    role models in, 185–90
    "toothache" in, 248–53
    work values learned in, 162–67
child-rearing, 99
"Children's Rhymes" (Hughes), 285
China, 144, 145
Chisholm, Wendy, 72–74, 105,
    193, 257
choice, 146
    see also decisions
Choklat, Aki, 114, 115
Choosing a Vocation (Parsons), 23

Chronicles of a Liquid Society (Eco), 54
CIA, 14–16, 65, 234, 276
Cisneros, Sandra, 223–24
cities, 41–42
Civil War, 41, 118, 182
Cleis Press, 281
Clift, Joey, 195, 256–57, 293–94
climate change, 144–45, 148, 219
climbing versus digging, 291–92
Clinton, Bill, 32, 150, 217
CNBC, 135
Cockerton, Judy, 158–61, 235–36
collective versus individual, 292–94
Columbia University, 186
Comedian and an Activist Walk into a Bar, A (Borum Chattoo), 173
communication and speaking styles, 125
community, 184, 185, 293
Conniff, Ben, 215, 257–58, 294–95
Conroy, Pat, 185–87
constructivism, 129
Conwell, Russell, 225
Copper Crow Distillery, 166, 276
Corrigan, Tom, 95
Cosmopolitan, 174
Coulter, Catherine, 70
Countdown, 52
Covey, Stephen, 22, 23
COVID-19 pandemic, 4, 64, 69, 232–33, 238, 269, 277
creativity, 187–88
Crime Scene Cleaning, 152

Crofter and the Laird, The (McPhee), 82
Cromer, Bruce, 120
curb cuts, 290–91
Curie, Madame, 187
curiosity, invention of, 36

Dark Angel, 133
Daufuskie Island, 185
Daunay, Ariel, 142–43, 192
Davis, Deniese, 219, 272–73, 288
Davis, Jefferson, 23
Davis, Ninah, 197, 200, 296
Davis, Shardé, 167–70, 214
Day, Dorothy, 172
Deadliest Catch, 74, 231
decisions, 158, 167
    looking back on, 218–19
    time and, 213–18
    wrong, gift of, 299–302
Defense of Marriage Act, 39
Delarato, Laura, 96, 105–6, 149
Deloitte, 251
Delsarte, François, 125
Democratic National Committee (DNC), 74, 163
Deuce, The, 121
Dev, Sonali, 69–70, 189, 278–79
"Digging" (Heaney), 139–40
digging versus climbing, 291–92
dignity, 187
disabilities, 72–73, 195–96, 216–17, 290–91
Discovery, 142, 215

Disney, 45, 46, 65
diverse workers, 22–24, 59, 71,
    125–26, 131, 169, 233, 291
doctors, 186, 187
Donovan, Chris, 113–15, 128–29,
    172, 210, 272
Douglass, Frederick, 135
doula work, 91, 259, 292
dramatis personae, 158
drinking straw, 290
Drucker, Peter, 22, 48
Du Bois, W. E. B., 135
Dunwoody College of Technology, 67
Dutton, Jane, 191–92

Eco, Umberto, 54
economy, 48, 60–61, 234
ecotone, 284
edge, centering, 284, 290, 291
edge effect, 284
Education, Department of, 238
Edwards, Blake, 190
Edwards, Cindy, 142, 230
"Elephant's Child, The"
    (Kipling), 153
Ellison, Ralph, 234
email, 290
Emerson, Ralph Waldo, 285, 292
emotions, 192–93
Emre, Merve, 122–23
entrepreneurship, 92
Entwined Destinies (Washington), 183
environments, 254
   see also where

Epic of America, The (Adams), 285
epitaphs, 264
escape, 249–50
Evita, 51, 52
experience-taking, 258

Facebook, 195, 238, 280
family, 99
Family Caregiver Alliance, 99
Fantoni, Carolina, 289–90
farming, 87–88
   agricultural economy, 35–37, 40,
    41, 47, 58, 82
Farr, Jamie, 52
Faulkner, William, 275
FBI, 44–45, 65, 210
Feiler, Edwin J., Jr. (author's father),
    180, 299–300
Feiler, Jane Abeshouse (author's
    mother), 180, 300
Figgins, Rusty, 276
firefighting, 281–82
fishing, 74, 201–3, 231
fitness, 267–69
Floyd, George, 236
Fly for the Culture, 189
Foley, John, 269
follow your bliss, 62–65
Forbes, 135
foster care, 159–61
Franklin, Benjamin, 111–12, 116–18,
    123, 256
Freud, Sigmund, 249
Friends, 167, 168

Friendship Missionary Baptist
 Church, 98
From Behind the Veil (Stepto), 135–36
From Mumbai to Maine, 172
Furstenberg, Diane von, 174
future, 153
 and being at a moment in life,
  218–21
 and best advice for oneself right
  now, 280–82
 in meaning audit, 136, 149–54
 place in, 237–41
 purpose and, 259–62
 what you want to do in, 197–200
 who you want to be in, 174–78
Future Forum, 233

Galbraith, John Kenneth, 22
Gallagher, Dan, 69, 163, 189
Game Management (Leopold), 284
Garbinsky, Emily, 152
García Márquez, Gabriel, 209
Garden Marcus, 165
Gates, Bill, 76
Gauthier, Andrew, 74, 163, 275
GE, 8
GE Healthcare Global Services, 278
General Hospital, 53
Genesis, Book of, 209
Gen X, 59–60, 286
Gen Z, 286
Glassdoor, 233
Gloria Dawn, 201
Gold, Morgan, 86–88, 92, 164

Goldman Sachs, 280
Gold Shaw Farm, 87–88, 164
Goodall, Jane, 197
Google, 176
Gore, Al, 144
Gotham Taxidermy, 79, 231
Green, Kirsten, 89–91, 259, 292
Greenlaw, Linda, 201–3, 221
Groening, Matt, 86
Gullah Sweetgrass Baskets, 128
Gutierrez, Sonia, 93
Gym-N-Eat Crickets, 79, 163, 216

Hannah Boden, 202
happiness, 65, 70, 94, 97, 113, 116,
 136, 193, 213
 and following your bliss, 62–65
 ghost jobs and, 101
 meaning and, 153
 side jobs and, 92, 94
Haring, Keith, 187
"Harlem (A Dream Deferred)"
 (Hughes), 212
Harlem Renaissance, 184
HBO, 121, 122, 219
Heaney, Seamus, 139–40
helplessness, 249–51
Here, Right Matters (Vindman), 206
Herold, Alexandra, 195–97
Heumann, Judy, 216–17, 221, 290
Hewlett Foundation, 272
Heying, Cathy, 66–68, 236–37, 257
Hirsch, Jacob, 78–79
Home (Andrews), 190

Homeland Elegies (Akhtar), 157
homelessness, 172, 259
Home Loan Company, 179, 180
Home Work (Andrews), 190, 191
Honest Company, 134–35
Hong, Cathy Park, 103–4
hooks, bell, 284
Horton, Maura, 196
Houdini, Harry, 186
House of My Own, A (Cisneros), 223
House on Mango Street, The
   (Cisneros), 224
how, 153–54, 263–82
   best advice for oneself right now,
      280–82
   best advice received about work,
      270–74
   and permission to change, 274–79
How to Win Friends and Influence
   People (Carnegie), 23, 125
Hu, Jing, 78–79
Huber, Richard, 117
Hughes, Langston, 184, 212, 285
Hungry Ocean, The (Greenlaw),
   201, 203
Hurricane Grace, 202
Hurston, Zora Neale, 184

Ibarra, Herminia, 203
IBM, 94, 105, 173, 232, 278
Idaho National Laboratory, 198
identity, 249
Imagine: A Center for Coping with
   Loss, 247

immersion, narratives of, 135–36, 142
Indigo Arts Alliance, 141
individual versus collective, 292–94
industrial and manufacturing work,
   37, 40, 41, 47, 83
injustice, 249, 251
internet accessibility, 73
intimacy coordination, 120–22, 129,
   214, 273
invention of curiosity, 36
inventions, 41, 289–90
Invisible Man (Ellison), 234
Irwin, Steve, 215

Jackson, Michael, 46
Jackson, Stonewall, 23
Japan, 207–8
Jaws, 189
Jenkins, Beverly, 181–85, 210, 293
Jepsen, David, 129, 130
jobs, 24–25, 54, 80, 81–107
   books about, 50
   caregiving, 25, 97–100
   changing of, 50, 203
   crafting of, 191
   creation of new types of, 42, 54
   first, 64
   ghost, 25, 101–6
   hope, 25, 93–97
   household, 85
   jobless, 88
   main, 25, 86–89, 92, 94
   number of, per person, 83–85
   quitting of, 3–4, 233, 266

jobs (*cont.*)
  redesigning of, 4
  roles viewed as, 84–85
  side, 25, 89–93, 94
  top-down model of, 191
  unpaid, 84–85, 92, 95, 97, 99
  use and definition of word, 83, 84
  see also career; work
Jobs, Steve, 77
Johnson & Johnson, 8–9, 278
Jones, Daphne, 105, 255, 278
Jordan, Michael, 188
Journal of Negro History, 182, 183
Junger, Sebastian, 202–3
Jurassic Park, 68
Just So Stories (Kipling), 153

kaleidoscope, 106–7
Kaufman, Geoff, 258
Kehrmann, Carrie, 263
Kennedy, Florynce, 297
Keynes, John Maynard, 83
Keystone Pipeline, 95
Kim, Sang, 92, 192, 216, 230
King, Martin Luther, Jr., 212
Kipling, Rudyard, 153
Kipling questions, 153–54, 180, 254,
  265, 280
  answers to, 297–99
  see also how; *what*; *when*; *where*;
    who; *why*
Kissinger, Henry, 205
Knight, Phil, 256
knowledge work, 40, 48

Kothary, Nishita, 194, 210
Krause, Aaron, 165–66, 256
Krause, Todd, 62–65
Kuehn, Kathleen, 95
Kwok, Wei-Tai, 143–45, 148, 152, 219

Labor Department, 60, 83
Ladies' Home Journal, 153
LA Underground Cat Network, 195
Lear, Norman, 79, 172, 173
Leaving Neverland, 46
Leonardo da Vinci, 47
Leopold, Aldo, 283–84
Levine, Jamie, 74–75
Levinson, Daniel, 170
Libby, Lisa, 258
life
  success and, 116
  work and, 63, 70–75, 85, 99, 116
Life Is in the Transitions (Feiler), 13
lifequakes, 2, 58, 71
life stories, 18
Life Story Project, 13, 18–19, 58,
  60, 146
Lift Garage, 68, 236, 237, 257
Likely, Nygil, 97–99, 278
LinkedIn, 141, 277, 301
Lion King, The, 69, 251
literature, 36–37
Lively, Kelly, 96, 105, 198–200
Living Playgrounds, 239
location, *see where*
Loewald, Hans, 162
Lorde, Audre, 106

Lorenz, Edward, 68
Louisiana State University (LSU), 32
Lowly Worm, 81–82, 85
Ludovici, Lisa, 214
Luke's Lobster, 215, 257, 294
Lutwack, Leonard, 228–29

Mad, 86
Madison Buffalo Jump, 94–95
Malik, Harmit, 96, 148, 295
management science, 41
Manalo, Annabelle, 188
Mansbach, Jodi, 238–39, 255–56
manufacturing and industrial work,
    37, 40, 41, 47, 83
Marden, Orison Swett, 123–24
Mary Poppins, 190
Massachusetts Small Business
    Development Center, 272
Mastrantonio, Mary Elizabeth, 203
math, 36, 41
Matthew, Gospel of, 246–47
McAdams, Dan, 130
McCallum, Jamie, 83
McClure's, 123
McNair Scholars Program, 168
McPhee, John, 82
meaning, 5, 26, 85, 106, 116, 249
    ABCs of, 146–49
    care jobs and, 100
    happiness and, 153
    main job and, 86
    money and, 78–79, 294–95
    side jobs and, 92

vacuum of, 152
and where we work, 233, 237
    see also why
meaning audit, 133–54, 266
    future in, 136, 149–54
    past in, 136, 137–43
    present in, 136, 143–49
mediumship, 93, 277
Mencken, H. L., 124
Mendez, Jasminne, 216, 256, 296
Mercer, 63
Merton, Robert, 186, 187
Metoxen, Kirby, 100, 250
MetricStream, 173, 232
MFG Texas, 69
Michigan State University, 181, 182
Microsoft, 73, 214, 257
Miles, Richard, Jr., 260–62
Miles of Freedom, 262
millennials, 60, 61, 286
minor feelings, 103–4
Minter, Daniel, 141, 287
"Mirrors, Windows, and Sliding
    Glass Doors" (Bishop), 241
MIT Sloan Management Review, 233
money, 116, 249
    in definition of job, 84
    in ghost jobs, 104–6
    meaning and, 78–79, 294–95
    success and, 75–80, 117, 128,
        294, 295
    superworkquakes and, 78
Montage of a Dream Deferred
    (Hughes), 212

moonlighting, 91
Morrison, Toni, 182, 292–93, 297
motivation, 181, 197, 214, 244
    see also why
MTV, 134
Mueller, Robert, 45
multidimensional workforce, 24
multilayered work and life
    experience, 24–25
multishaped work experience, 25

Napoleon, 264
narratives, 13, 54, 103, 143
    of ascent, 135–36, 142
    autobiographical, 13, 129–30
    in career construction, 26
    grand, 54
    of immersion, 135–36, 142
    in psychology and psychotherapy,
        6, 18, 129, 249
    see also story, storytelling
NASA, 8, 9, 199
Natal+Home, 197
National Bank of Canada, 79, 163
National Career Development
    Association, 129
National Museum of American
    History, 264
Native Americans, 94–95, 118, 166,
    182, 195, 250, 292, 293
Negro History Week, 182
Neo-Futurists, 231
Netflix, 195, 293
network, 40

neuroscience, 129
New Thought, 123
New York City, 42, 231, 235
New York Daily News, 217
New York Times, 88, 121, 153–54
Nichols, Lauren, 69, 93, 209, 277
Night Song (Jenkins), 184
Nike, 256, 268
9/11 attacks, 45, 52, 63
Nineteen Eight-Four (Orwell), 209
Ninja Sex Party, 214
Nixon, Richard, 143, 145
Noel, Karen, 105, 194, 236
nomads, 58
Northwest Renewable Energy
    Institute, 238
Nowland, Wynne, 176–78, 194, 211
NPR, 279
numbers related to work, 34–37, 54,
    82, 116, 294

Oculus, 280
Olbermann, Keith, 52
Oliver, Mary, 26
O'Loughlin, Brian, 251–52
One Hundred Years of Solitude (García
    Márquez), 209
Orlando, Connie, 272–73
Orwell, George, 209
Outside, 202

Paradise Lost (Milton), 248
parenting, 99
parents, 26, 187

stories inherited from, 189–90
values learned from, 162–67, 187
Park, Meroë, 14–16, 25, 65, 234–35, 276
Parsons, Frank, 23, 42–43, 49–50, 125, 129
Partnership for Public Service, 276
Parton, Dolly, 51, 101
passion, following, 62–65
past, 153
    best work advice received in, 270–74
    favorite places in childhood, 228–32
    in meaning audit, 136, 137–43
    role models in, 185–90
    start of work story in, 207–12
    "toothache" in childhood, 248–53
    values learned from parents in, 162–67, 187
pastoralists, 58
patents, 41
Patti + Ricky, 196
Peale, Norman Vincent, 23
Peloton, 269
Peña, Brijette, 1–3, 25, 65, 79
People, 134, 184
Perfect Storm, The (book and film), 202–3
permission to change, 274–79
personal archaeology, 137–43, 149, 153
personality
    character and, 122–23
    success and, 119–26, 131
    tests of, 48

Personality Brokers, The (Emre), 122–23
Peterson, Nathaniel "Coyote," 189, 215
Philadelphia (magazine), 210
Pierpont, Tim, 137–39, 141, 152, 214, 276–77
Pierpont Painting, 139, 276–77
place, *see where*
plan, ten-year, 65–70
Plath, Sylvia, 209
Plato, 42
Playboy, 215
PNC Bank, 211–12
policing, 220
Power of Positive Thinking, The (Peale), 23
present, 153
    best and worst things about your work in, 190–97
    in meaning audit, 136, 143–49
    permission to change in, 274–79
    stories in, 253–58
    taking next step in, 212–18
    waymaker in, 167–74
    where you want to be now, 232–37
Presley, Elvis, 102
Project HOME, 172
Project Runway, 115
ProShares, 87
Proverbs, Book of, 212
Prudential, 246, 247
Pryor, Richard, 52
psychology and psychotherapy, 6, 18, 129, 249

purpose, 259–62
  see also why

Queer Cosmos, 174, 231
questions, *see* Kipling questions
Quinlan, Larry, 251
Quinn, Aaron, 148–49, 281–82
QVC, 166

Rae, Issa, 219, 273
Ragged Dick (Alger), 118
Rainbows for All Children, 246, 247
Ramirez, Ebony Peay, 280
Ravilochan, Teju, 258, 289
Ray, Derrick, 74, 192, 231
reading the clock, 213, 216, 218
reading the room, 213, 214, 218
reading your gut, 213–14, 218
real estate, 226–28
Reeves, Jordan, 235
Refinery29, 281
refugees, 38–39, 65, 296
Rendell, Ed, 259
representation, 188
résumés, 44, 47, 49–50, 54, 152
Rich, John, 102
Richard Miles Act, 262
Ringgold, Faith, 297
risk, 216, 218–20
Robert-Houdin, Jean-Eugène, 186
Roberts, Ed, 290
Robinson, Mary, 244–48
Rock, Chris, 52
Rodgers, Daniel, 116–17

Rodis, Alicia, 119–22, 128, 214, 273
Rodriguez, Carolina Guillen, 225–28
Rodriguez, Ericka, 197–98, 200
role models, 27, 254
Role of Place in Literature, The
  (Lutwack), 228–29
romance novels, 70, 183–84, 278–79
Romance Writers of America, 184,
  278–79
Rosehaven (Coulter), 70
running, 267
Running Wolf, Michael, 94–96, 292
safecracking, 240

Salk, Jonas, 154
San Diego Seed Company, 2–3, 65
Santore, Charlie, 239–40
Sapelo, 142
Saudi Arabia, 52
Savage, Courtland, 189, 192–93, 209
Savickas, Mark, 130–32, 186
Scarry, Richard, 81–82
Schkolnick, Meyer, 186
Scott, Cherie, 171–72, 210
Scott, Cornell, 105
scripts, 5, 131, 189–90, 253,
  254, 262
  work, 5, 253–54, 291
script theory, 253
scriptures, 6, 22, 26, 55, 135, 190,
  229, 254
  work, 5, 137, 158, 291
Scrub Daddy, 166, 256
Scullion, Mary, 172, 259

Seasons of a Man's Life, The
(Levinson), 170
sedentists, 58
Seinfeld, Jerry, 57
self-care, 104, 105
self-employment, 92
self-reliance, 292–93
Sessions, Hudson, 92
7 Habits of Highly Effective People, The
(Covey), 23
sexual harassment, 74
Sforza, Ludovico, 47
shape-shifting, 147
Shark Tank, 166
Shaw, George Bernard, 83
Shaw, Pauline, 42
ShearShare, 176
shelter, 180, 185, 191
Sherr, Sara, 210
Shut Up and Run, 268
side hustle, 91–92
sidewalks, 290–91
Simpsons, The, 86
Sinclair, Upton, 48
skills, 54
slavery, 35, 36, 118, 128
sliding glass doors, windows, and
mirrors, 241
Smalls, Michael, 126–29, 210, 234
Smart, Leah, 141, 277, 301
Smith, Shelby, 79, 163–64, 216
Smithsonian Institution, 184,
264, 276
Sound of Music, The, 190, 191

Soviet Union, 204, 206, 207
Spatrisano, Issa, 37–40, 65, 100,
271, 296
Spaulding, Laura, 149–52, 192, 250
Spaulding Decon, 151–52, 250
speaking and communication
styles, 125
Spence, Harry, 160–61
Spielberg, Steven, 189
Springsteen, Bruce, 244
status versus story, 295–96
Steinbeck, John, 22
Stephens, Vivian, 183, 184
Stepto, Robert, 135–36
story, storytelling, 6, 87, 88, 129, 153,
253–58
life, 18
Life Story Project, 13, 18–19, 58,
60, 146
status versus, 295–96
see also narratives; success stories;
work story
straw, drinking, 290
Stumpf, Bill, 290
success, 4–7, 11, 12, 16, 136
books on, 23
definitions of, 5, 6, 129, 131, 132,
288, 295
emerging kaleidoscope of, 24–26
history of, 116
money and, 75–80, 117, 128,
294, 295
work and life in, 116
writing your own story of, 26–27

Success, 123–24
success, four rules of, 289–91
  climbing versus digging, 291–92
  individual versus collective,
    292–94
  means versus meaning, 294–95
  status versus story, 295–96
success stories, 12, 111–32, 136,
  225, 249
  Alger, 118–19
  character in, 113–19, 131
  Franklin, 111–12, 117
  personality in, 119–26, 131
  sameness of, 5, 22–24
  writing your own, 26–27,
    126–32, 154
Sull, Donald and Charles, 233
Sun Microsystems, 138
Supreme Court, 39, 74

Tang, Ken, 188–89, 252–53, 293
Taylor, Frederick Winslow, 41, 43
Taylor, Troy, 7–9, 25, 70, 288
Te, Bouy, 93
TED, 53, 235
Terkel, Studs, 24
Thomas, Danny, 52
time
  decisions and, 213–18
  see also when
Time, 172
Today, 217
Tomkins, Silvan, 253
tonglen, 195

"toothaches," 243–44, 248–54
transitional figures, 170
Transportation, Department of, 69, 93
Treehouse, 161
Trotter, Lloyd, 8, 9
Troubled Waters (Abeshouse), 264
Turrentine, Dominique, 194, 272
Turri, Pellegrino, 289–90
typewriter, 290

Ukraine, 204, 205
Unapologetically Ambitious
  (Archambeau), 232
Uncharted, 258
Union Bank, 138
University of California, Berkeley, 290
University of California, Los Angeles
  (UCLA), 188
University of California, Santa
  Barbara, 167–68
University of Connecticut, 169
University of Pennsylvania, 179
unknown known, 130–31

values, 117, 132, 141
  learned from parents, 162–67, 187
  role models and, 187–88
Vasquez Heilig, Julian, 100, 175
Vélez-Villar, Eric, 44–47, 65, 79,
  210, 295
Venturelli, Nate, 141, 194, 210
Venturelli, Susan, 97, 100, 220, 221
VideoOut, 235
View, The, 219

Vindman, Alexander, 204–7
Vindman, Yevgeny "Eugene," 204, 206
Vishwananda, Swami, 77
Vocation Bureau, 42–43
Vohs, Kathleen, 152
von Furstenberg, Diane, 174
Vox Media, 96, 105, 149

Wagoner, Porter, 101
Walker, Candice, 191–92
Wall Street Journal, 176
Walt Disney Company, 45, 46, 65
Walters, Barbara, 219
Warner, Isiah, 31–33, 70–71, 255
Washington, Elsie, 183
Washington, George, 111
Water Is Wide, The (Conroy), 185–86
Watts, Duncan, 158
waymakers, 167–74
Wecht, Brian, 214
Weinstein, Harvey, 121, 214
Welles, Orson, 295–96
Welty, Eudora, 224, 274
Wharton School, 179
what, 153–54, 179–200, 229, 254, 266
    best and worst things about your
        work today, 190–97
    role models in childhood, 185–90
    work life in the future, 197–200
What Color Is Your Parachute?
    (Bolles), 23, 50
What Do People Do All Day? (Scarry),
    81–82
when, 153–54, 201–21, 229, 266

being at a moment in life, 218–21
    start of work story, 207–12
    taking the next step, 212–18
where, 153–54, 223–41, 266
    favorite childhood place, 228–32
    future place, 237–41
    present place, 232–37
White, Alton, 68–69, 104–5, 214, 251
white-collar work, 48, 50, 232–33
who, 153–54, 157–78, 229, 254, 266
    parents, in the past, 162–67
    waymakers, in the present, 167–74
    you, in the future, 174–78
why, 153–54, 243–62, 266
    childhood "toothache" and, 248–53
    preferred types of stories and,
        253–58
    purpose right now, 259–62
Wilson, Karléh, 96, 291–92
windows, mirrors, and sliding glass
    doors, 241
Wizard of Oz, The, 270
women, 23, 24, 47, 99, 105, 118, 149,
    219, 233, 291
    Black, 23, 24, 105, 168–69, 183–84
    workquakes of, 59–61, 71
Wooden, John, 188–89
Woodson, Carter, 182
words related to work, 34–37, 54, 82,
    116, 294
work, 10–14, 53, 54
    in agricultural economy, 35–37, 40,
        41, 47, 58, 82
    defining, 34

work (*cont.*)

ethic of, 116

existential crises around, 152, 218

history of, 35–36, 116

industrial and manufacturing, 37, 40, 41, 47, 83

leisure and, 116–17

life and, 63, 70–75, 85, 99, 116

mobility in, 58

knowledge, 40, 48

number of hours engaged in, 82, 83

numbers related to, 34–37, 41, 54, 82, 116, 294

reasons for changing, 193

remote, 233

résumés and, 44, 47, 49–50, 54, 152

schedules of, 83, 88

scripts of, 5, 253–54, 291

scriptures of, 5, 137, 158, 291

success and, 116

360-degree circle of, 85, 97, 106

toxic cultures at, 233

unpaid, 84–85, 92, 95, 97, 99

words related to, 34–37, 54, 82, 116, 294

see also career; jobs

work, bad advice about, 61–80

always keep your eye on the bottom line, 75–80

follow your bliss, 62–65

keep your personal life out of your work life, 63, 70–75

make a ten-year plan, 65–70

Working (Terkel), 24

workquakes, 7, 19, 25–26, 55, 57–80, 136, 144, 149

collective, 233–34

first, 59

nonwork, 71–75

number and frequency of, 59–61

personal archaeology and, 140

questions to ask in, *see* Kipling questions

superworkquakes, 77–78, 152

work story, 6–7, 35–36, 54, 129–31, 136, 154, 158, 180–81

questions in, *see* Kipling questions

see also story, storytelling

Work Story Project, 1–27, 71, 136, 244, 302

lessons of, 22–27, 35

Work Story Interview in, 16–19

World Wide Web Consortium, 73

Wright, Chely, 101–3, 192, 209

Wrzesniewski, Amy, 191–92

Yahoo, 135

Yellowstone Club, 166

Yes, and . . . Laughter Lab, 172–73

Yogananda, Paramahansa, 76–77

Young, Kara, 96–97

Young, Michael, 167–70

YouTube, 87–88, 152, 189, 214, 215, 219, 254, 265, 272

Zayid, Maysoon, 50–53

Zelensky, Volodymyr, 205